Also By Jennifer Holik

The Tiger's Widow

Engaging the Next Generation: A Guide for Genealogy Societies and Libraries

Branching Out: Genealogy for Adults

Branching Out: Genealogy for High School Students

Branching Out: Genealogy for 4th-8th Grades Students

Branching Out: Genealogy for 1st-3rd Grade Students

To Soar with the Tigers

Stories of the Lost

Written by Jennifer Holik

Generations Publishing

Copyright Information

Editor: Heather Gates Reed

Cover Designer: Sarah Sucansky.

Cover photo of flag draped caskets provided courtesy of the American Battle Monuments Commission.

Holik, Jennifer, 1973 –
     Stories of the Lost / Jennifer Holik. Includes bibliographical references and indexes.

ISBN: 149748099X
ISBN-13: 978-1497480995

Printed in the United States of America

Dedication

This book is dedicated to all of the men and women who served our country and fought for freedom, both past and present.

Acknowledgements

This book could not have been written without the support of several people. First to my boys, Andrew, Luke, and Tyler. You listened to me talk about these men, their stories, and my ideas for several years. Thank you for your patience while I researched and wrote my book and lectures. Through you our family's stories will live on.

Thank you to my cover designer Sarah Sucansky for an incredibly moving cover. Thank you to my outstanding editor Heather Gates Reed for her editing skills and guidance.

To my parents, Patricia and Thomas Holik, for always seeking information on each trip to Europe for my stories. Thank you mom, for writing about your cemetery visits for inclusion in this book. To my best friends Patti Fleck, Karissa Christensen, and Matt Zakowski, for always reminding me that I can do anything! Thank you to my friends, fellow writers and genealogical colleagues Connie Yen, Terri O'Connell, Stephanie Pitcher Fishman, Lisa Alzo, and Jennifer Alford for your constant support and encouragement.

Thank you to the late LeRoy Privoznik, and Jim, Chris, and Krysta Privoznik, for sharing James' stories, books, and artifacts with me so I could more completely write his story. James made sure you had the best clues to pass to me to find his story. Your support and cheerleading throughout this process has helped immensely.

Thank you to Barbara Mrenna Geisler for telling me the story of Private Frederick Goempel and sharing your knowledge of the Graves Registration Service. Your recommendations and resources have been very helpful with several projects, including this book.

I am very grateful to Norm Richards, a historian for the 90th Division Association, for his dedication in helping me locate records at the National Personnel Records Center. Also for answering every question I ever asked about military records. I could not do the work I do without your assistance. You are my favorite military researcher!

To my friends in Europe, Norbert Morbé and Romaine Fraiture, thank you for honoring the 90th Division in Luxembourg and sharing your photos, knowledge, and love of those soldiers with me. Mike Boehler for putting me in touch with people who could help locate information on James Privoznik's military service and always answering my questions. Martijn van Haren and Jasper van Haren for sharing their stories of grave adoption. Joy DesRosier, the Assistant Superintendent of the American Battle Monuments Commission Luxembourg Cemetery for sending numerous photos, the cemetery history, and answering many questions.

Thank you to Robert Rumsby for suggesting numerous books to read so I can learn more about the men of the Graves Registration Service and the work that continues by countless individuals today to bring the remains home of our fallen.

A big thank you to staff at the Pritzker Military Museum and Library in Chicago, Illinois. Pritzker Military Library became a second home while I researched and wrote parts of this book. I'd like to thank Teri Embrey, Chief Librarian, who provided many resources for this volume and read through James Privoznik's draft for me. I'd also like to thank Paul Grasmehr, Reference Coordinator, for answering a million questions and talking through certain aspects of World War II with me on numerous occasions. You both helped make this process much easier.

Michael Mercier and the Camp Butner Society for help in the identification of some photographs from James Privoznik's life and information on the Camp during the war years. I also appreciate the photograph for the James Privoznik's story. Thank you for all you are doing to preserve the history of Camp Butner.

Christian Levaufre, for providing a drawing and the history of La Cambe Cemetery where members of the 29th Infantry Division were temporarily buried.

Joseph Balkoski, the former historian for the 29th Infantry Division for locating records on Frank Winkler. 29th Infantry Division WWII Veteran Ralph Windler for telling me his story and answering my questions.

Thank you to Margie Wilson and Karen Prasse for their help locating information on Skagit County, Washington, and the Civilian Conservation Corps' Camp Lyman.

I am thankful to have been able to call upon the expertise of Willis Cole and George Ciampa when I researched the Graves Registration Service. And Lisa Budreau for information concerning World War I burials.

When I wrote Robert's Flying Tiger story, I had the assistance of many people including Robert's widow, Virginia S. Davis; the late Charles R. Bond, Jr., and the late John Richard Rossi for corresponding with me in 1997 about their memories of Robert; Charles Baisden, 3rd Squadron Armorer in the AVG, for sharing his memories of Robert and answering many questions during the course of my research; Jo Neal, President of AVG-FTA for answering numerous questions for me; Brad Smith for providing a photograph taken by his father, R.T. Smith, of Robert in 1942; Karen Halla and Mary Ellen Jenicek with the Morton East High School Archives, who provided information and several photographs of Robert from high school; the reference staff of the Hawthorne Works Museum, located at Morton Junior College in Cicero, who helped me locate information not only from the Hawthorne Works archives but also from the Morton Junior College archives.

And, thank you to my readers for keeping the memories of these valiant men alive.

Table of Contents

1

Introduction

Have you considered?

Men and women returned home from both World Wars changed. Some were blind, paralyzed, had missing limbs, were altered mentally and suffered from what we now know is Post-Traumatic Stress Disorder (PTSD.) It was not death, but they were lost to their loved ones and the life they lead before the war.

Those who did not return, the Soldier Dead, were forever lost. Soldier Dead is a term used to describe someone in the military who died in service. At the beginning of the United States' involvement in World War I, there was no official policy to repatriate the bodies of those who died during service. The United States wanted to bring the fallen home but it would not happen immediately. There were many other political issues to deal with such as United States policy and Allied countries' policies on such matters.

In 1919, the War Department decided it needed to find out if the American public wished for the remains to be brought home or left overseas in United States cemeteries. Both sides of the debate were heard and some felt since the government took their sons to war, it was their responsibility to bring them home again, even if they had died.

On March 4, 1921, Congress passed Public Law No. 389 which established funding to repatriate the remains of the fallen. This law was met with some resistance as government officials visited the temporary cemeteries in France and were appalled that these "shapeless things" were being dug up for reburial or repatriation. Keep in mind by this time some of these soldiers had been buried up to three years. Despite these opinions, the United States military continued to give families the option of repatriating their soldier dead's remains.

The Graves Registration Service, which was part of the Quartermaster Department, established policies and procedures to identify, record, and bury the fallen. These records were used at the end of the World War I and World War II when it was time to create permanent overseas cemeteries or repatriate the fallen.

We are so far removed from both World Wars we may have forgotten it was not a group of elderly men and women who fought. It was men and women primarily the ages of those just out of high school and college. Yes there were others in their 20s, 30s, and beyond serving, but the majority of those who served were very young.

Stop and think for a moment what your life was like at this age. Try to put yourself in their shoes.

I suspect we forget this fact because our World War I veterans are all gone now. Our World War II veterans are dying by the hundreds every day. When many of the veterans really began telling their stories in larger numbers in the 1980s, they were older. So in essence, we have been conditioned to think of these men and women as elderly, not the very young people they were when they fought and died for our country.

The Parents

Consider for a moment that you are the parent of a child going off to war. How do you feel? Did your son enlist or was he drafted? Are you scared? Do you have a foreboding feeling he will never return? Do you feel he will be wounded, return missing a limb, or somehow changed?

You send your child off to basic training for sixteen weeks. After training your soldier gets a few days of leave before shipping out overseas. Letters come sporadically. Sometimes they stop all together and you wait and wonder. Fearful the worst has happened. You begin waiting for the dreaded telegram to arrive. One day it does. Your child is Missing In Action (MIA), taken as a Prisoner of War (POW), or worse…Killed In Action (KIA).

What you do not already know is if he dies overseas it may be weeks or months before you receive confirmation of this fact. It will be years before the military tells you where he is buried overseas in a temporary military cemetery. And it will be much longer before you have the option to repatriate his remains or have them buried in an official American cemetery overseas.

What you do not know is the military will not tell you everything surrounding the events of your soldier's death. The military will not tell you how bad the wounds were and if there were personal effects to send home. They will not tell you which items were taken off the dead. You may not find out until years later if someone did take something off their buddy who died. You may only discover this when the soldier reached a place of peace or remembrance and felt he could return it to you.

When your soldier's remains are brought home the grief begins anew. You go through the feelings of hearing again that he has died only now it is very, very real. You have proof, a body. A body which does not resemble the man or woman you sent off to war. And now it is time to finally lay him to rest.

Notices are placed in the newspaper about the arrangements. The family and friends gather and pay their respects. The funeral procession moves from the home or funeral home to the cemetery. A gathering takes place to honor the soldier dead as he is placed in the ground. Family and friends gather after the service to reminisce but things are not over. Now it is time to do the paperwork to request a military headstone and the grief begins anew.

If your soldier or sailor returned home he may be mentally scarred for life. All those who served returned home changed in one way or another. For some, the mental grief and anguish of what they saw and did was too much. For others, it was shut away into a box in their mind to be released many years in the future or never at all. The mind is a powerful instrument and sometimes we just cannot speak of certain things.

The Soldiers

Consider for a moment you are a 18 year old soldier going off to fight. Did you enlist or were you drafted? How did you feel about the choice to enlist? How did you feel about being drafted? Are you scared or are you confident you will go overseas and beat the Nazi's? Have you considered the fact you may come home wounded, missing a limb, blind, unable to ever walk again? Have you considered the many ways you could die?

Have you considered \ war is hell and you may not have the comforts of home? No warm showers, hot meals, family and friends surrounding you? Have you thought about missing birthdays, holidays, and other family celebrations while you are off fighting? Are you leaving someone behind? Parents, siblings, girlfriend, boyfriend, fiancé or spouse and children? Have you considered what will happen to them if you do not return?

Have you thought about the effect your service and possible death will have on your family and the rest of the world? The families will feel great pain, the pain of losing a son, brother, fiancé, husband, father and the pain of not knowing where he is buried or when his body will return. The pain of knowing he is not the only one and there will be more.

Each one of us has an impact on the entire world. Together, fighting with your countrymen for freedom, impacts everyone. What you do matters and your service is important and will be remembered.

There may not be a choice when it comes to serving our country. It was war and in most cases you either enlisted or were drafted. You went for love of family, freedom, adventure, and love of country. The resounding feeling across the country was, We are the Americans! We will go over there and show 'em what we've got! We will not be defeated! With this attitude, how could you lose?

For Those Reading Today

When I first started writing this book series I decided to base it off my very well received lecture, *Finishing the Story*. In the lecture I talk about Michael Kokoska, Frank Winkler, and Robert Brouk. I thought writing as set of books incorporating those stories would be a good idea.

I then was inspired to re-write the introduction to my Finishing the Story lecture in March 2013. The introduction captured the audience in a way I had never experienced in all the other times I had given the lecture. I knew then I had to rework the book and the stories. In telling their stories, using creative non-fiction techniques, I wrote them each in a different way to illustrate there is more than one way to tell a story. I also included my previously published book *To Soar with the Tigers* with a slightly different ending. I wrote this book in 2010 and it includes Robert Brouk's Flying Tiger war diary. His story is the only one which has such a document.

One of my goals is to encourage researchers to dig deeper through the research process. Anyone can pick up a book about World War II or the Battle of the Bulge and skim the surface of events. It is safe there, more comfortable for us. We are more detached from what really happened.

Basic research is important so you have an overview of events, however, you must dig deeper. Entrench yourself in the mud and snow, pain and grief, death and dying of war. Feel what the men felt. Experience the battle through their senses. Witness what the family felt upon hearing of their loved one's death.

Tears will be shed as you research and write. Strong emotions will surge through you as you try to place yourself in their shoes to write their story as accurately as possible. You may even feel they are whispering in your ear as you write, guiding you, sending you here or there to look for a new piece of information. People talk about genealogy serendipity – I believe these soldiers are working with us to tell their stories.

I experienced this serendipity. I sat in Starbucks many mornings to work on my book. You can't cry in Starbucks right? Wrong! But working there does take the edge of a little as you really start to write and get into the extreme pain of battle. I'd write a little, go online to look something up, go back through my notes and write a little more of the story.

The week of January 7, 2013, I was working on James Privoznik's story. That Friday, January 11th was the anniversary of his death. On Monday the 7th, I was writing a description of his death and the condition of his body upon interment and disinterment. It was heart breaking. When my writing session was over for the day, I felt completely sick to my stomach. But the piece had been drafted.

That afternoon I went to meet some colleagues and one brought his wife's great uncle's World War II memorabilia with him, a uniform, photographs, medals, pieces of a shell and shrapnel. This could have been pieces of something similar to what hit and killed James. I held these two bronze colored heavy pieces about two inches long and maybe an inch or so deep with sharp jagged edges. Holding them gave me a much better idea of the hell of war. I could more easily picture how something like this could have damaged James' body so badly it killed him. For a moment I was there picturing the scene. Later I wrote more.

As the writing progressed I read oral histories and spoke to a World War II veteran. I encourage you to listen to their words, their pain, and their joy. What can you draw from their stories to add to your story? You do not necessarily have to talk to someone or listen to an interview a soldier who served in exactly the same unit, but try to for someone within that general area of fighting. You need an idea of what the weather was like, the action, and the events which surrounded the battle.

This book series is not for the faint of heart. Neither is researching the stories of your military ancestors. You may uncover details you had never considered. You may unravel a family story which was passed down and now appears to be incorrect. You will be faced with things we take for granted today which our men lived through or fought for.

When we think about the family stories we've heard there is something to keep in mind. The family was so close to the event the details they might have known may have been lost in their grief. Details may have been lost as the family waited for their loved one to return or their Soldier Dead's remains to be brought home. The families were also not told everything surrounding the death of their soldier.

Details and stories surrounding those who returned may also be sketchy because some things were not discussed. Some things were hidden. Some aspects may have been too hideous, painful, or difficult to explain, yet were burned into the memories of the veterans. There was no escape for them. Looking at the history of the events which surround the deaths of each soldier and those who survived provides a different perspective.

Today we are able to gain a glimpse into the life our soldiers led while serving their country. Accommodations we often take for granted like hot showers, warm meals, and protection, were not a part of the everyday life of these men and women. It also offers those of us enjoying our freedom today, the opportunity to look at things we may take for granted which our soldiers fought and died preserving.

So where do you start in telling the story? Have you written down what you know? Do you know where to locate records for your military ancestors? Have you heard no records exist?

Most everyone has heard a major problem in researching our military ancestors is the lack of records. There was a fire at the National Personnel Records Center in St. Louis in 1973. Over 80% of the Army and Air Force records were destroyed. While this is a devastating loss, there are other record sources you can consult to help fill in the gaps of military service and life.

Will you ever tell the full story? No. You were not there to experience it and can only write based on what you know and find in the records. Does this mean you should forget writing the story all together? No. There are enough resources available to paint a picture of the soldier's life. You can still explain what his service may have been if he had been in a specific unit at a given time.

When you write the stories of your military ancestors, both those who returned and those who were lost, consider the feelings of those involved. Research if possible, the events which surrounded the decision to fight if the individual enlisted. Learn about the training the men went through in boot camp. Research the histories of the units in which the men served to have a more complete picture of the events that took place and the impact on the war and the world.

Put emotion into your writing and really think about how the parents, wives, children, siblings, and friends felt about losing someone in the war, or having them return ..... altered.

Tell the Stories of the Lost the best you can with what you know. You will make them proud. Their stories will live on forever and their sacrifice will never be forgotten.

He who once was lost, will now be found and remembered always through your stories.

Want to know more? Visit my Generations Blog to read detailed analysis of what the World War II records contain. In the month of May I am featuring "Military Memories" writing prompts to help you start writing. You can find it at http://blog.generationsbiz.com. Also watch for a new book series out this fall from Generations which will further analyze these valuable records.

2

On a Foreign Shore

We stand on a foreign shore surrounded by a thunderous, deafening noise. War is definitely hell. Men are screaming in agony and shadows of death can be felt and seen everywhere. You can smell it in the air. Corpses lie scattered, bloated, and rotting on the land.

We are somewhat in shock. The fear we feel is overpowered by the ferocious desire to fight and live through this hell.

In training they used words like 'determination,' 'courage,' and 'sacrifice.' Training is one thing but the reality of war is a different experience. Will I be able to rise to the challenge when faced with danger or will my fear overtake me?

Destruction surrounds us as we march. Do we march toward our death? Is God watching us and protecting us with his shield? Or has he abandoned us completely? Some say there is no God. There cannot be a God who allows death and destruction on this scale.

My thoughts move from God to those I left behind at home. If I return, will they listen to my stories of war? Will they understand all this? Will they understand the danger, death, sound, taste, feel, smell and horrors of war? They are not here standing in my shoes so doubt clouds my thoughts. How could they possibly comprehend all this? I have trouble processing this even as I stand here amidst the rubble and death.

So many thoughts race through my mind. I think of my parents, wife, siblings, children, and friends at home. Will I return unharmed, unchanged, and whole? Or will I sleep forever in this foreign soil.

Will I be among the lost?

If I am, who will tell my story?

And, will anyone listen?

3

The Doughboy
Michael Kokoska

32nd Division, 127th Infantry Regiment, Co. L

(1891 – 1918)

The Family Story

My grandmother told me that my great grand uncle Michael Kokoska, who was the brother of my great grandfather Joseph Kokoska,
fought in World War I. Michael served in the 32nd Infantry Division.
He died in France in 1918. Only a snippet of the life of Michael Kokoska remained in our family lore. His story begged to be told.

The Early Years

My name is Josef. My wife Majdalena and I immigrated from the
Pilsen area of Bohemia. Our ship, *Fresia*, left the port of Hamburg,
Germany on August 31, 1881 en route to Le Havre, France, and arrived on September 22, 1881 at the Port of New York.[1] We came to
the United States for a better life, a life full of plenty, peace, hope,
and love.

Less than a month after arriving in the United States, we were
living in Chicago. Majdalena and I were married by a Justice of the
Peace on October 11, 1880.[2] Soon after we exchanged vows, the
children began to arrive. We had 11 children in total and counted our
blessings that 10 survived
to adulthood.[3] In those days,
disease was rampant and babies and children often died
at a young age.

My seventh child Mi-
chael was born September
28, 1891 in Chicago.[4] He
was one of four sons who
served during World War I.
Michael was the only son to
go overseas and the only one
we lost.

We lived within the
Pilsen neighborhood of Chicago with other Bohemians.
I worked as a laborer in a
lumber yard most of my life.
Our family moved around
a lot in the early years. In
1900, we had moved into our

*Michael Kokoska. Photo courtesy Charles
Kokaska.*

final home located at 988 W. 18th Place, Chicago. Majdalena and I remained there until our deaths.[5] When the Chicago street numbers changed in 1909, the house number became 2122 W. 18th Place.

As a boy, Michael attended school and learned to read and write English. After finishing school, he worked as a coat maker in a tailor establishment.[6] In 1917, he became a truck driver at Coonley Manufacturing.[7]

The World Is Changing - Michael

In 1914, I was 23 years old. I was tall, slender, confident, and had my entire life ahead of me. Don't we all feel that way when we are young? The world was changing as war erupted in Europe on several fronts. News of the war littered the papers and was the talk on the streets. Many of us began to wonder how long the U.S. would stay out of the war. We were lucky so far, our country had stayed out of the war. Men were dying by the hundreds daily. If we entered, would I be sent to fight? Could the government make me fight? Would I want to fight?

Joseph and Michael Kokoska
Photo courtesy Charles Kokaska

The United States avoided becoming involved until after the sinking of the *Lusitania* by the Germans. This was something which could not be overlooked and the country had to fight back. As a result, the United States declared war on Germany on April 6, 1917. The government then passed the Selective Service Act in May of 1917 in order to raise thousands of troops to prepare for war. It looked like the questions I had asked a few years earlier had been answered.

Everyone was required to register for the draft. I registered for in Chicago on June 5, 1917. At the time, all men between the ages of 21 and 31 were required to register.[8] I chose to enlist in the Army and was inducted on

August 10, 1917.[9] I was now 26 years old and felt a duty to protect my family and country. I also felt a sense of adventure and did not want to be looked at as a coward. I was unmarried and could come and go as I pleased. My parents were nervous about my decision but I was a man and had to make my own choice.

Initially, I was assigned to the 343rd Infantry Division, Company D.[10] I then transferred into the 64th Infantry Brigade, 32nd Division, 127th Infantry, Company L, on December 17, 1917 where I remained for the duration of my service.[11]

I went through basic training at Camp Grant in Rockford, Illinois which was built specifically for World War I training.[12] The first troops of the National Army were received at Camp Grant on Labor Day, September 3, 1917. Thirty-seven thousand troops were reported as having marched through the Rockford cantonment.

Camp Grant was a military city comprised of areas for the soldiers and areas for training. There were 126 barracks which were to house 200 men each with sleeping areas, mess, and bathing facilities, 130 lavatories, 15 regimental infirmaries, a base hospital with 63 buildings, and 10 general stores for the needs of the soldiers. The hospital was built with the intention of not only attending to the sick and injured at Camp Grant, but those returning home from France in need of medical care.

To accommodate training, there were 40 regular stores which allowed for one for each battalion, 10 miles of road, a rifle range, drill grounds which were 1,000 feet by one mile in length, and a maneuvering ground which was 2 ½ miles long and ½ a mile wide.[13]

The contractors ensured no refuse was left in the camp as it was built and the construction workers resided there. Health was a concern for all involved as everyone learned more about diseases and their causes. The facilities were always kept clean.

Fire safety within the camp was another major concern which the contractors took seriously. The buildings were built on streets 100 feet wide with a 50 foot alley separating each building. Every nine buildings formed a brigade and at the end of each was a 300 foot separation or "firebreak." There were water buckets spread all over the camp and over 250 high pressure water hydrants in case of fire. At the time of opening, three firehouses were being completed which contained the latest in fire fighting equipment and vehicles. Men from each regiment would be trained as firefighters at Camp Grant to ensure the safety of the others.[14]

After basic training, additional training for the 32nd Infantry Division was held at Camp MacArthur near Waco, Texas. The Division underwent 16 weeks of training which included learning to use new weapons, grenade training, the correct use of a gas mask, and trench warfare.

Trench warfare was a different type of war than the U.S. troops had seen before. In this type of combat, each side dug trenches and fortified the sides with wooden beams. The men lived in these trenches rather than in tents out in the open. Trenches were dug for front line fighting, to hold reserve troops, emergency supplies, communication lines, and living. There was no way to irrigate the trenches so when rain water or snow accumulated in the trenches, the men had to build walkways to navigate. There was the constant threat of having wet feet and fear of getting trench foot, a condition which could lead to gangrene. It was important to try to keep our feet dry.

Just outside Camp MacArthur, a system of trenches was constructed for use in training. By November and December 1917, our Division was visited and deemed ready for action overseas. Now all we had to do was wait for the order to ship out.

32nd Division Red Arrow Patch

On January 2, 1918, the 32nd Infantry Division Headquarters staff moved from Waco, Texas, to Camp Merritt, New Jersey. The staff then traveled to the Port of Embarkation at Hoboken, New Jersey, where they set sail for France.[15] By January 24, 1918, the advance party of the 32nd Infantry had arrived at Brest, France. We were the sixth American Expeditionary Force to arrive.

Much of the 32nd Infantry Division was made a replacement division in early March 1918, where it set up headquarters at Prauthoy, Haute Marne, France.[16] The 127th Infantry Regiment was not included in this change. The 127th Infantry Regiment was part of a group moved from base ports to Bordeaux, Dijon, St-Nazaire and Vaucouleurs for duty with the Services of Supply division.[17] Our regiment was ordered to rejoin the 32nd Division, at the end of March.

By April 10, the entire 32nd Division was removed as a Replacement Division and sent to the 10th Training Area to prepare for the Front.

Conditions in the early part of 1918 in France were horrible. The weather was cold and damp. As a result, we were freezing, soaked, and exhausted from training in bad weather and digging and building trenches. Despite the weather, we still trained on the rifle ranges, and practiced trench warfare tactics.

I sent a letter home to my Sister dated April 12, 1918.[18]

Dear Sister,

I sent you a souvenir for your trouble a few days ago but I forgot all about your friend. I thought it would be a good thing if you and her would have the same. I know that she has a fellow in the Army, but maybe she didn't get something like this from him.

Michael Kokoska, WWI. Photo courtesy Charles Kokaska

I will send each & one of you a souvenir just as soon as I get a few French money again. I got a quiet [quite] a few letters to answer but I got so much work to do that I don't get time to write.

I whish [wish] you will excuse me this time & as soon as I get time to write again I will tell you all about the pretty French girls I got out here. I whish you'll tell Joe that I didn't get the Bible he send [sent] me. I think that I will get it pretty soon for some of the boys told me that the mail boat land in port again. Well I will have to remain for it is getting late & I don't no [know] what to write any more.

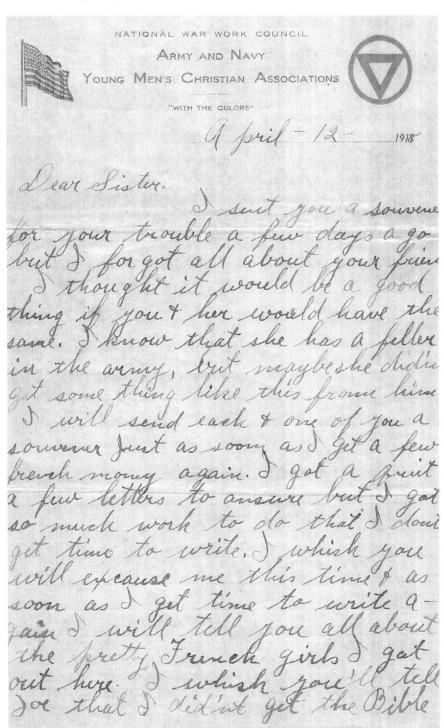

NATIONAL WAR WORK COUNCIL
ARMY AND NAVY
YOUNG MEN'S CHRISTIAN ASSOCIATIONS
"WITH THE COLORS"

April - 12 - 1918

Dear Sister.

I sent you a souvene
for your trouble a few days a go
but I for got all about your frin
I thought it would be a good
thing if you & her would have the
same. I know that she has a feller
in the army, but maybe she didn
get some thing like this from him
I will send each & one of you a
souvener just as soon as I get a few
french mony again. I got a quit
a few letters to answer but I got
so much work to do that I dont
get time to write. I whish you
will excause me this time & as
soon as I get time to write a-
gain I will tell you all about
the pretty French girls I get
out here. I whish you'll tell
Joe that I did'nt get the Bible

NATIONAL WAR WORK COUNCIL

ARMY AND NAVY

YOUNG MEN'S CHRISTIAN ASSOCIATIONS

"WITH THE COLORS"

_____1917

he send me. I think that I will
get it pretty soon. for some of the
boys told me that the mail boat
land in port again. Well I will
have to remain for it is geting
late & I dont no what to write
any more.
        Whishing you all
my best regards.
            From Private
                Michael Kokos
        Co. L. 127th Inf.
A. E. F. Via New York.

Whishing you all my best regards.

From Private Michael Kokoska

Co. L. 127th Inf A.E.F. Via New York

By May 14, 1918, the 32nd Infantry Division was moved to an area of the French 7th Army near La Chappelle-sous-Rouge Mont.[19] A few days later, the 32nd Infantry Division was given the order to move to the region of Belfort in Alsace, Germany. The 32nd Infantry Division became the "First on German Soil."[20]

Between June 15 and July 15, 1918, the 32nd was in tactical command of not only their troops but also of the 9th French Division as well. We were responsible for the sector from Aspach le Bas to the Rhine-Rhone Canal. During this time in Alsace, training continued and there were a few raids but no major offensives. Some considered it a "quiet sector." Patrols went out nightly into "No Man's Land" and American control was kept. As the French troops were slowly withdrawn, however, the American Expeditionary Force became more active in this area. It was no longer considered a "quiet sector."

I was stationed on the front lines, "quiet sector" in Alsace only 12 days. One of my duties was to patrol the trenches. I carried a heavy rifle slung over my shoulder. It swung side to side as I patrolled the trenches. My jacket protected me from the elements and my boots protected me from what lied or scurried about in the trenches. We had a huge problem with rats in the trenches. They gnawed on us if we slept and we had to fight to keep them out of our rations. Sometimes the guys shot rats in the trenches to thin out the population. It didn't seem to help though as there were always more.

Today is June 27, 1918 and I am on patrol at dusk in the trenches of the "quiet sector." I heard someone approaching, yelled halt and stood with my gun ready. I saw Private Howard come around the corner. He stopped and stood in the ready position, it was the last thing I remembered.

Josef and Magdalena's Grief

I cannot believe my son is dead. Majdalena and I were notified of Michael's death by Western Union Telegram on August 10, 1918. The telegram stated,

Deeply regret to inform you that it is officially reported that private Michael Kokoska inf Died June twenty seven from accidental gunshot wound.[21]

My heart stopped and I could barely breathe when I received the telegram. But a man has to be strong for his family. I could not let them see how much it affected me.

My son died almost two months ago and we are just hearing about it now. How is this possible? Is it so hard to send a letter across the ocean? It seems the news travels fast enough so why not a notice about our dead son? What really happened? Accidental gunshot? Why is that all we are told? Did he suffer?

The war ended and we waited for word on Michael. Where was he buried? When would his remains come home? How long would it take? We sent three sons to war and Michael was the only one we lost.

It would be years before anyone would know the real story, which is what Sergeant Elmer J. Black reported and signed almost a year after Michael's death.[22] It is unknown if Josef and Majdalena ever knew anything beyond the fact that Michael's death was accidental. Based on the records and paperwork, it appears they were never told anything else.

"While we were in the trenches at SS Manspach, Alsace at GC 65, Kokoska was standing guard just about dusk about the 27th or 28th of June, 1918. Just then Pvt. Richard Howard came around the corner of a traverse trench and Kokoska halted him with his gun at the position of ready. Howard admitted later that he had been shooting rats and that he had reloaded his rifle and forgot to put on the safety lock, and when halted came to the ready position, accidently pulling the trigger, and shot Kokoska thru the neck. I helped to put Kokoska on a stretch and Kokoska's last words were, "Let me at those Germans." I do not believe that Kokoska knew that Howard shot him. When I last saw Kokoska he was unconscious but not dead."

How can I explain the pain associated with losing a child? We lost Emilie when she was just a baby. We loved, raised and held Michael close for 27 years. His light extinguished much too soon. The pain slashes our family like a knife. It's too close and too heartbreaking to discuss very often. Yet his mother and I do discuss it. I often think it hurts her more than anyone else.

Michael Kokoska, photo courtesy Charles Kokaska

We became concerned we would never be able to claim his body and it would remain forever buried in foreign soil. With the fear in my heart that I would never again have my dear son home, I wrote a letter to the Graves Registration Service.[23]

Chicago, IL
Dec. 17, 1919

Chief Graves Reg. Bureau, Wash. D.C.

Dear Sir

Please be so kind and furnish us with the location of Our Dear Son's Grave. Name Michael Kokoska Co L. 127 Inf. Died of accidental gunshot wound June 27 1918.

Please also let us know if we will ever be able to claim his body. He gave his [life] to France we are proud of that but would like to have his body honor our cemetery lot and as we are old and know we have not much more years or days to live we think we could die happily to know Our Son is resting with us.

We had four sons in the Army he is the only one we ever lost. Please answer as soon as you can for although he is dead a year and a half we do not know where he is buried.

Thanking you in advance we remain

Joseph & Madg. Kokoska
2122 W 18th Place, Chicago, IL

The Army did not reply for a month. In a letter dated January 19, 1920, the Grave Registration Service finally provided us with the location of Michael's grave.[24]

Office of the Quartermaster General Graves Registration Service, Washington, D.C.

January 19, 1920

Mr. Joseph Kokoska
2122 W. 18th Place, Chicago, Ill.

In reply to your inquiry we beg to say that the records of the Graves Registration Service contain the following information as to grave location:

Case of: Pvt. Michael Kokoska,
                  #275180
                  Co. L. 127th Inf

*Place of burial: French Military Cemetery, Morvillars,
Department of Ter-de-Belfort.*

*The grave has been registered and suitably marked for
present purposes, pending the adoption of a more permanent
monument by the National Fine Arts Commission, which now
has the matter under consideration.*

*While it is a sad duty on our part to convey information
concerning the burial of men who were our valiant comrades,
it is a satisfaction to answer the queries of those who suffer
so grievously by the casualties of War.*

By authority of the Quartermaster General:

*Charles C. Pierce
Colonel, Q.M. Corps, Chief, Graves Registration Service*

The Chief of the Graves Registration Service also included a
booklet about the return of the war dead for our information.

More time passed and it was June 1920. I sent another letter to
the Graves Registration Service again asking about Michael's body.[25]

Chicago, Ill

June 7, 1920

*War Department, Office of the Quartermaster General,
Graves Reg. Service, Wash. D.C.
Charles C. Pierce*

Dear Sir.

*We beg to inquire of the body of Our Son Pvt. Michael
Kokoska #275180 Co L. 127th Inf. Place of burial: French
Military Cemetery, Dept of Ter-de-Belfort.*

*As we read by the papers about the bodies of our soldiers
being brought here and of some that are from our own City
we would like to hear from you. It is over a year now that*

we received a card to fill out if we want the body of Our Son home we answered yes we have been waiting patiently ever since. We have bought a burial lot on our Bohemian National Cemetery.

A certain paper stated those wanting the bodies of their Soldier boys home to write for them. Hoping that this is the place to write to. We are asking if Our Sons Body could be sent home soon. As we are getting old we feel bad about seeing and hearing of others sent home and not Our Son.
Any answer from you will be appreciated.

Sincerely,
Mr. J. & Madg. Kokoska

The time from learning of Michael's death until we were able to receive his body in our home in Chicago seemed like an eternity. We were seeing and hearing of so many Chicago boys coming home and we could not understand why our Michael had yet to be returned. I received no reply to my letter.

Summer passed and fall arrived. The children were in school again and Majdalena and I had still not heard about Michael's body. It was time to write another letter.[26]

Oct. 21, 1920

Charles C. Pierce, Major U.S. Army Chief Cemeterial Division

Dear Sir:

In answer to your letter of the 18th. Michael Kokoska is not survived by widow or children. He was a single man living with parents at 2122 West 18th Place. I am his father.

Joseph Kokoska
Mother: Madg. Kokoska

We waited and there was no response from the Army. Another year drew to a close and 1921 dawned with the hope that we would soon have our dear son back with us to bury in our cemetery. But it was not to be just yet. I had to write another letter asking about Michael.[27]

Chicago IL
Feb. 15, 1921

Cemeterial Division, Washington D.C.
Dear Sir,

Am asking about the remains of Our Son Michael Ko-koska Co L. 127 Inf.

I've wrote several letters asking to have them sent home you ans [answered.] They would send them home after Sept 15, 1920. Several remains arrived here by not my Sons. Please let us know if our papers were not filled out correctly or if we made some mistake. Because some of the remains sent here were of Soldiers that died of a later date than our Son. We would like to have him at home already because we think he should have been here already.

Please let us know if there is a way in which we could get him home soon. Thank you in advance for whatever informa-tion or advice.

We remain.

Respectfully,
Josef & Madg. Kokoska

Finally at the end of February I received a response. But yet we were told they needed more information and we would have to con-tinue to wait.[28]

February 28, 1921

From: The Quartermaster General, U.S. Army (Cemete-rial Division)

To: Mr. and Mrs. Josef Kokoska
2122 W. 18th Place, Chicago, IL

Subject: Return of Body

In reply to your letter of February 15, 1921, you are advised that your request that the body of your son, Private Michael Kokoska, Company L, 127th Infantry, be returned to you for private interment is on record in this office and your wishes will be complied with in the event that the deceased is not survived by a widow or child. It is, therefore, requested that you advise definitely whether or not such relatives survive, and if so, that the name, or names, and address, or addresses, of each be furnished this office without delay.

The bodies of the American soldier dead are returned to this country according to a plan based on the geographical location of the cemeteries in which they are buried and not according to the date of death of the soldiers.

Operations incident to the removal of the American soldier dead are in progress in the French Military Cemetery at Morvillars, Department of Ter-de-Belfort, in which the remains of your son are buried. It is impossible to state definitely when this particular case will be reached but the legal next of kin will be notified by telegram from our branch office at Hoboken as soon as possible after receipt of information from Europe that the remains have been shipped. He is again notified by telegram from Hoboken upon shipment of the remains from Hoboken, New Jersey.

By authority of the Quartermaster General:

Charles J. Wynne, 2nd Lieut., Q.M.C.

I filled out the card the Quartermaster requested and returned it giving permission to have his remains brought home. I also send another letter once again confirming that Michael was a bachelor and had no children.[29]

Chicago Ill.
March 3, 1921

Charles J. Wynne
2nd Lieut. Q.M.C.

Dear Sir,

There is no such relatives as (Wife or Children) surviving Michael Kokoska. He was a Single Man and live with us his parents.

Joseph & Madge Kokoska
2122 West 18 Place, Chicago, Ill

A few days later I received a letter that Michael's remains would be sent to us. It seemed the long wait was finally about to end.[30]

> *March 11th, 1921*
> *File No. 293.8 Cem. Div., Cor. Branch.*
> *(KOKOSKA, Michael)*
>
> *Dear Sir:*
>
> *Remains of the late Private Michael Kokoska, Serial Number 275180, Company L, 127th Infantry, to be returned to the United States and shipped to you at 2122 West 18th Place, Chicago, Illinois.*

After we received word that Michael's body would arrive soon, I sent a telegram to the Graves Registration Service in Hoboken, New Jersey which acknowledging their letter.[31] [32] We then received a telegram in May that his remains would be delivered soon. We were overjoyed.

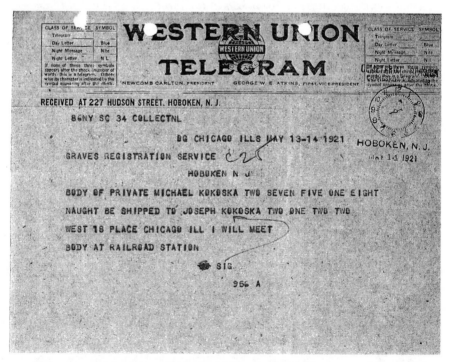

When we knew his body would be back, I placed a death notice in the *Denni Hlasatel* newspaper in Chicago. [The obituary was written in Czech and the translation reads,]

*With deep dejection and grief we announce to all rela-
tives and friends that, brought to us from far France were the
remains of our beloved Son and Brother, soldier MICHAEL
KOKOSKA from Company L, 127th Infantry where he was
interred from 27 June 1918 at the Morvillars Ter-De-Belfort
Cemetery. The dear departed was born in Chicago where he
was a member of Lodge Praha M.W. of A. 12042. The funeral
will be held on Sunday 29 May 1921 at 2:00 P.M. from the
Funeral Home 2122 W. 18th Place and then to The Bohemian
National Cemetery. JOSEF & MAJDALENA KOKOSKA,
Parents; Josef, Frank, Karel, Vaclav, Albert, Edward & Emil,
brothers; Mary Darda & Anna, Sisters. Those wishing to attend the funeral come to the Funeral establishment of Marik
and Sons. Telephone Lawndale 3972.*[33]

Michael's Return

It is May 27, 1921 and I wait on the platform at the rail depot listening for the deep thunderous rumble of the train coming down the
track. Although there are many people waiting for this train and their
dead soldiers, I feel isolated from them. Alone. Invisible.

A slight breeze caresses my cheek as if to say hello, you are not
alone. The skies are cloudy and dark as if the heavens are preparing
to shed their tears along with mine. I hear a distant whistle, a groan
of thunder, and my heart cracking. The train and the pain are close
like a storm about to explode in the sky.

Today is the day my son arrives back from the war. He arrives
not walking off the train, but carried off in a flag draped casket.
Dead almost three years now and buried in a foreign land. We did
not know where he was buried for almost two years after he was
killed. This was the land his mother and I left years ago. How ironic
he should die there when we came here to give our children a life of
hope, plenty, and most importantly .... peace.

The clouds gather close as the train arrives, slowly, slowly, grind-
ing its brakes as it grinds pain into my heart. Finally the train comes
to a stop. My heart stops too for a moment. The doors open in front
of me as if in a dream. Soldiers march in formation off the train and
stand guard in a present arms state outside the baggage car doors as
the families wait silently. Breaths are held as we await the unloading
of our soldiers. I see tears silently sliding down the faces of some of
the women as they place their hands on their hearts and bow their

heads in solemn prayer. I feel their pain and my chest aches. It is becoming more difficult to hold back the tears.

The grief I first felt when I learned of Michael's death has returned with a vengeance. It is as if the storm brewing in the air is brewing inside me just waiting to be released. The grief consumes me as it explodes once again in my aching chest. Sadness seeps from me through the air to the boxes holding the caskets which carry the soldiers. Can the soldiers feel my pain? It's so real you can almost touch it.

Box after box is carried off the train. Soldiers appear carrying my son. They place Michael's box gently on the floor next to the other boxes which are laid side by side in the train station lobby. The soldiers await orders on where to transport the boxed caskets from here. The grief of all the men, women, and children standing in this room waiting to sign for their soldier is thick and oppressing like high humidity and I can hardly breathe. I wonder how long this pain will last.

I sign the receipt of remains for my dear son and give directions on where the casket should be delivered. I turn to depart the train station and leave a piece of my heart behind as I go.

Caskets of Soldier Dead awaiting delivery. Photo courtesy American Battle Monuments Commission.

The next day our dear son was laid in state at home in our parlor. His mother and I waited so long for this moment. Visitors file into our home throughout the day on May 28, and pay their respects. There is no laughter in the house today. The grief filled the room. Something we could not have avoided no matter how hard we tried.

May 29, 1921 arrives and soon it will be time to bury our son. It is a beautiful day, fair, sunny, and warm.[34] A white carriage stands in front of the house. The street is filled with family, friends, and neighbors. Men from all branches of the service enter the house to remove his casket. They load his casket in the white carriage.

Michael's funeral. Photos courtesy Charles Kokaska.

A military band leads the solemn procession down 18th Place from our house. We follow the carriage in more than 12 cars. We make our way north to Bohemian National Cemetery where a full military burial service is held.

Michael's funeral. Photo courtesy Charles Kokaska.

The white carriage stops next to the area where Michael will be buried. A military chaplain awaits us. An honor guard acting as pall bearers gently extract his flag draped casket from the carriage and carefully laid it next to the open hole which will serve as his final resting place. The chaplain begins speaking, although I hear very little of what he has to say. My thoughts rest on my dear son lying quietly in the casket at my feet. The chaplain finishes speaking and a group of rifleman fires a salute.

After the boom of the guns, an eerie silence descends upon us all. Then the mournful sound of a trumpet and Taps is played. The family gathers close and sadness washes over us like an ocean wave.

When Taps is finished, the deathly silence envelopes us all as the flag which covered Michael's casket was taken off and folded very precisely. With her heart shattering and head bowed as her tear filled eyes are fixed on Michael's casket, Majdalena weeps, the tears staining her cheeks. She raises her head and looks at the soldiers standing before her with Michael's flag. She stretches out her arms to receive the flag. Pulling it close to her heart she bows her head again and sobs knowing she will never again hold her son.

We say our last goodbyes as Michael is lowered into the ground and finally laid to rest. Maybe now that he is home with us the pain will begin to subside. Maybe now we can all find some peace and begin to heal.

The last of the dirt is placed upon the grave and people begin to depart. Our family stands there a bit longer to reflect on our dear son and his sacrifice which allows us to live free and in peace. We are proud of our son and his service.

As we walk away, I turn one last time to say goodbye to Michael. He was named after Michael, the archangel patron of protection and love. Our son now lies near a tall monument with a statue of an infantryman standing guard and protecting us all.

Michael Kokoska's grave 1920s. Photo courtesy Charles Kokaska.

4

The Replacement
Frank Winkler

29th Infantry Division, 115th Infantry Regiment, Co. G

(1924 – 1944)

The Family Story

My grandmother told me a story about my cousin Frankie Winkler, saying he enlisted in the Army when he was 19. He had started college but chose to enlist because of the guilt he felt for not fighting. His father, Frank Sr. did not approve of his choice. It was said that Frank Sr. was very protective of his only living son. So protective he wouldn't let him even ride a bike for fear he would be hurt. Family lore also said Frankie's uncle, Frank Kokoska, would join the fight and watch over Frankie.

As the story continued, my grandmother said Frankie came ashore on Omaha Beach on D-Day with the 29th Infantry Division. He spoke German and was doing reconnaissance work. I wondered how they would have known he was in reconnaissance.

My grandmother also told me Frankie died on June 24, 1944 of head wounds received on D-Day. A photo appeared in Life Magazine of a soldier sitting on a beach on D-Day with his head wrapped, holding a cigarette in one hand and a pack of smokes in the other. The family to this day swears it is Frankie.

I've seen this photo and I'm not sure it is him. I can see some resemblance and can understand why the family chose to believe it was him. That photograph was something for them to hold on to. Hope that he was still alive. Hope that he would emerge alive from the war.

The story continued and grandma told me when Frankie's remains were returned to Chicago, his mother was too distraught to view them. Instead, Frankie's uncle and

Frankie's parents, Frank and Jennie Winkler.
Photo courtesy Blanche Branecki.

father went to the funeral home. After viewing the remains they did not think it was Frankie. This did not make sense to me. Why would they not have thought the remains sent home were his?

I listened to my grandmother's story, took notes and left it at that. It was not until my parents European vacation in October 2010 in which answers to my questions began to emerge. My parents visited several American Battle Monuments Commission cemeteries. They asked many questions about the war and where to locate information on Frankie's service. Using the information my parents provided, I spent two years researching his story and discovered many twists and turns. In the end, the story I uncovered is different from the family lore.

Thoughts on the Research

Frankie's story is one which has evolved over many years. I had the family lore, facts based on records I located, and the words of a veteran of the 29th Infantry, 115th Regiment. Yet, the puzzle I was piecing together kept changing.

Unfortunately, Frankie's service records burned in the 1973 fire at the National Personnel Records Center in St. Louis. His exact whereabouts between October 1943 and June 24, 1944, are unknown. To complicate matters further, there are Morning Reports which show his entrance into the 29th Infantry, but they do not say where he specifically came from upon transfer. His footsteps cannot be traced backwards from his entrance into the 29th Infantry Division through other records.

At the writing of this book, I feel confident in my assessment of the information available through military records, World War II history, and the events which unfolded after D-Day in France. Of course, there is always the possibility new information will surface in the future which will change his story. Only time will tell.

What follows here is the story based on the long winding road of records I encountered. There are multiple dates given at times for the same event. It came to the point where I had to create a table to make it all make sense. Not all soldier stories are created equal. We need to keep in mind as we research; the records were created by humans. Humans make mistakes, especially when they are under a great deal of stress. There is one report created within the company which contained the most accurate information, and it was the Company

Morning Report. This is the report I used on which to base Frankie's death date.

Errors in dates occurred during war time because of many reasons. There was a lag between when a soldier was in a unit, then perhaps missing in action or killed in action. There was a lag between the time he or his remains were recovered and the reports within the company were updated. There was a lag between when an event occurred and the military notified the family of the event as well as a lag between when the military notifies the newspapers of the event. Dates may be transcribed incorrectly or reported wrong because there was so much chaos and death.

We were not there and can only write our stories based on what the records tell us. And when information differs between reports, we have to navigate that carefully and explain our reasoning for using certain pieces of information.

I wish I could go back in time and talk to Frankie's parents. I would tell them what happened to their son based on what I know today. I would explain why they received so few personal effects. I'd try to ease their pain. If I could go back in time, I'd ask them to sit on the sofa, get comfortable, and listen to a story about an Infantry Replacement Soldier named Frankie Winkler. This is what I would tell them.

The Replacement Soldier

Frankie Winkler circa 1925. Photo courtesy Blanche Branecki.

Frankie Winkler was born on November 1, 1924 in Chicago, Illinois, to Frank and Jenny, nee Kokoska, Winkler.[1] In 1940, prior to the start of World War II, Frankie was 15 years old and attended Farragut High School.[2] As a 15 year old, Frankie probably did not pay much attention to the fact Hitler was invading countries in Europe and taking control. He probably did not give it much thought whether the U.S. might ever be involved or if he would.

Frankie graduated from Farragut High School in January 1942 and began college.[3] By this time, the world as he knew it had changed and everyone knew it was only a matter of time before he too would be required to fight.

You didn't want Frankie to go fight. He was attending college. You were afraid yet another one of your children would die. You had lost so many already. Yet, people came into your butcher shop and asked why your son was not fighting. Was he a coward? Why was another person's son sent off to fight and your son was not?

You know it wasn't a matter of cowardice. It was a matter of college, age, and timing. So you told people Frankie had enlisted in the Army but it was not the reality of the situation. He was drafted into the Army on

Frankie graduation. Photo courtesy Blanche Branecki.

September 29, 1943 at the age of 18 years and 10 months of age.[4] By late 1943, the U.S. Army's draft age requirement had changed. No longer did the Army want fresh 18 year old men.

> The family said he enlisted but his serial number was 36695605. Two pieces of evidence discredit the enlistment story. First, a search of the National Archives database, Electronic Army Serial Number Merged File, ca. 1938 - 1946 (Enlistment Records), does not list a Frank Winkler that matches my Frankie.[5] Second, according to the numeration of serial numbers, those assigned to World War II draftees ranged between, 31,000,000 and 39,000,000.[6]

I heard from Jennie's sister Rose, my grandma, their brother Frank Kokoska would watch over Frankie if he enlisted. However, when I looked into Frank Kokoska's records, he was already involved in the fight. He was part of the 33rd Infantry Division, 108th Combat Engineers. He had no pull with officials to determine where Frankie would end up for training or if he would go overseas.

In October 1943, Frankie was sent to basic training and stationed in Camp Wolters, Texas. The U.S. Army had been planning a massive invasion into France for months. The Army knew there would be a need for Army Infantry replacements and camps were established around the U.S. to train replacements. Camp Wolters, Texas, was one such camp.

After basic training, the men were transferred either overseas to the Pacific theater or England or Ireland for additional training and placement in a Replacement Depot.

The U.S. Army had a replacement policy for World War II. A replacement depot with soldiers was available to replace a combat unit with as many men or as close to as many men as were lost in battle. These replacement soldiers were supposed to have the same job or "Military Occupational Specialty" (MOS) as the soldier they were replacing.

The units which needed the replacements were on the front lines for weeks or months at a time. The Army thought if they could replenish these units from a group of replacement soldiers there was no reason to take them off the front lines. The 29th Infantry Divi-

Frankie 29th Infantry. Photo courtesy the late Blanche Branecki.

sion was one unit which constantly received replacements.

Unfortunately, veteran soldiers in these units felt the effects of the 'repple depple' or replacement depot syndrome.[7] The unit veterans were exhausted by combat and their morale was low due to weather, constant fear of death, and the very visible aspects of war. Adding replacement soldiers who were inexperienced in combat did not bring confidence to these veterans.

The men who were classified as replacements were trained in the U.S. and then shipped overseas to enter a replacement depot. The men they trained with were usually not the ones they ended up with in the replacement depot. And the friends they made at the replacement depot were not usually the ones they were sent into battle with when they were needed to fill a combat unit.

Because of this, the bonds they formed with other soldiers were broken and they became what some would consider as orphans of the military. They had no group of soldiers with whom they had a bond and no cohesive unit to consider "home." Many of these men entered a unit and were killed or reported Missing In Action within 24-48 hours before anyone knew their name. Unfortunately, this appears to be what happened to Frankie.

After training, Frankie was sent overseas to Ireland. I suspect he sent a letter home which said what country he was in, otherwise how would you have known this? It is impossible to know just where Frank was stationed in Ireland. There were many Replacement Depots scattered throughout that area. Frank's Company Morning Report for June 25, 1944, did not state which Depot he came from, just that he was assigned from 29th Division Headquarters.

Frankie did not enter France on D-Day like you thought. He arrived a few days later with a group of replacements for the 29th infantry. Replacements were brought into France through Omaha Beach after D-Day. Because of the fire which destroyed many service records, there is no information as to where he entered France and how he ended up where the 29th Infantry Division, 115th Regiment, Company G was stationed on June 23, 1944.

I spoke with the 29th Infantry Division Historian, Joe Balkoski about Frankie. Joe felt Frankie was likely sent out on a patrol the 23rd of June and never returned.

You received a telegram on July 25, 1948 from the War Department saying Frankie was listed as Missing in Action. He was not. This was some sort of error in paperwork. The Morning Report dated July 4, 1944, stated Frankie was killed in action on June 24, 1944.[9]

France, after the D-Day invasion, was filled with American Troops constantly on the move fighting the Germans. The company clerks did their best to keep track of their troops but reporting accurately on a daily basis was almost impossible due to the movements. There were also so many casualties and wounded, it was difficult to process them all in a timely manner. It is likely Frankie wandered unknowingly behind enemy lines and his body was not recovered immediately. This could account for an error in the paperwork also.

The Report of Death filed by the Graves Registration Service stated Frank was killed in action on June 24, 1944 and the War Department had received sufficient evidence of this death by August 4, 1944. This information also terminated his Missing in Action status.[10] You were likely notified of his death after August 4, 1944. The Chicago Daily Tribune reported Frank's death in the November 3, 1944 issue, roughly three months after the War Department received confirmation of his death.[11]

Some of Frank's personal effects were recovered and sent to you. These included 620 Francs, 2 cents – U.S., 4 souvenir coins, papers, and ring.[12] These effects were registered with the Army Service Forces Army Effects Bureau on August 30, 1944. With the effects, you were sent a letter and asked to sign and return one copy confirming receipt. You complied and also sent a letter back to the Army asking about additional effects.

November 19, 1944

Dear Sir,

A few days ago our family received the package with our son's personal property. Those few things that we did receive belong to our son but what we want to know is if they are going to send any more.

We know for a fact that he carried more personal things on him and we are wondering why we didn't get them. For one thing, he always carried all his papers and identification cards in his wallet which we did not receive, and he also always wore his wrist watch. We neither one of these along with other things I need not mention.

Could you please tell us if what we have is all that we are to receive or if we are to get more.

Also, could you tell us if these things we did receive were found on his body.

We shall appreciate your giving us any further information that you can, for as you know, we can't help but want to know all we possibly can. Thanking you very much, we are —

Very truly Yours,

Frank Winkler

The letter stated,

November 19, 1944

Dear Sir,

A few days ago our family received the package with our son's personal property. Those few things that we did receive belong to our son but what we want to know is if they are going to send any more.

We know for a fact that he carried more personal things on him and we are wondering why we didn't get them. For one thing, he always carried all his papers and identification cards in his wallet which we did not receive, and he also always wore his wrist watch. We neither one of these along with other things I need not mention.

Could you please tell us if what we have is all that we are to receive or if we are to get more.

Also, could you tell us if the things we did receive were found on his body.

We shall appreciate your giving us any further information that you can for as you know, we can't help but to want to know all we possibly can. Thanking you very much we are.

Very truly yours,
Frank Winkler[13]

The government responded there were no other effects located for Frankie.

Frankie's remains were interred in France until the war ended. His Report of Burial stated he was buried in La Cambe Cemetery located 17 miles north of St. Lo, in France, in grave number 146, row 8, plot F. To his right laid M.J. Cenar and to his left laid J. Van-Loon.[14]

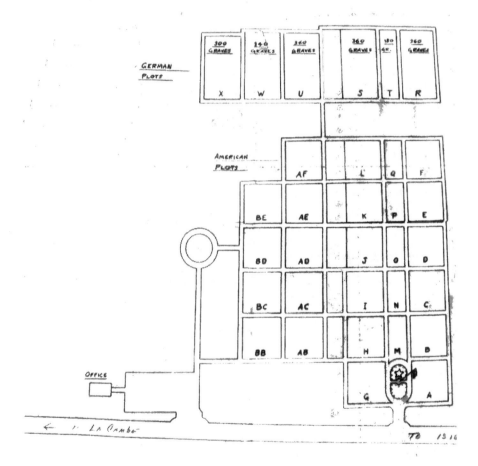

La Cambe Cemetery Plan, 1944, Drawing courtesy of Christian Levaufre, La Cambe Cemetery, France.

You were not notified of his grave location until December 2, 1946, a year and a half after his death.[15] It took this long to notify you because only after the war had ended, the Army was able to being the process of final interment of our country's Soldier Dead. Sadly, the newspapers never really talked about the work of the Graves Registration Service and the temporary cemeteries overseas. You would not have known why there was such a delay in news about Frankie.

On July 31, 1947, you received a letter from the Quartermaster General stating you had the option of having the government repatriate the remains of Frankie or have him buried in a permanent American Cemetery overseas. You chose to have him repatriated.

A Disinterment Directive was completed on October 15, 1947 and Frankie's remains were disinterred at La Cambe Cemetery on October 31. His remains were described as advanced decomposition

Disinterment Directive for Frank Winkler.

because he had been buried almost three years at this point. His remains were then prepared and he was dressed in fatigues and placed in a new casket on November 6, 1947. His remains were prepared for shipment to the United States.[16]

You received a telegram on May 3, 1948 from the Chicago Quartermaster Depot stating Frankie's remains would be delivered on Monday, May 3, 1948 at approximately 1:30 p.m. accompanied by military escort. The remains were received by A. Linhart & Sons Funeral Home.[17] Frankie was interred in Bohemian National Cemetery in May just after his remains were returned.

You applied for a military headstone on July 14, 1948. Unfortunately you wrote that Frankie was part of the 129th Infantry but this was incorrect. There was not a 129th Infantry, just a 29th Infantry. [18] I imagine you were very distraught at the time you completed the application. The Office of the Quartermaster General did not catch this error or compare the information to other records. Frankie's gravestone was incorrectly carved. Even though something is "written in stone" does not always make it accurate. The stone ordered was upright marble with no emblem.

The full details of Frankie's military service may never be known. Sadly, as you were experiencing everything, the government wasn't giving you much information. They kept much out of the news and in some cases, just did not think the families could handle everything. War is hell as we all know.

I hope I have brought you some measure of peace by explaining what happened. Nothing can bring Frankie back, but we can preserve his memory for eternity through his story.

Frankie Winkler grave. Author's photo.

5

The Tiger
Robert R. Brouk

American Volunteer Group (Flying Tigers) and

Captain in the U.S. Army Air Corps

(1917 – 1942)

The Family Story

Around 1996, my uncle showed me a photograph of a flying cadet. He told me the pilot was Robert Brouk and he had been a Flying Tiger. I had no idea what a Flying Tiger was at that time.

The story was Robert joined the American Volunteer Group and when they disbanded in July of 1942, returned home to Chicago a hero. After returning home, he met and married a woman named Virginia Scharer. About three weeks after they married he was killed in a plane crash in Florida. No one knew what happened to Virginia.

By the time my uncle told me the story, Robert's parents and brother had passed away. There was no one left from that part of the family and at that point, no way to finish his story.

The Tiger

Robert Ralph Brouk was born September 2, 1917, in Oak Park, Illinois. His father, Peter Brouk was a Bohemian immigrant, who arrived in the United States January 5, 1900, at the age of 10.[1] His mother, Emily Novak, was born in Chicago to Bohemian immigrants.

Peter and Emily had three children, Peter, born September 4, 1915, died April 1, 1922[2]; Robert; and Harold, born October 6, 1923, died December 23, 1983[3]. Harold joined the United States Army during World War II and was sent to Fort Warren, Wyoming, for training.[4] During World War II, Fort Warren served as a training base for U.S. Army Quartermaster Corps Soldiers.

Robert's father Peter was a sign painter, and took great pride in his community.[5] As a business owner, he was a member of the 22nd Street Business Men's Association in Cicero, where he served in the role of Secretary in 1931. The organization's goal was to revitalize and encourage growth of the businesses along 22nd Street in the villages of Cicero and Berwyn in the 1930's.[6]

As a child, Robert attended Woodrow Wilson grammar school. From 1931 to 1935, he attended J. Sterling Morton High School in Cicero, where he was active in campus clubs. Robert like many in the family was musically inclined. He participated in the Drum and Bugle Corps his freshman, sophomore, and junior years.

Yearbook photo - J. Sterling Morton Drum and Bugle Corps 1932
Photo courtesy Morton East High School Archives.

Yearbook photo - J. Sterling Morton 1934 Wrestling Team. Robert is on the
top row, fifth from the right. Photo courtesy Morton East High School Ar-
chives.

J. Sterling Morton 1935 Chemistry Club. Robert is on the top row, first person
on the right. Photo courtesy Morton East High School Archives.

Robert also had an athletic side and was a wrestler his Junior and Senior years. He also served as Vice-President of the Chemistry club his senior year; and played Intramural Sports his junior year.[7]

Robert graduated from J. Morton Sterling High School in 1935.[8] After graduation, he attended Morton Junior College, in Cicero, for two years. While attending Morton during his freshman year, Robert participated in the Chemistry Club, Engineer's Club, and continued with his wrestling.

Seated: E. Seyk, A. Jantar, S. Bourbaki, G. Thomas, C. Hosek, C. Wankat, E. Stantejsky, C. Sellen, S. Solopolous, V. Lameroux, C. Benes, J. Vendel. First Row Standing: E. Mosna, M. Molik, H. Grillot, J. Koveckis, T. Erdelyan, R. Brouk, H. Kerber, E. Sisul, J. Javorsky, O. Vasak, H. Vyletal, J. Vltek, R. Burg, J. Braun, M. McIntyre, A. Buboly, H. Gass. Second Row Standing: A. Novy, J. Koneeny, A. Wild, G. Tugana, E. Wassel, M. Kokoska, K. Brensten, M. Hlinsky, S. Palansky, W. Smaus, E. Kanak, J. Martinek, A. Yuska, O. Warning, H. Widiger, W. Plourd, E. Michl.

Yearbook photo – Morton Jr. College 1936 Engineers Club
Photo courtesy Morton Jr. College Archives.

The Engineer's Club was a very active club which took field trips to engineering departments at the University of Illinois and Purdue, the Argo Starch Company, and Universal Oil company refinery, and other similar companies. The Morton Junior College club was part of a larger group, the Midwest Engineers' Club which consisted of five other area junior colleges' clubs. This allowed ideas to be shared freely for everyone's benefit.

The Chemistry Club also took field trips to chemical laboratories of area colleges and Abbott Laboratories, in addition to conducting experiments and sharing ideas. Robert served as the secretary-treasurer during his freshman year.[9]

Fit in mind and fit in body, Robert was mentioned in a Morton wrestling article, in the Morton Collegian, because the college had the largest squad in years, and "Competition rife in the 135 lb. division with Robert Brouk..." seems to speak to Robert's competitiveness and skill. [10] The Morton Junior College Wrestling Team exceeded expectations in 1936 by winning against several four year colleges in the Chicago area.

Yearbook photo – Morton Jr. College 1936 Wrestling Team. Robert is on the bottom row, middle. Photo courtesy Morton Jr. College Archives.

Also during 1936, Robert was inducted on June 21, as a Master Builder in the Cicero Chapter, No. 12, Order of the Builders.[11] The Order of Builders is still today, a part of the Masons, for boys ages 9 to 21, and its purpose is to teach the members the principles of democracy and ideals of Freemasonry, while participating in various social, athletic and civic projects. To be inducted, the boy must be a close relation to a current Masonic member. Robert's father, Peter Brouk, was a Mason in Cicero.

During Robert's sophomore year at Morton College, he again participated in the Chemistry Club and the wrestling team.

Yearbook photo – Morton Jr. College 1937 Chemistry Club. Robert is on the bottom row, middle. Photo courtesy Morton Jr. College Archives.

The Wresting Team, in its second successive season, did not win as many matches as it had the year before. However, Robert was listed in the Pioneer Yearbook as one individual who consistently won the matches in which he competed.[12]

In the *Morton Collegian Prophecy* article about the sophomore graduating class, it was predicted that Robert would be, "Research expert for the We Chew Your Gum Co," which speaks to his probable sense of humor.[13] In the Pioneer Yearbook for 1937, it lists Robert Brouk as a Pre-Engineering Student who was, "athletic, scholastic and sociable."[14] Robert graduated from Morton Junior College on June 13, 1937.

After graduation, Robert attended Lewis Institute of Technology (currently the Illinois Institute of Technology or IIT.) It was here that Robert joined the Army Air Corps.[15]

Robert was stationed at Randolph Field in Bexar County, Texas, in 1940 where he was a flying cadet.[16] Robert graduated from the United States Army Air Corps Advanced Flying School on August 20, 1940, at Kelly Field, Texas. Upon graduation, Robert received his commission as a Second Lieutenant in the Army Air Corps Reserve.[17]

Later, while serving at Mitchel Field, Robert learned about the formation of the American Volunteer Group (AVG.) Mr. 'Skip' Adair of Central Aircraft Manufacturing Company (CAMCO) visited Mitchel Field to recruit pilots, mechanics, and armorers to join the AVG in China. The AVG was being formed by all volunteer pilots and ground crew under the leadership of Claire Lee Chennault.

In 1937, Chennault was a retired Captain of the U.S. Army Air Corps. He was working under the leadership of Madame Chaing Kai-shek between 1937 and 1941 to help China build an air force similar to the U.S. structured Army Air Corps. China was on the verge of war with Japan and needed assistance building a solid program and defense system.

After consulting for many months with the Chinese Air Force, Chennault handled the strategic planning of air raid systems, air fields, and pilot training. He flew many missions with the Chinese pilots against the Japanese and developed new combat strategies. He took this knowledge and proposed the formation of the AVG.

In Chennault's mind, the purpose of the AVG was to defend China and Burma's main roads and supply routes from Japanese attack. He also wanted to attack Japanese staging areas and supply depots. To accomplish this, he needed a well-trained group of pilots and ground crew.

Without support from the U.S. Army Air Corps or U.S. Navy, who did not want to see volunteer American pilots in China, Chennault enlisted the aid of President Roosevelt. The president sent out an unpublished executive order on April 15, 1941, encouraging pilots and ground crew to join the fight. These men would be honorably discharged from the U.S. Army Air Corps or Navy, to join the AVG and were hired by the Central Aircraft Manufacturing Company (CAMCO.) The president also authorized specific individuals to visit air fields to recruit pilots and ground crew. Mr. 'Skip' Adair of CAMCO visited Mitchel field in late April and early May 1941 where Robert was stationed. It was at here that Robert decided to join the AVG.[18]

Why were the men of the AVG known as the Flying Tigers? Chennault explained it was simply because they painted the shark toothed design on the noses of their planes. This design was not original to them, but something they copied from a R.A.F. squadron that served in the Libyan Desert. Walt Disney's company then created insignia of the plane flying through a 'V' for Victory. The design and name caught on and people all across the country were calling these men the Flying Tigers.

This story is the history of the Flying Tigers from the words and perspective of Robert Brouk. Robert proved to be an avid recorder of events and kept a diary of his experiences during his time as a pilot in the American Volunteer Group. His diary provides a graphic account of events in China at the beginning of the war. His diary is presented unchanged and in its entirety with editors comments bracketed.

"What's Next" War Diary of Robert R. Brouk

April 1941 – July 4, 1942

April through June 1941

During April and May of 1941, a Mr. 'Skip' Adair of CAMCO, came to Mitchel Field and talked to the fellows in regards to flying in China for CAMCO, mainly to protect the Burma Road. After much hullaballoo and studying pros and cons, and finally getting all the Army matters straightened out, a group of 11 of us left Mitchel around the first of June. There were Atkinson, Dupouy, Harris, Sawyer, Walroth, Little and myself from the 33rd Squadron. Kelleher, Olson, Cook and Martin were the others. We were to report to Los Angeles the 12th of June. The first group of mechanics from Mitchel sailed about the first week of June.

I arrived home in Cicero on Memorial Day and due to a hold-up in sailing, was notified to report the 18th. My mother, brother, cousin and I left Cicero on the 9th of June by car. We drove through the Southwest, stopping at main points of interest, such as Will Roger's Memorial, Painted Desert, Grand Canyon, Petrified Forest and arrived in Los Angeles the 14th. After reporting on the 16th at Harlow Aircraft in Alhambra, I learned sailing was again delayed. Those fellows already present were staying at the exclusive Johnathan Club in L.A. so I proceeded to do likewise. My family left for home on the 20th.

July 1941

After an interesting stay in L.A., seeing points of interest and going to places of amusement, along with 30 other early arrivers, we left L.A. at 6:30 A.M. Sunday, July 6th for San Francisco, which was traveled to in about 12 hours. There we met the rest of the group. On the 7th, about half of us were given quarters on our ship, the Jagersfontein, and the rest came aboard on the following day. The group consisted of approximately 50 pilots, both Army and Navy, and 73 Mechanics and other enlisted men.

Sailing from S.F. was at 1:20 P.M. Thursday, July 10th. The first day out, we ran into a small swell which enabled us to get our sea legs and ascertain (sic) our stomachs to the toss and roll of the sea.
From the first night, we practiced blacking out and were very strict to its adherence.

The second day out was rather calm so our most delicious food was thoroughly enjoyed. A boat drill was also held in the morning.

On Sat., the 12th, Dr. Samuel Pan, a fellow traveler along with 17 other Chinese exchange students returning from the U.S., started a Chinese language class which a group of us started.

Sunday started a group of lectures by the Chinese travelers on China and customs of the Chinese, which they thought would prove interesting and helpful to us. That evening an informal quiz program was held in the Social Hall. Beer served for prizes.

Monday's warmer weather brought into use the outdoor pool which many of the fellows made quick use of.

Hawaii – the land of hula and palm trees. It came into view Tuesday morning and the port was entered about 9:30 P.M. The passengers had deserted the ship by 10:30. All were in to see or do (sic) the City of Honolulu. The next morning was also spent in part, and not having much time, I did well to see Waikiki Beach and do a little necessary shopping. We sailed at 1:00 P.M.

The next morning found us out of sight but not memory of Hawaii, but in sight of two Navy cruisers; which were to act as convoy for the journey. The lectures and classes in Chinese continued as the next stage of the journey began in earnest.

Friday was needle day. We all received our first shot for cholera and also smallpox or vaccination. Our course was almost due South which caused a lot of prophesying on our next stop, but nobody was "in the know."

The next week passes as prototype as the usual day. (sic) Breakfast around eight, then a thorough sun bath on the deck, sometimes reading and interrupted around 11:00 for the morning cool, refreshing drink served by the barefooted turbaned Javanese boys. A little side light is that these boys, around 33 years of age, make only one of(sic) two trips a year as they can live on $30.00 for almost six months. Their pay is from tips from the passengers. Most of them cannot speak any English, but are well trained in their jobs. Luncheon is at 1:00 for the officers, enlisted men ate at 12:00 noon. The luncheon consisted of a vegetable salad, soup, entrée, dessert and fruit. The coffee was served afterward in the Social Hall.

From two till four was Chinese language class. I'm taking it with the hope of using it, but like any other language, the further you progress, the more intricate and complicated it becomes. Class was usually ended by the "boys" again making the round of the ship serving tea and cookies.

From four till seven was usually spent in reading, especially books associated with China, Japan, or its associated complexities.

The most interesting episode during these last few days was the conversion of "pollywogs" to "shellbacks". This is a time honored custom of the many of initiating all new sailors who cross the equator for the first time. It consists of a group of Shellbacks, those who have already crossed, acting as prosecutors and administrators of justice. This administration of justice consisted of a thorough shellacking of the "body stern," coloring of the body, a hit of pungent fish, shave with a wooden razor, and finally a "helped" entrance into the pool with a triple ducking for good credit. It was fun watching and participating even though it left its memorial marks.

The evening meal was not to be outdone. With olives and celery followed by salad, fish dish, the entrée, dessert, fruit and again coffee in the Social Hall.

Most evenings were just spent sitting on the darkened deck with only the blue lights showing the lifeboat stations, and the occasional glow of a cigarette. No lights were permitted to be shown, as were matches forbidden to be struck outside. Many are the fellow who blindly ran into a deck chair or a fellow passenger. But safety is safety.

Bob on the Jagersfontein en route to China. Photo courtesy Virginia S. Davis.

August 1941

Somewhere above Australia we slept through a day. That is, went to bed on Friday and woke up on Sunday. That and the fact we changed two U.S. Cruisers for one Dutch cruiser on the 3rd of August was the only bit of excitement for the past week.

For the first time since leaving, we had a "no blackout" night. With our escort we anchored off a small island and picked up an Australian Straits Pilot. The next day we passed many small islands in the afternoon passed close by a fortified entrance to the opposite end of the Straits of Torres. There we left off our Pilot and continued on our journey.

Since then we have been seeing scattered islands on both sides of us, each fellow expressing his guess to its name and position.

My daily routine now usually consists of two hours Chinese class in the afternoon; the sun bathing in the morning with about an hour of elementary hand balancing or wrestling just before noon. The latter part of the afternoon is spent reading.

This time also marked the end of picture taking for a while as all cameras had to be turned into the purser's office. It seems all the governments don't relish photos of their islands' fortifications turning up in unwelcomed hands, so – no pictures!

Journey still moving along at its 15 knots, more islands, more guesses as to their position and names. One, somewhere very near Java or Bali, we spent the morning about three miles off shore while the Dutch Cruiser "Jana" went in closer and oiled up. Our first indication of our first stop was posted on Saturday the 11th, where it stated we would dock early Monday morning in Singapore and should have our baggage ready for disembarkation.

Monday, August 11, we arrived outside the harbor of Singapore about 7:00 where the quarantine officer and pilot came aboard. We finally docked around 8:00 but due to a little difficulty with the immigration department, we did not leave ship until after 2:00 P.M.

Robert sightseeing in China
Photo courtesy Virginia S. Davis.

After spending almost an hour trying to declare money, mail, get a return pass (which we finally found out was not needed) we left the gate into the Humdrum of Singapore; the melting pot of the Orient. Our first bit of orientation was a short ride on the "Tram," then came the long waited surprised(sic); a ride in a real rickshaw pulled by a typical Chinese cootie.(sic)

That ride was about the most interesting and enlightening ride I have ever taken. It started out in a typical Chinese section with the stores running into each other; their wares almost intermingled and their odors certainly were. Most of the shop keepers were young Chinese and in a few cases, the shops were run by other Orientals than Chinese; somewhat sconitic(sic) in appearance. The trail then ran along these streets, strewn literally with humanity; Indians with their skirts and turbans, Chinese women with their babies on their backs in papoose style, the Sheiks or Indian policeman who are almost all over 6 feet and real strapping fellows. Here and there were whites doing either business or rubber-necking; every ten feet it seems the coolies had to dodge a stunted automobile. Here most cars are of European; mainly British built, and are small; comparable to the Austin. All cars here have right hand drive and travel along the left hand side of the road. I never did get used to looking in the opposite direction before crossing the street, although it seems as if no one else does from the manner in which jay walking is carried on.

Soon we came into the more modern section with its newer buildings, larger, cleaner and more spectacular window displays. Here also the traffic became much more dense and dodging really came into being. A river, or rather Singapore Canal, was crossed and traffic on this canal was literally stopped by the great number of junks and sampans reaching from one bank to another.

Another prevalent means of transportation in Singapore is the bicycle. There are almost no women riding them, but every male from young boy to the old Indian with his skirt and turban fluttering in the breeze is ducking in between rickshaws and pedestrians. First comes the automobiles, then the rickshaw, next the bicycle and finally the poor pedestrian. He hardly stands a chance.

Besides all the shops and interesting shop keepers, another human took up quite a bit of notice.

The soldiers in Singapore almost seem to outnumber the civilians. All kinds of nationalities seem to be represented. The Indians, Australians, New Zealanders and even quite a few Brishers(sic) are noticed strolling along. There are also quite a number of sailors, although now they were mostly at sea for any emergency.

Our little ride ended in front of a curio shop where we entered and did a little rubber-necking ourselves. There were very many intricate and delicate pieces of hand carved wood made out of a single piece. Also many pottery, (sic) china and silverware. This place did not happen to have any jade though.

A short walk back to the post office to purchase some stamps and then we found a cab driver; a Malayan who spoke English. We hired him and his 10 H.P. Ford, to drive us around town and show us some of the interesting sights. We passed the famous Raffles Hotel; but more of that later. Saw several convents and girls schools; thru more real Chinese sections and out into the suburbs where we came across new, modern, larger and beautiful homes. These belonged mostly to Consular workers or rich businessmen. We also saw a few of the Army Officers' homes, which were very nice. Finally we came to the Botanical Park. It is a large, very well kept park containing many variety of plants, trees, shrubs and flowers. It even had its water lily pond and to my surprise, a large number of monkeys. The monkeys were rather tame and would take peanuts out of the hands of their feeder. Every one bought peanuts and fed the little fellows. We did happen to see a young mother monkey with her offspring clinging to her chest as she scampered from spot to spot or partook of peanuts we fed her.

Our next stop of interest was at the Tiger Balm Museum. It is a fully furnished house, unlived in of course, but richly decorated with real Chinese decoration. All the rugs, tapestry, and handiwork was(sic) very colorful and pretty. Throughout the house were innumerable Jade carvings. That alone must have amounted to over a million dollars. From there we drove out to the Civil Airport; now taken over by the R.A.F. We talked to a young New Zealander, R.A.F. Sergeant. We found that a friend of Howard, who was my traveling companion, was stationed here as an observer, but was not there at the present. So we stopped for a cocktail before we left for the Raffles Hotel for dinner. Upon walking in, the first person we saw was Howard's friend, Price, and several of our bunch so we promptly joined them. From there it was back to the Airport Restaurant for dinner and then out for the evening.

We went to the famous New World, which is somewhat of a Chinese amusement park. It contains a cabaret, several movie houses, and even more outdoor play houses where we saw real Chinese drama being presented. One interesting sidelight is that there are not acts. It is continuous and when they want to change scenery, the actors turn their back to the audience and young boys change the scenery. Also only men take part in these plays and young boys take the high pitched women's parts. We looked around a bit and then went to the cabaret where we had a few dances with the Chinese hostesses. These girls are mostly all pretty, speak English and highly prize these jobs. From there we went back to Raffles for the last few minutes before the 12:00 curfew on bars. There we met more of our group along with three R.A.F. pilots who saw service over London; all had several confirmed victories. And so then back to the ship via an open air midget cab.

The next morning we loafed close to the boat, buying bananas, milk, ice-cream, cigarettes and sun hats from the traveling Chinese Merchants.

We left the dock at 2:15 P.M. with two of the group missing. As we were clearing the pier, they came up and quickly went to the end of the long pier and got a taxi boat. They came aboard outside the harbor as the harbor pilot left.

And so on our way to Rangoon.

The mouth of the Irrawaddy River came into sight on the afternoon of the 15th; we picked up our pilot and started our trip down the river to Rangoon. As soon as we entered the river, it started raining ala Burma. It soon became dark so(sic) with the rain and darkness we had our last night's sleep on the Jagersfontein.

At 5:30 A.M. the breakfast gong awoke us for the last time. After a short breakfast we transferred to a lighter and were taxied to the wharf among the numerous water taxies and sampans.(sic)

A short bus ride and we were dropped at the Silver Brill for a fine breakfast. From there we had a quick ride through the quaint streets of Rangoon, somewhat like Singapore, to the railroad station.

Amongst the many Indians and Burmese, we sorted our baggage and broke up into groups of six for a second class railroad compartment. On our narrow gage, small engine train, we started a very interesting ride at 1 P.M. Saturday, August 16th.

The coach itself was rather small with two fixed seats on each side with the center section folding out from the side of the coach to form a bed or place for three during the day. A drop bed which laid flat against the side and made a double bed above the seat bed, so the compartment held six day or four night passengers. They were not very comfortable, but sufficed for the short journey.

The train made very good time and rode very smoothly. The railway ran through many villages, some rather large with railway sidings, a large station; somewhat of a main street and a few larger stores. Other villages were nothing more than a few bamboo homes and a mud road. All along were numerous rice fields, all under water and many natives pulling out the ripe stalks, none(sic) stopping to watch the train; others going on nonchalantly with their work.

The peoples passed were mostly Burmese(sic) or Indians. They all wear their dress like cloths wrapped around their lower portions and a shirt of various colors and designs. The Indians wear turbans and the Burmese and a few Chinese have larger bamboo sun hats. The land was very flat and as afar as the eye could see were rice fields and a few spots of thick jungle-like growth of shrubs and trees. Many large and small birds were seen throughout the trip, large swan-like birds called "Paddy Birds" were seen on all the rice fields. A few larger, black buzzard birds were also seen. Water buffaloes were as prevalent as cows back home. They would lie in the water ditches along the rice fields, irrigation canals, rivers, and small puddles of water.

Another object of interest all along the way were the numerous idols. Some were large busts of Buddha, as high as 50 feet, enclosed by brick walls with only the face showing, and the front section open to show the whole front of the bust. Other objects were intricate towers topped by gold kraft(sic) work. Some were a part of a large bird, who sat on the ground like a boat. These birds were about 100 feet long and the towers about 30-50 feet high.

We stopped at about 3 o'clock at a larger village and were each given a lunch box, which was not too appetizing, but proved rather welcomed. At this same stop, some of us took off into the village proper. We saw a native having a shave with a straight razor and no lather whatsoever, just dry, and as clear a shave as you would want. Whenever we came into view all the women would run away or hide their faces. The other populace would just stare back. Most of the houses were upon piles above the water which was everywhere, but on the road. The animals lived along with their owners in the same rooms.

The Burma Road, which we followed all the way from Rangoon to our destination also ran through this town, so we saw several convoys of American trucks pass thru on their way probably to China.

Our next stop several hours later brought us another group of station well-wishers, who seem to spend all day at the stations, either just watching, selling their wares, or begging. The small children begged for money and would scramble when coins were tossed to them. We saw a few Buddha priests in their yellow robes and shaven heads.

At about six o'clock we came to Toungoo where we saw several fellows who were already at the outpost. From there it was only a few minutes ride to where we stopped at a small village and our baggage unloaded into trucks and we were driven in station wagons and Plymouths ('41) about eight miles to the R.A.F. Field.

So after 36 days on a boat, a bus ride, train ride and a station wagon ride, a trip half way around the world was at a halt. From sunny California to rainy Burma. Blackout ship, rickshaw rides, strange people and customs; these all filled the otherwise dreary days.

The field here, built by the R.A.F. in the spring of '41, is well laid out for an air post. It was cleared from semi-jungle into a large scattered post. The roads are of stone and clay, hand made by the coolie workers. The buildings are of frame construction with laced bamboo matting for sides and roof. The builders were at least 1000 yards apart. The officers' quarters were of the barracks type; one long room with 16 mosquito net covered beds, a dresser between each set of two; there was a shower room 50 feet away as well as separate springs again 50 feet. The water was chlorinated at the well before distribution so it was all drinkable. Of course, there was electricity, but no radio as yet. A phonograph served for entertainment, in our particular barracks. The other officers' barracks as well as enlisted men's were the same.

There were separate mess halls for officers and enlisted men. The hangar was almost two miles from the mess hall; so it was either a long walk or a bumpy ride in one of the station wagons, of which there were about three and also three '41 Plymouths.

The hangar was of timber and sheet metal; capable of about 18 planes. (sic) Scattered around the hangar were bomb proof shelters as well as dugouts for planes. The petrol dump was about a mile from the hangar; between the mess hall and hangar.

There was a part exchange, laundry, barber and other small conveniences on the port, so we were not altogether away from civilization.

Since we arrived during the rainy season, we were well initiated. Black clouds would soon appear, a heavy rainfall, a sudden stop; this would continue for hours.

The meals became more inviting, or we became more accustomed to the food served in Burma. The days were usually well spent with a few details to be taken care of at the hangar, an evening spent in Toungoo, exercise or sunning during the day.

I was supposed to leave for Rangoon on Friday, August 22, but no planes were ready for ferrying, so my packing went for naught. The same Saturday, (sic) but Sunday we did leave here about 11:30 in the Beechcraft with a Major of the Chinese Air Force as pilot. The weather was rather poor with mostly instrument flying.

Since it was Sunday, after we arrived, there was no one waiting for us, so we had a quarter mile walk to where we caught a local Rangoon

Robert in Burma. Photo courtesy Virginia S. Davis.

bus, filled with its usual melee of passengers; Indian, Burmese, and others unbeknown to me. About half way into town a '41 Chevy pulled up behind the bus and honked the horn. It was the company car which missed us at the airport and caught up to us. From there, we were taken to Minton Mansions. It was supposed to be the second best hotel in town; but was rather old and not too pleasantly decorated or furnished; but offered a suitable place for sleeping quarters. After a quick shower and change of clothes, a not too delicious or appetizing luncheon, we drove into town to the Strand Hotel where Mr. Pawley was living. We discussed a few points of discussion; had a drink with him, then one at the bar and proceeded to see some of the town. We had use of Mr. Pawley's car for the day, so we drove, or had our Burmese driver drive us to the Shwe Dagon Pagoda just outside of town.

It is one of the largest Pagodas in the world, covering about four square blocks, surrounding a 100 foot, gold plaited shrine. This pagoda is almost 2500 years old, built over hairs of Buddha's head. There are numerous smaller shrines which are gifts of private families, and depending upon their wealth is the many jewels or richness of shrine.(sic)

All visitors must go through this Pagoda barefooted; so after we got through, we stopped at a pharmacist on the way back and bought Potassium Permanganate to bathe our feet in.

After this very interesting sight into the religious nature of Burma and Buddhism, we proceeded back to the hotel for dinner. We started out for the theatre, but found out the show did not start till 9:30; so back to the Strand for a drink and then to bed.

The next day was spent in town shopping and finding out some information regarding passage back to the states for some of the fellows who contemplated going back home.

It was raining too hard to fly back so the afternoon was spent with a Mr. Gibson who was a former Navy pilot, but is now a pilot for Brewster Co., and testing the R.A.F. "Buffalo" here at Rangoon. That evening we did make the show and saw "Flame of New Orleans".

Tuesday morning was again spent in shopping and general sightseeing. The planes were grounded because of foreign material on the flight controls. So no ferry trip home. The Beechcraft brought two more ferry pilots; Swindle and Merritt, so after dinner we all went to another show and saw "Scarlet Pimpernel".

Robert's Plane was number 85.
Photo courtesy and copyright Charles Baisden.

Wednesday, August 27, I had my first flight in the Curtis 81-A Tomahawk or China Fighter.

I took off from Rangoon at 10:30 and after flying thru several squalls and never over 1000 feet; usually at less than 200, I arrived back at Toungoo about 11:15 o'clock.

After lunch I again had a half hour flight during which I got familiar with the plane and had a merry time doing vertical slow rolls and flying on my back.

A distribution of the cake and candy I brought back brings me to dinner time.

We started flying in earnest with three or four planes in commission with as many chutes. For the past week averaged almost two hours each per day, most of the time spent in individual combat, going up above the overcast thru any small hole which could be found in the vicinity, and taking on any single, pair or formation of ships. Many times two planes would start combat and within five minutes there would be four or five planes winging in and out of each other's way. It sure kept one's eyes open to keep all planes in view and still trying to get an advantage on one. By the time you would be thru fighting and get ready to land, you would have to acquaint yourself and try to figure out where the field was. Usually if you could find the railroad and Burma Road, you could figure out where the field was.

Authors Note:

Chennault provided training for all his pilots. He called his training "Kindergarten." The pilots were required to log "60 hours of flight training and 72 hours of lectures."[19] Japanese flying tactics were taught and the AVG pilots were instructed how to attack based on the type of plane they were flying and the way in which the Japanese fighters attacked. He instructed the pilots to "fly in pairs – stick together.....enter combat with the altitude advantage...dive, hit, and run."[20] Chennault told the men, "[Japanese] pilots have been drilled for hundreds of hours to fly in precise formation.......break up their formations and make them fight according to our style."[21] All the training provided helped save many of the pilot's lives and Chennault's tactics were proven to succeed as the AVG downed plane after plane.

September 1941

This last period also saw September 2, come and go, which was none other than my 24th birthday – I felt magnanimous enough to buy drinks for the fellows who came from Mitchel – all in return sang the Birthday Song at dinner.

Besides flying everything is about the same except an earlier schedule for breakfast and work in the morning – 6:30 breakfast.

Today, Saturday September 6th, we had another insight into the industries of Burma – Teakwood. We traveled about 11 miles out of Toungoo in one of their famous dilapidated busses with hard seats and wooden windows. The elephants they use for movement of the trees, work only in the morning, but through a company official we had it arranged so that one elephant would be available in the afternoon to put on a show. The trip to the farm was thru the city and then into the most dense jungle growth I've ever seen. One could not see beyond the first foliage group. Not only did the many trees block the view, but wires would grove between the trees and shrubs making a curtain of Greene foliage. The road was of dirt, one way, and wound up and around a climb of only about 500 feet, but because of the dense growth, made it long and treacherous. Many were scared going around curves with a drop into impenetrable jungle on the side. One noticeable feature was the absence of flowers and colorful plants – everything was Greene – trees, vines, shrubs, plants and grass. We did see a small plant like an ordinary pot shrub, which would close its leaves and droop whenever it was touched or brushed against.

We had a little difficulty in finding the exact spot where we would find the elephant, mostly thru language difficulties, but as we were driving along, we suddenly noticed the elephant just inside the foliage, next to the road. We called for the elephant boy who lived in his small bamboo thatched hut along the edge of the road. He went to where the elephant was seen and called him out. He then proceeded to make the elephant kneel down, sit down and do various maneuvers. He then rode him to this house where he had a scaffold under which the elephant stood while he placed mats on his back and strapped on his harness for chains in order for the elephant to drag logs. Two interesting maneuvers these two went thru was that the boy dropped a loop in front of the elephant which he put his trunk thru then one foot at a time so that the boy had a rope around the elephant which held the mats down. He also had a loop of bamboo about 12" in diameter which he hooked over the elephant tail while he held his tail out.

The boy then took the elephant to a siding where several logs were already placed and had the elephant pull a log about three feet in diameter and 20 feet long. He also picked up smaller logs with his trunk from the road up on a bank about six feet high. He also thru(sic) a smaller log along the road.

Several of us had our pictures taken alongside of the elephant and one fellow ventured on top of the elephant and had a short ride. We passed the hat around for the elephant boy who had put on a good performance with his well-behaved beast.

A seemingly long ride on the hard seats brought us back to our little community.

Monday, September 8, was a real black Monday. While we were sitting at the luncheon table with empty dining room, we heard that two planes crashed in mid-air. After a process of elimination, it proved to be Bright and Armstrong, both Navy men. By one o'clock Bright had been located hanging from a tree in his parachute, unscathed, but mildly shocked. At first Armstrong's plane was not found but soon it was located almost buried in the jungle, both planes within five miles of the filed. Armstrong never did know what hit him.

Tuesday morning we had our first formation flight. We had five ships starting out in a three ship element and then followed by a two ship element, cross over, turns, string, back into two ship elements, three ship elements and practiced a Lufbery circle. There was no flying in the afternoon due to the services and burial of Armstrong. The services were held in the Officer's Mess Hall with all members present. From there we all drove into town and had the burial services at an English Cemetery. Chaplain Frillman officiated at both services. There were a fine bunch of flowers at the grave and a most impressive ceremony – a bugle call given by one of the Burmese soldiers.

An episode of interest happened today, Wednesday. We started out in a four ship flight of two, two ship elements to visit the alternate airport north of here about 125 miles. We did not quite get far enough north due to unpredicted drift, so buzzed a boat on the Irrawaddy and proceeded back home. The drift again took us to our left so we passed the field and after a while, we all became a little anxious as to our position. We then were far enough south to hit Rangoon, but not knowing our exact whereabouts, the formation broke up into every man for himself. I thereupon headed due north, following the railroad and Burma Road. After running on gas tank completely empty and just running dry on my second, after 25 minutes of flying due north, I saw the field and switched over to my last tank of 30 gallons. The surprising feature was that as I made my traffic pattern to land, I saw all three of the other planes, so my wonder as to their predicament was brought to a good end. We all landed with approximately 20 gallons of gas after 2 ½ hours of flying.

The Third contingent of pilots and mechanics arrived on Monday, September 15, almost a month to the day after us. They left San Francisco on July 22, went to Honolulu, Sydney, Australia, Manila, Batavia, Singapore, Rangoon and here, so they had a longer and more diversified trip than we. They were 53 days at sea, or on their way. There were 16 pilots, 6 Navy and the rest Army. The others were Mechanics and armament men. Those already here waited up for them to come in about 10 p.m. and have a few drinks with old friends. I knew two who were with me in Flying School. Tuesday they looked around and did a little shopping in Toungoo. Wednesday they started checking out – one got a prop when he used the brakes too energetically. Wednesday night we also had the first of our movie pictures here on the field. We are to have our own projector and 12 pictures a month coming up from Rangoon. They will be American pictures – just a few months old. I saw my first one Friday night. It was "Lillian Russell" – rather entertaining!

Saturday morning our long awaited visitors came in. We were expecting several English visitors for a week and spent three days practicing a review formation for their benefit. They arrived about 9 o'clock in a Blenheim, Lockheed Hudson, and our Lockheed '12. There was Sir Robert Brooke-Popham, a General, and several other ranking British Air Ministry Officers. We flew an 18 ship formation, first came over in three ship veer off the three squadrons of two elements each. The second pass the first squadron was in a two ship element; the second in company front, and our third was in string. It turned out fairly well. The visitors left about 11 o'clock and everything resumed normally.

Monday morning proved to be another "Black Monday" with poor ceiling rain all around, low clouds and a thorough day. Death came again. Maax Hammer was listed as missing after he did not land at 11 o'clock; there was no news of him, so at 3 o'clock with poor conditions, ten ships were sent out as a searching party, but about 5 o'clock a call came in that a plane was seen to have crashed about seven miles from Toungoo and the pilot was killed. Several cars departed with the aid of several native guides, a tough trek thru jungle brought the crashed plane into view. It was believed that Hammer in an inverted spin, could not pull out with such a low ceiling. The memorial services were postponed from Tuesday till Wednesday afternoon as Rev. Frillman was down at Rangoon and had to come up. There were memorial services in the Officers Mess and at the cemetery(sic) as was for Armstrong,. Maax was with me in primary at St. Louis and at Randolph and Kelly.

Monday morning also brought the Air Vice-Marshall of Far East Air Force of England to our home base. Due to bad weather that afternoon, Tuesday and Wednesday (a late monsoon period) we did not fly a review for them till Thursday morning. It was the best yet.

I was also relieved as S-4 (Supply) and made Assistant Operations Engineering Officer.

Mr. Alsop, a newspaper journalist came up here with our group to act as a publicity man later on. He was formerly in Washington doing political writing.

Another newspaper man who just stopped here on his way into China was Mr. Leland Stowe, of the Chicago Daily News, war correspondent staff. He has been in Norway, Finland, England, Spain, etc. and in the Far East where he saw some real action. He stayed here for two days and gave us a short talk on his experiences and view on the war situation.

October 1941

Flew down in the Beechcraft on Thursday, October 2, supposedly to get a P-40 to ferry back, but there were only two ready, so only two of the four of us could fly back; Moss and I were left out so we came back on the Beechcraft in the afternoon without even leaving the airport. The trip was therefore a failure as far as I was concerned.

The week from the 6th went by rather slowly due to Wednesday being maintenance day and there being no flying. Also had a couple of days of rain which further held up flying. Thursday I was in the Airdrome office, spending my time in the tower watching everything from the outside looking in.

We were also honored with a visit of several ranking officers from the U.S. Army mission on their way to China – General Scott was among those present. At the same time, there were two air Corps members of the Chinese American attaches, Major Rosendorf was one, the other was a Captain.

The Major incidentally was once with the 8th Pursuit Group when it only consisted of the 33rd Squadron; back in 1932.

Saturday a group of us went into Toungoo to see a traveling show. There were a large group of small open stores selling mostly foods – open air restaurants. The natives would be squatted on the ground around the large tray of many varieties of food and eating as if they were alone in a palace. The main tent was of bamboo. It was about 100 x 200 and sloping roof of matted bamboo held up by a few bamboo poles.

The whole area was covered with small bamboo mats about 3'x5' with a larger numeral in one corner. We finally found out that those were the reserved seats! The patrons brought a rug, pillows, and thermos jug and probably food. They would come at 7 p.m. and stay till 7 a.m., the next morning, watching a continuous performance. The first thing to catch our attention was the orchestra.

The main piece of music was a circular row of skin-metal drums, ranging from 2" in diameter to about 10". There were about 20 of them and the musician; squatting on a table in the center, would twist around tapping the drums with his fingers; sometimes hitting two or three with one hand, his fingers being outstretched enough to strike several small drums. There was also a similar cage with cymbal instead of drums. There was also a regular drummer, with three or four large tom-toms; a symbol player, two squeaky horn players, and the oddest of all were three men who played a split bamboo instrument. These instruments were about four feet long and four inches in diameter. They were split lengthwise and tied together at one end; the musicians would pull apart the opposite end and let go and a resonant "clap" would be heard. The whole orchestra playing together was a weird sounding affair, the melody and rhythm being hard to follow as each man seemed to play at will.

The stage was of the usual size with appropriate Burmese scenes depicted on the curtains. The first scenes consisted of a group of Burmese girls on one side and men on the other, kneeling, facing a statue of Buddha and they sang several songs.

Then followed several scenes of the girls dancing and singing. After that followed two acts of comediennes which we could not appreciate. We seemed to have seen enough by this time, so after a peek behind the stage where we saw the space divided into a sort of dressing room, we left.

From the "Opera" we went to the railroad station to welcome the latest newcomers into our ranks. We said "Hello" to most of them, had a glass of tomato juice and left for home.

Sunday, the 12th, was sightseeing day. Doc Priso got a station wagon and seven of us piled in with a box of canned and bottled goods and took off about 10:30 a.m. We drove out of Toungoo, east into the mountains. After 30 miles of hairpin curves, narrow roads, and plenty of dust, we reached the summit of that particular mountain, 4368 feet above sea level. Because of the cloudiness, we were at times looking down on top of the clouds, stagnant in the valleys. We stopped there at the P.W.D. house and hungry consumed our "canned" dinner. It was very tasty at that! From there we drove a little further to a tea mill. There we saw where the tea is laid out to dry in a constant temperature room (85 deg. F.), washed and rolled, left on a cement floor to ferment for about six hours; then dried in ovens; separated in size by machines, hand cleaned, sifted once more and then packaged. Some of the tea after sifting is pounded by a very primitive method of two women stepping off and on a fulcrum pile driver while a third woman took care of the hammer and tea. The tea would be pounded into a very fine dust which would dissolve almost immediately. There were four grades of tea depending upon size of the leaves. The English manager took us on a tour of inspection thru the three story wooden mill.

On the way back home, we were met by a native servant along the road who directed us to Mrs. Cote, M.D., M.B.E. This woman is about 89 years old and has lived in Toungoo for the last 20 years. She was in Rangoon practicing medicine for 30 years previously. She originally came from Canada. Her wit and speech is of the finest; knowing all the latest word information and topics of interest. Her Indian maid, who speaks good English, made us donuts and tea which was very enjoyable, not having any such delicacies for some time. The M.B.E. is an honorary title given her by Britain. Member of British Empire.

And so back down the winding cloud hidden road to Kyedaw Airport, supper and a show – "It's a Date" with Deanna Durbin.

Sunday also proved to be a surprise in that upon returning from our little journey, I found a letter awaiting me from home. The first letter since leaving home. Sure was welcome.

Bob sightseeing. Photo courtesy Virginia S. Davis.

Thursday, October 16, we were again honored by a visit of English officials. This time it was the Right Honorable and Mrs. Duff Cooper. They came up in the Lockheed and as soon as they landed and got out of their plane, 18 of us, six from each squadron took off and passed twice in review. The first time we were going north. The three squadrons were in elements of V's. The second pass was going south. The 1st Squadron was in company front, we were second in string, and last was the 1st Squadron in three elements of twos in V. It seemed a very good review from the air and were told it looked fine from the ground. The visitors were only here for several hours making a short tour of inspection of the airdrome.

Colonel Hoyte, now a member of the American Observing Corps in China, formerly a commanding office of several pursuit groups back in the states, was here for several days and also gave us a little talk on cooperation and teamwork.

Due to Bob Walroth's leaving, I was made Engineering Officer temporarily. We had a good scare Saturday the 18th when, at about 4 o'clock two foreign looking planes flew overhead and we could not make out their type. We were of the opinion of their being Japanese observation planes, but found out Sunday that they were the new British training planes. For this reason and because of the new crisis of the Japanese War Cabinet collapse and reforming, we started arming our planes and having several fully loaded and ready to go. We are to start an alert set up – just in case.

By the following Tuesday, we had our first alert staff working. There were a total of 12 planes, four from each squadron. All of these were fully armed and loaded. Each day a new squadron would furnish six pilots and reliefs for these six planes. The other six planes would be taken by the first pilot to get it.

Our Squadron #3, had its first taste on the next Thursday. We awoke at 4:45, got a truck at the pilot's mess and were ready to take off at 5:30, if necessary.

The mechanics arrived at about 4:45 to check and warm the planes up. We were brought hot coffee and sandwiches about 6 o'clock and then went for breakfast at 7:30. That day we had maneuvers with three Blenheim bombers. The alarm was sounded about 9:30 that the rats had left Rangoon. Our six alert ships took off along with 12 others. Three groups of six each, were sent out to intercept them. About 10 minutes out, I sighted the three rats about 10 miles to our left and 3,000 feet lower. I called the flight leader, Olson, and said "Three rats at 3 o'clock." I then caught up to him and wobbled my wings to get his attention. As soon as I got it, we started in their direction, but by then I had lost sight of them. We continued on the course for several minutes and then saw a bi-motor ship about 6000 feet above and to our right. We quickly climbed, but soon saw it was the CNAC [Chinese National Aviation Corporation] Douglas DC-2. By then we lost all track of the real enemy and started down to get ready to land when we got another report of the position of the enemy so we took off again in pursuit of them, but soon received the report that the field had been reached by the imaginary enemy and blown to bits. So there was nothing for us to do but go back and land. None of the other squadrons had not seen anything of the enemy so I lost my chair of being "here of the day" and instead became goat by losing sight of the enemy. Nothing much was said except a little ribbing by some of the fellows. It was a lot of fun even if we did not prove successful in our mission. At least I learned something.

Our squadron also had its first major plane catastrophe on the same day after the maneuvers when Hodges ground-looped and tore off both wheels and skidded on the belly onto the grass alongside the runway. He was not hurt at all, but the plane was a washout.

A fancy dress ball in aid or war charities, with Major General J. Bruce Scott, M.C., at the railway institute on Friday, October 24, was the event of interest for the week. To prove its worthiness, I put on my tux for the occasion. There were quite a few people in costume, the women mostly trying to represent some phase or form of peace, even to one with angel wings. About half of the people were Burmese so I had an opportunity of dancing with several of the locale belles. Of course, I was particular and fortunate enough to dance with only the prettiest of the girls. With several drinks to hasten and enlighten the frivolity, the evening was most enjoyable and was almost sorry to leave at 1 o'clock except for being slightly tuckered out after so new an evening of entertainment.

Black Saturday, 25th of October. They say accidents happen in threes – well, we had our third mortal catastrophe and I hope our last. While acting as relief at the alert station about 9 o'clock, Pete Atkinson took off on a test hop. About 15 minutes later, we heard a terrific whining sound and glanced up into the blue sky to only see an airplane disintegrating into a million pieces. The whine continued for a few seconds as the pieces of the plane floated down while what looked like only the engine section plunged onward at a terrific speed – another second of quiet followed by a loud roar as if a bomb had exploded as the motor hit the ground. A wing continued floating down and other small pieces tumbled down among them, as we later found out, was Pete still strapped in the seat, plummeting earthward to crash thru a tin roof of a house and unnecessarily complete his final landing. Another friend and good pilot had landed his last plane.

From other persons observation it appeared that the plane was diving at a great speed, the prop over running considerably, making as loud a whine as anyone ever heard; the plane started to pull out of the dive and the plane started disintegrating; the tail section coming off, then the wing, then the whole plane coming apart like a fire cracker shot off in the air. The almost indestructible diving plane just gave out at the wrong moment and took away another test pilot.

There was no flying scheduled besides test hops, but all flying was called off and all planes grounded till the tail assembly and wings were inspected.

The following day we held the last rites for Pete. At the Pilot's mess hall, we had 24 pilots and crew chiefs form a honorary pall-bearer double line thru with six of us pilots from the old 33rd acted as pall bearers. The services were given by Paul Frillman and after the very impressive ceremony at which almost every man attended; we formed a long procession of seven cars, three station wagons and two buses into Toungoo to the cemetery. There we again had the double line and at the grave alongside the other two concrete slabs of former pilots, services were again given. This time by a Catholic priest as Pete was a rather devoted Catholic and wanted it that way. So at 5 o'clock of the afternoon of October 26, 1941, a great friend and pilot passed from the level of this earth to a better one beyond.

For the next few days, there was quite a scramble getting the tail assemblies of all the planes inspected, which caused very little flying to be done.

Once again the English High Command paid a visit to our training base on Thursday, October 30. This time it was General Wavell and his staff of about three other Generals, including Gen. Scott of Toungoo. They were flying in a DC-2 accompanied by a Blenheim. They were here only a few hours, but long enough for us to hurriedly gather together 18 inspected planes and put on a review. Because of rush, it was not as good as might be expected, and also offered a little excitement when, while landing, Sandell got a wing tip but took off and circled the field and landed. Sawyer also had a little bad luck in blowing out a tire, but doing no damage to the plane otherwise. Moss also had the same thing happen just before the party arrived.

The previous evening another contingent of pilots and clerks arrived from the U.S. after 58 days out of Frisco. We got three pilots. They started flying Friday and since they all came from the Navy and were flying big boats, they had some difficulty. Conant, one of our gang, landed 15 feet up in the air and when he did hit the ground, he ground looped, tearing up an airplane, but not doing any damage to himself.

November 1941

Sunday morning we went for a swim up in a rushing mountain stream about 20 miles up from Toungoo. There were eight of us in a station wagon. We brought sandwiches from the mess and bought some canned fruit and had several thermos jugs of an ice cold fruit drink. It took about half an hour to get up to the 500 foot altitude of our little swimming hole. The stream at this spot is about 50 feet wide and about 30 feet of it is over eight feet deep for a stretch of another 50 feet.

The current is almost too strong to make any headway against it, so it is quite a workout to just hold your own. After a swim and a little lunch, we continued up to Than dung and the tea factory on top of that mountain. On the way back, we stopped at Dr. Cotes for tea and donuts.

If Sunday was a day of peace and quiet, then Monday was a day of disaster and rumpus because with seven accidents, it could not be very peaceful. Among the affected was Conant, who after cracking up on his first flight, nosed one up after overshooting on his second flight this date. Another rather avoidable one was caused when a mechanic rode a bicycle into an aileron and damaged it enough to be replaced. The third casualty to our squadron was when McAllister nosed one up tailing to the line. One of our new pilots left his prop switch on maneuvers, dove over, ruined the prop and burned out the bearings. Then in the afternoon a mechanic of the 1st Squadron taxied one plane into another damaging one pretty badly and putting the other out of commission for several days. Then Squadron Commander Sandell got his third ship – he nosed one up off the runway. Those are the seven and one minor one – a flat tail wheel on Sawyer's plane at Lashio on a cross country finished the day of woe.

They came thru with several more ships Tuesday and on Wednesday Conant got his third one – he blew a tire on a touch and go landing and held it straight for a while, but a landing gear gave way and he ground looped right towards a ship being bore sighted with about six mechanics working on it. He stopped about 20 feet from it.(sic) This plane was really washed out. All we got Thursday was a blown out on a ship taxiing so not much damage done except that we are running out of spare tires which we are getting from wrecked planes – also no spare props.

On Thursday an order came out of naming Squadron C.O. vice C.O. Flight Leaders and Wingers – I was named A.F.L.!!! Should mean a raise in pay I hope!

That Saturday, three Blenheims and six Brewster Buffaloes flew up on their way to Hayhoe. The pilots were those we met at Singapore and now they were transferred up here. They remained here only several hours, gassing up and having lunch. They flew over the field later in the afternoon on their way back.

Tuesday I was incapacitated with a slight touch of dysentery, so I spent the day in bed and did not fly the next.

Thursday got in an hour flying for a change and Friday I got my first gunnery practice. Between the iron sight and half the guns not firing, I did not do so good. The rest of the morning I spent as Airdrome officer in the control tower. Also test a ship with vanes on the dust pan of the wheels to try to get them spinning before landing, but the experiment was not very successful.

Robert sightseeing. Photo courtesy Virginia S. Davis.

On Sunday morning I received a post card from Grace and Gus from Albuquerque mailed September 18th. Also took a bicycle ride to a nearby pagoda to take a few pictures. It is a small compound, a stone shrine and several small stone shrines – one building with a golden Buddha but not many jewels on it. Another alabaster statue and several old objects like drums and bells. On returning to the field, we watched the Beechcraft land with Gen. Magruder, one of the American Mission to China. He stayed overnight and caught the CNAC the next day.

One day the next week, two Brewsters came up and Shilling took one on in a dog fight and beat him three out of three. This morning, Friday, another group came up, four of them, and Bacon split one for on. It seems the Tomahawk can hold its own.

Last Thursday, Olson, Howard, Neal and Shilling flew up to Kunming to look the place over. They made it in about 2 ½ hours, averaged 245 mph. They returned today.

The next few weeks passed by like greased lightning. Nothing happened but the time went very quickly.

December 1941

Monday, December 8th will probably prove to be an outstanding day in my aviation career for upon arriving at the line about 6:30, we were met with the astounding news that on December 7, Japan had attacked Hawaii, Philippines Islands, Wake and Cream Islands of the United States Territories. They attacked Hawaii early in the morning and without any opposition did considerable damage to the airfield,

killing over 200 soldiers and about 3000 casualties were due to the
bombing of the cities. There was a naval battle near Honolulu when
Pearl Harbor was attacked and it was rumored that the Oklahoma
and West Virginia, both capital ships, were sunk or badly damaged.
Several Japanese ships were shot down in the melee. The attack upon
the Philippines was very similar and here they tried to land parachute
troops on several of the islands, Tuzon in particular. Both Nichols
and Clark air fields were severely bombed and a good number of
dead and casualties. The Clipper was shot at and burned. Here also a
few Jap planes were brought down and a German pilot was found in
one of them. Wake and Guam islands met similar fates.

The Japs also attacked the Malaya Straits, simultaneously bombing Singapore and Hong Kong. There were rumors of parachute
troopers being landed above Singapore on Malaya Straits.

Thailand also felt the force of the Japanese army when it held
off the attack for five hours, then resistance stopped, but again drove
back the Japs.

It looked like a well planned Blitzkrieg for Japan. They seemed
to have won the first round, but the fight is far from finished.

Here at the field, all the ships ready to go were put on the alert
fully loaded, oxygen lined up and even kept warm. Nothing happened here at the field but a lot of post mortems and prophesizing
went on. The Navy boys took quite a verbal beating for letting the
Japs attack without holding them off or letting them thru.

Tuesday brought more reports repeating the previous happenings
and a few confirmations came thru although many reports of new
naval battle, sinking of ships, landing of parachute and land forces
came over the radio from all parts of the world.

That afternoon about four o'clock after an otherwise calm day
(besides getting up at 4:30), an observation plane was thought to
have been near and immediately about 20 planes took off in search
for it, but none located any foreign ships. A night alert group of six
was put in effect and almost came in use. About 3 o'clock the next
morning we were awakened by the shrieking of the siren, denoted
an air raid – in a few minutes we heard the six ships taking off. By
then we were dressed and outside our barracks next to the five bomb
trenches constructed for such a purpose.

We could hear our own ship flying overhead, but even with a
bright half-moon and a clear sky, we could not follow their course.

I went to the field about 3:30 to await developments. By then most everyone had congregated there for the same reason as I with the thought of a bombing in sight. However, discounting several flashes thought to be flares and others thought to be bombs, nothing happened, and after a half hour the all clear signal was given and the runway was fairly lit by hard lanterns. Soon the planes were seen to turn on their wing lights and come in to land. The first two made it fine, but the third with Tex Hill overshot and went into the brush; working the plane out, but doing no personal damage. The other three ships landed in good order. Soon it was time for breakfast so had a not too hearty breakfast after that small alarm. The rest of the day passed as per usual, but for the tenseness in the air. The radio was listened to with interest and everyone expressed his views on the happenings and consequences. There was a report of Jap planes seen 20 miles off San Francisco. There were no further reports of the battles in the Pacific.

There were also no reports or confirmation of any bombings in Burma so we must have been mistaken in our little escapade which cost us one great P-40.

That afternoon, we also sent out a camera ship with two escorts over Thailand for a reconnaissance flight, but they returned with no important news. That day we also heard the rebroadcast of President Roosevelt's Fireside Chat, which all the fellows seemed to acknowledge. An alert crew has held that night but although there was no alarm, there was the telephone, tenseness and other precautionary noises to cope with for a none too pleasant night.(sic)

Thursday morning the reconnaissance flight took off for Jevoy and refueled and then flew over Bangkok at 26,000 feet for pictures. Upon returning and developing the pictures, 93 planes were counted on the field. Seems like they took Thailand over and moved right in. More news of the sinking of several British ships off Singapore. About 3 o'clock, I heard our squadron was to go down to Rangoon to help the R.A.F., but because of bad weather, could not take off. We did get off at 9:30 the next morning and 18 of us made the flight without any trouble. The truck convoy that left the previous evening with the ground crew was there waiting for us at Mingaladon.

A "Yank with the R.A.F." might now be my nickname. We got our planes dispersed, gassing facilitated, room and board taken care of and got ready for action. We were fortunate enough in not getting any the first date, but on Saturday after being kept up most of the night with a mild case of diarrhea, I had tea for breakfast, straightened out a few matters and returned to the barracks, but was awaken by the siren. There were two observing planes seen overhead, but except for several Brewsters giving chase, no other action was taken. Back to bed. At about 1 o'clock the shrill blast of the siren, the call of fellow pilots that they were coming, and I was out and dressed in no time flat. I missed the car and by the time I walked to the line, all the planes had taken off. The report was that there were 27 enemy planes coming. Within 15 minutes, there were 18 Tomahawks and about 16 Brewsters up and after them. Two of the 40's had to return because of prop trouble. This alarm again proved to be in vain because the enemy turned back about 100 miles from here. Hope they do it every time. We quickly serviced the planes just in case they returned, but not till about 9:30, just after I got to bed and about to fall asleep – thinking of some good air tactics when the shrill siren sounded and roused me from my semi-sleep – fumbled the mosquito netting, grabbed my clothes I had set next to my bed for just an emergency, threw them on quickly, grabbed my gas mask, helmet and gun and dashed out the door, down the stairs and next to a bomb trench where I was already beaten by several others. Soon it became very quiet except for someone calling, "Put out that light". After about a half hour of this tenseness, waiting for something to happen, the all-clear siren sounded and back to bed. This time I really slept.

My stomach still bothered me for the next few days, but except for a half-hour check hop on Tuesday, we did not do any flying, so I had no cause of worry about flying. We have a three shift alert now, of two groups, from 5:30 to 8:00; 8:00 to 1:00; and 1:00 to 5:30. This gives each fellow a chance to get a little sleep when he is on the 30 minute alert. The five minute alert remains on the line, keeping the planes warm and in readiness.

We did get a chance to go into Rangoon Sunday night after a rather hectic trip in. There were no taxies out at the field so five of us rode atop a gas truck into Insien where we took a local train into Rangoon and a bicycle rickshaw to the Savoy for supper. Took about 2 ½ hours from the time we let the barracks till we got to the Savoy. As my stomach was upset, I only had a brandy to try to calm it and a bowl of soup – at about 9:30, Haywood and I got a taxi and I came back out, not a too eventful trip.

At first I really thought I missed hearing the alarm and a Jap bomber had buzzed the field, but as I became more fully awake from my afternoon resting, and did not hear any bombs, I thought it was a formation of Brewsters. Someone on the porch said a consolidated

B-24A had just passed over, so I quickly ran out and saw it disappear below the trees preparing to land. Several of us quickly dressed and ran out to the runway just in time to see it turn around and taxi back to the line. We took one of our little Stud. "Champions" and drove down to the plane. With high hopes and feeling elated over meeting the American crew, but only one fellow was known to any of us. He was the navigator in Hodges class and later I found out he knew Chuck Beves very well. They had left Bolling Field and proceeded via Miami, Puerto Rico, Brazil, over the South Atlantic to Africa and up to Cairo, Egypt, where they picked up General Brett. The plane stayed overnight and then took off for Calcutta for safety. Most of the officers, including the General remained here.

The next morning, Thursday, I went up on my first patrol. The British were expecting an important convoy and wanted some fighter protection. We only had four ships up at one time; two at 10,000 and two at 15,000. We were first at 15,000 for an hour then at 10,000 for the second hour. We only had a 30 mile strip to patrol; about 20 miles East of Rangoon between the coast and Thongwa. Nothing happened during the tour, except a sore fanny from the ride.

Another patrol Friday at 17,000 feet for a couple of hours, but nothing sighted. We have the alert now from dawn to dusk. Same schedule Saturday.

Since I was to have Sunday off, I went into town Saturday evening. Several of us went to see "Hold That Ghost" with Abbott and Costello, which was quite a scream. Then we went to the Savoy for a steak dinner and a few drinks. From there I went to the Silver Grill, where I met Kennedy with his girl, which called for a little Bird-dogging, so I had two or three dances with her – the first real dancing since Los Angeles, except for the Dress Ball up at Toungoo. I left for home rather early – Kennedy had the CAMCO station wagon, so he was kind enough to take me home. A rather pleasant evening was had. I had a notion to go into town Sunday morning to spend the day there, but was unable to get a taxi, so Hedman and I didn't go in till after luncheon. We went to see "Mr. Jordan Returns", then had tea at Savoy and we went to a show again. I saw "Bittersweet" and he saw Abbot and Costello. Afterwards we met at the Savor for another spot of tea where we met Overend and Older. We all came about 10 p.m. Monday passed as usual.

BUT – Tuesday, (12-23-41) Now, that was the day – war came to Rangoon in the form of 38 bombers and 27 pursuit.

The 3rd Pursuit Squadron. Photo courtesy of the San Diego Air & Space Museum.

We received an alarm about 10 o'clock so six of us took off for 17,000 feet. Dupouy had three and then Martin and I and Jernstedt the last three. At about 10:30 we were at 17,000 when I saw 21 bombers in a beautiful tight V of V's, coming in towards Rangoon at about our altitude about 10 miles away. We climbed about 2000 feet and then dove on them in a string. I aimed at the leading formation and from a front quarter diving attack, was able to sweep the whole formation with no apparent results. After diving down and away, I turned around and got more altitude from which I again followed Martin in a rear quarter diving attack. I made the mistake of again sweeping a formation instead of picking out one ship. No results again. Since we had broken formation by then, I started looking for someone to hook onto. I thought I saw a group of about six planes which I thought were another of our group, so I started toward them to tack on. Upon approaching closer I saw the planes had fixed landing gear. I thought this odd and upon getting closer I saw the large red circle on the upper wing starring me in the face. I quickly turned and gave it full guns as I saw two planes take after me. They only followed me up a few thousand feet and then dropped back down into formation. I kept climbing up to 20,000 feet where I looked around for someone to hook on. I couldn't find anyone so after a half hour, I went down and landed. Although the bombing was terrible and devastating, but it was a picturesque sight to see the large bombing formations of 21 and then another of 18 that came in a second wave. They held a beautiful close formation and you could see the black particles of smoke on their bombs hit Rangoon. The spots were scattered and about 10 or 12 fires were started, bellowing smoke straight up and forming a mushroom at about 3000 feet. There were also many bombs dropped along the docks but it seemed as no damage was done – only splashes of water as the bombs hit. Around the formation were black spots as the anti-aircraft were being fired upon the bombers. Out towards the airport I could see several fires as petrol dumps were hit – one in particular was giving off a black tower of smoke which rose perfectly vertically and formed a head about 3000 feet. Spots were also seen on the runway where small craters were made by dropping bombs. Throughout my flight I could not see any pursuits, but upon landing I heard the other fellows' stories. Most of them seemed to be by themselves in their attacks – getting in close enough to see their hits go home. There were about six fellows claiming hits. We were missing three planes but after about 20 minutes, Greene came back in a car rather banged up. His plane had been badly shot and he bailed out. His chute was loose and jarred him and scratched his neck and face. He was stiff all over. On the way down he was strafed but luckily enough not hit. Someone had seen Martin hit and dive in, but no confirmation. Gilbert's plane was found with him shot and burned – not much left of him. So we lost three ships from being fired upon and crashed and two others shot up too badly to be serviceable. Reed upon landing in an afternoon patrol, hit a bomb crater damaging a wheel and wing; which leaves us with 12 serviceable ships. By the by – Greene was using my plane when he got hit, so I feel sorry about that, but happy to know my chute worked!

While one squadron of bombers hit Rangoon, another bombed the field putting many direct hits upon hangars, petrol dumps, operations buildings and the runways. The pursuit ship came down and strafed the field. They did a great deal of damage, burning up grounded planes and ruining many buildings.

On the humorous side was the fact that most of the bearers and cooks and servants left the field and never returned. We had to make our beds, get our own food from the kitchen and mostly we had cafeteria, buffet style of serving. The rest of the afternoon, we kept up at least six planes on patrol, but nothing was sighted.

There were eight bombers and one fighter confirmed, but there were probably more that did not get back to their bases. I think I put enough lead in some of them to sink them.

My reactions throughout the day were varied. When we first sighted the enemy I marveled at the beauty of the formation, and as I charged my guns and turned on the switch, diving down on them for the first time, I had a slight feeling of exultation and mostly wonderment – wondering if I would bring anything down. The next pass I made as casual as on a target ship, not even worried very much about return fire. But as I passed, I really stuck the nose down expecting to be hit any second. My greatest scare came when the two Jap pursuit ships started after me, but after I lost them, I just kept my eyes rolling like a (expletive), looking for enemy. I think I'll do better hereafter using more discretion and less caution.

After just retiring that night, a false alarm came through which caused us the unpleasant necessity of going out to a trench.

Wednesday brought no news of Martin or more than nine confirmations. We kept up a patrol all morning with six ship flights – around noon a report of nine enemy planes came thru – everyone took off, but nothing was sighted. We patrolled all day till dusk, putting in five to seven hours each. The mess facilities were not much better, but we did get some food.

"CHRISTMAS IN THE TRENCHES" or more appropriately, "War in the Air". The morning started out pretty calm, even though the Japs promised us over the radio that they would give the Americans and Rangoon a real Christmas present. About 10:30 we got a call to scramble to 15 angels – I was on Bishop's wing in Dupouy's flight. We took off first, but Bishop did not wait for the rest of the flight. We got up to 18 angels and cruised around for a half hour, then not hearing anything on the radio, Bishop and I dove down over the field. We just about got to 2000 feet when I heard the radio say not to pancake. We started climbing again and as I got about 4000 feet, I looked around and saw a burst and then bombs exploding on the field. We must have been directly under the bombers and did not see them. I expected any moment to hear some ships diving on us as we were slowly climbing. I quickly gave it the gate and climbed as fast as possible. I got to 18,000 feet unmolested and I then saw a tight 30 ship Jap bomber formation going southeast over Rangoon at about 20 angels. I started towards them and as I got closer I noticed a single Jap Navy #96 pursuit ship, with fixed landing gear. I had about a 1000 feet height advantage off to his left, so I turned into him on his rear and dove down below his rear and climbed up his blind spot under his tail. As I closed into within 50 yards, I opened fire with all six guns. I could see the bullets entering his ship and he suddenly made a very quick wing over to the right, and I had to turn the opposite direction to miss him. I turned around to see if I could find him, but he was probably going down too fast. I didn't follow him down so cannot say exactly where he fell, but from my close fire, he could not have possibly escape destruction. I dove down for speed and then climbed up to 16 angels – I could not see any planes so I came in to land. Pending confirmation, I think I have my first plane.

The other fellows did very well – Hedman accounting for four, McMillan got three and was shot down himself. We thought he was a goner when he did not return, but after supper about 8:30, he walked in the mess hall with a bandaged arm and hand. He made a crash landing in a rice paddy and finally got the natives to help him. He got a horse and rode about 10 miles to Toungoo where the police took him to Rangoon on a police boat and then in a police car up to the field. He had a Jap Saber which he got from a bomber shot down on the first raid. We sure were glad to see him walk in. Overend was also reported shot down and missing, so we did not expect to see him anymore, but at about 9:30 that night, we got a telegram from a small village that Overend was safe and we should pick him up at Rangoon about 10 p.m. He was not hurt at all, but shot down while shooting a bomber down. He also had a crash landing.

Our unofficial account was 10 fighters and nine bombers. The R.A.F. got six planes and lost four. This was their first loss in personnel.

The two ships shot down and Smith's and Hedman's were pretty badly shot up. Dupouy shot down one model "0" and in getting away, hit his wing tip against the wing of another causing the enemy to spin in and Parker came in alright with his right wing tips off and half of his aileron missing. Another McMillan feat. Older and Haywood stuck together and counted four together. Some of the fellows thought they saw some Me 109's but not positive.

The damage to the field was about the same as before with larger holes caused by bigger bombs. Only one Petrol dumb was hit and two casualties on the field. The greatest damage to the personnel was via food. We were very low on food and, of course, were without any kind of Christmas Dinner. In the afternoon, Mr. Bill Pawley came out with a car full of canned food and drinks which was really welcomed. So another day under fire passed with experience gained and ships lost. A sidelight of interest was that just after the air raid sounded, the British General – Wavell D.C. – 2 landed with her and General Brett of the U.S. Air Corps. They both had to take shelter in a trench and saw the raid first hand.

Friday morning we had an alarm and sent up about seven ships on patrol. We were up at 22 angels for two hours, but nothing was noted.

We expected them back Friday, but except for the alarm none came. There was a rumor circulating around town that there were pamphlets dropped over Rangoon that the Japs would drop 3000 parachute troops that night, so we all went to bed ready to pull a strategic retreat in our cars just in case. However, except for a very slight sleep, we were spared the wild ride that would ensue.

The worst part about Saturday was the utter lack of digestible food. Breakfast consisted of bread and tea – dinner was salmon, apricots and coffee – supper was bread and cheese with tea. The cooks had all gone and no food seemed to be in sight – somebody slipped up some place. For safety's sake we took six ships over to Satellite Field at Regu at dusk.

While we were in readiness at the alert tent during the afternoon, we saw two large impressive looking cars with a flag flying from the radiator cap. They came to us and saw it was the Governor of Burma, Sir Dorman Smith, with General Brett and several other high British officers. The Governor expressed his best wishes and thanks for our cooperation and the General gave his opinion as of the air service. It helped the morale of the troops!

Sunday we heard that we were to be relieved by another squadron from Kunming, so we felt a little relief. There were no alarms or patrols for us so we got a little rest. About 10 o'clock we were surprised to see one of our CAMCO trucks pull up in front of the tent with the mechanics of "B" Squadron. There were three pilots in with them so we got some of the news from up North. We found out the official dope on the 3 CW 21's which got lost between Lashio and Kunming. Mangleburg crashed on a forced landing and was burned. Shilling and Merritt crashed their ships, but did not get hurt. Since there was not any missing facilities, the fellows took a train back to Toungoo where they had dinner at the railway station and then took a train back to arrive at Mingaladon again about 10 o'clock. We did not have any alarms or patrols again, but were packed ready to go whenever the other squadron would arrive, which it did not that day, except for Newkirk and Bacon who came ahead to get things in shape.

Finally on Tuesday morning, 15 more of "B" Squadron planes came in so after a couple hours of hot-air blasting, we took off for Toungoo. McMillan had engine trouble so did not get off, so only 10 of us got up to Toungoo about 1:30. Had the first good meal in about a week.

The next morning we had a breakfast of eggs – the first in one week – got weather reports from up country and got ready to take off at about 10:30. I just got off the ground when I noticed oil on my windshield. My oil cap was loose and oil was frothing out. I came right back in to have it taken care of. The others saw I was O.K. and went on their course. I was fixed up in about 15 minutes, so I took off. I thought I might catch them so I gave it plenty of mercury, in fact I had a hard time checking my check points because of my speed. However, I hit Mandalay all right and headed for Lashio. Just as I got over the field, I saw that about six were on the ground and a couple more in their traffic circle, so I let my wheels down and started coming in. As I was just on my last leg, I saw Smith, who was top cover man, coming down so I beat him in for a perfect timing flight. The country up to Mandalay was flat and had lots of towns and roads, but from there to Lashio was a little rougher. There weren't very many check points and the course was over a very narrow valley, with rough mountains on either side.

At Lashio we were taken into town for a bite to eat while our ships were being gassed. We took off about 2:00 with a bad broken overcast. About 10 miles out we went through a large cumulus cloud for several minutes and when we came out, we were all scattered, but finally rejoined. The country over which we flew was perhaps the most beautiful and most dangerous I have ever been over. We were at 15,000 feet and every now and then only five or six thousand above the top of some rugged peaks. There seemed to be sheer drops of several thousands of feet between cliffs – no landing places for miles on end. As it was fairly well overcast, we could not see very far, except down, and that was not all enlightening. The strange thing was that in the remotest part of nowhere on the ride, top, or valley of a range would be a green patch of vegetation of some farmer. How they ever knew what was even 50 miles away was hard to conceive. There were places about eight to ten thousand feet completely covered with clouds which looked like a snow covered lake between two mountains. Large billowy cumulus clouds started in a valley and rose about peaks like smoke rising above pipe. Besides being somewhat jittery about the flight path, it was rather cold and it was a great sigh of relief when the lakes at Kunming came into view. We dropped down, circled the large grass field with a runway being built through the center, and then landed 6500 feet above sea level. It was the first time, besides Lashio at 2500 that I landed over two or three hundred feet above sea level.

We were rushed to a ready shack where it was warm and were brought tea and cakes, and then some winter flying clothes to keep us warm. About an hour later, we were driving from the field to our hotel on the other side of Kunming, thru the bomb blasted streets, with a milling throng of heavily dressed Chinese, out on the streets with their wares displayed for sale. Others carrying produce in baskets hung from a bamboo pole across their shoulders. I was surprised by the great number of American cars each trying to out blow their horns.

Our hostel consists of three narrow buildings, three stories high, of white or grey brick with red tile roofs of Chinese design with painted ends and carvings all along the edges and top. The Administration building is in the center with rooming houses on either flank. The enlisted men sleep on the south and we on the north. My room is on the first floor, of white calcimine, about 20x20x12 with a canvas bed with a soft quilt mattress, a dresser, locker and writing table – two windows for fresh air and light, and a small clay charcoal burner for heat, and not too much of that.

The service is very good and the food almost equals that on the good old Jagers frontier!

Authors Note:

The end of 1941 proved the American Volunteer Group could fight and beat the Japanese. Chinese and American newspapers announced the victories against the Japanese. These announcements gave the people of the United States heroes to honor as the World War was progressing against the Japanese in the Pacific.

The Chinese Newspapers "heralded their victories and dubbed them 'Fei Hu,' the Flying Tigers." This was an important designation because since the 1911 founding of the Chinese Republic, the Tiger was the national symbol. The name, Flying Tigers, was the highest accolade that could be bestowed on the American Volunteer Group by the Chinese Government.

During the last days of December heard the exploits of the American Volunteer Group were broadcast on many U.S. radio stations and through these broadcasts, the Flying Tigers became national heroes. They were known as the most dedicated and hardworking fighters to serve anywhere. The Flying Tigers became heroes and legends at a time when Americans needed that most.

January 1942

The first day here, incidentally, January 1, 1942, we slept till about 7:30. Had three eggs for breakfast, then drove into town to exchange some money and send a radiogram home.

Most of the people in Kunming seem of the poorer class, wearing almost all a blue cotton quilt long dress with tennis shoes, and varied colored long stockings seen thru the split in the bottom of the dress. The women work as hard as men, carrying their babies, a la papoose, carrying baskets on their shoulder poles, have large bundles on their backs held by chest and head straps. I get the impression their work is terribly hard yet they endure it without any wailing. Men carrying in tremendous loads, looking as if they might not last another step, keep trudging on till they deliver that load to get another.

The shops along the brick streets are of mud bricks or wooden, one upon the next, with wooden doors, open during the day for an entrance, and closed at night for their home. Most all shop keepers live right in their shops. There are a few larger buildings and some on a more modernistic design, but there are also many just barely standing, after direct hits from bombs. Many a wall is standing with an interior.

The first week was spent in a most leisurely manner. We were having our planes checked and had no duties so we were on our own, getting up about 8 o'clock, taking plenty of time eating breakfast, then just sitting around the charcoal stove in the bar, playing Acey-Deucy or reading. The afternoons were usually spent getting flying equipment or just riding around getting familiar with the lay of the land. One afternoon several of us took a little side trip about 20 kilometers away up on top of one of the mountains overlooking the lake. There we saw the "Temple of 500 Faces". It gets its name from the fact that the main idol building, besides the five main statues in the center, are numerous life-like images of people. These small images, about three feet high are in full detail (plaster of Paris) with vivid coloring. They range from grotesque dwarfs to beautiful looking women – some seem to depict scenes – there were three walls covered with them from floor to ceiling, and there looked like more than 500 to me – closer to a thousand. They were like a Christmas display of brightly dressed and painted dolls.

The temple itself seemed to be built on a plateau of a cliff, rising 2000 feet straight from the lake. It gave a marvelous view of the lake, city and ranges of mountains surrounding the valley of Kunming. On the way back we stopped half way down the mountains to practice our gunnery with a 22 cal rifle and my .38.

Monday the 5th, we had the night alert of six, so I happened to be chosen and spent the afternoon getting details settled. We used mostly the 1st Squadron ships as ours were not finished as yet. We were on duty from 6 p.m. to 5:30 a.m. Nothing happened except I had a slight case of diarrhea which kept me awake most of the night, whereas we might have slept. I also was on the alert Wednesday night, but this time I slept better. Thursday afternoon, Sawyer, Greene, and I went in the Beechcraft to Yunnanyi for a three day vacation. Sawyer was told to take a rest and to take two fellows with him, so Greene and I were the fortunate associates. We left about 2 o'clock and started flying west along the Burma Road, only after about 30 miles, it divides and true to form, the pilot took the wrong fork and came to a field which he thought was it. We landed and found it was Shungshee about 20 miles northwest of our course and 50 miles from Yunnanyi. We gassed up and took off. After crossing several ranges, we came into view of a large valley with numerous lakes and small villages. There seemed to be about 40 lakes and as many villages. The field stood out like a sore thumb, especially the new stone runway coolies were building by hand. There are several hundred coolies just breaking large stones into little ones and placing each in place by hand. It is a sight to see – comparable only to the Burma Road construction gangs doing the same slow tedious work. They get paid 10-20 cents a day, while those on the road only get food from the Government.

We finally landed about four o'clock and were met by the three instructors stationed there along with Capt. Carney. We went to the house belonging to Skip Adair where they live. It is situated on the side of a hill about three miles from the field and overlooks the whole valley a splendidly situated spot. We had a bit of tea, then went to our hostel, where we were to stay. It consisted of about six wooden buildings of six rooms each, holding two to a room – not too spacious but comfortable. After supper we went back to their house where we met two members of the British Embassy; an American who we called Sak; and Dave Olsen. Sak is an American citizen though, born in Colorado, went to the same military school, New Mexico, as Greene, so these two had a few things in common. Sak also went to Colorado University and to Harvard. He almost has his Ph.D. He was about 35, but has the wit of G.B. Shaw. He traveled over quite a bit of Europe and Japan, and Far East. He is somewhat of a Socialist, I think, and is very much interested in China. Very interesting to talk to, especially Political Science. They brought several bottles of Scotch, which is at a premium up there, so a good time was had by all; except I wasn't too well so did not indulge. That night I also had the runners. I slept all next morning and went walking up in the hills in the afternoon, lying on the top, listening to the wind whistle thru the pine trees. That evening the gang of us got together again for a friendly game of Black Jack. No more liquor was had! Saturday, Sawyer and I spent the forenoon out tramping with our 22's, but did not get any birds. After noon the six of us, Sak and Olsen left to find the rest of their convoy they lost somewhere, went duck hunting. We tramped at least 10 miles and only got one goose and two teals. I got one of the teals with my trusty 22 after stalking him for 30 minutes on one of the lakes. That evening we were invited to Capt. Carney's house for a real Chinese dinner. His woman, Rose, a pretty Chinese woman, fixed up a most delicious Chinese dinner, and at first I had quite a time with my chop sticks, but soon caught on. Thereafter, I enjoyed it immensely. The main dish was chicken soup with egg foo young; almond dish, sweet and sour pork, chicken paddy; cabbage; two meat stews; and several other dishes. It really was good and I had my fill. The evening was spent playing records and drinking the Captain's whisky.

Sunday morning was spent mostly in bed again. After dinner we stopped at Loanes, Shepards, and Shemlin's house till we heard the Beechcraft coming in for us. After Hennesy and Mickelson, the pilots had dinner, we took off, and what a take off. We just cleared the trees and just tipped the tops. Not enough oomph in the old bus.

We got back at Kunming about 3 o'clock after a real restful sojourn ready to get back to work. I would like to spend about a month doing what we did up there – rest, go duck hunting, and a few delicious Chinese dinners. Nothing for us to do till night alert – Monday night.

Seems that the second squadron down at Rangoon base had a little combat. They had one raid which shot down fire, but Bright, Paxton and Christman were shot down, but not hurt. On the strafing job at Tak, Newkirk, Hill and Howard got seven ships – no damage to self. They went back with nine 40's and five Brewsters, got 24 at Tak, but Matt was seen shot down – not definite of outcome or him. Hope for the best.

The Japs now call use cruel, barbarous, blood thirsty Americans. One of the pilots shot down called us pugnacious, unorthodox. The radio at Tokyo also said the AVG is Japan's No. 1 Enemy.

Monday night Greene and I were on alert with nothing more to do than catch up on a little sleep. Having Tuesday off, several of us got a car and took a drive to the other side of the lake where a natural landslide left a sheer vertical drop of over a thousand feet. Many large boulders measuring 30 feet on a side were along the river's edge, some partially submerged. There was a small village amongst the rocks where the people lived that broke the rocks into smaller pieces, loaded them on sampans and sailed across the lake to the city for disposition. There also seemed to be some kind of kilns there that burned the rocks and gave forth voluminous black, sulfur odor smoke and left a black coal like residue. We could not find any interpreter around so could not find out what process was involved.

The next day, Wednesday, I was on day alert and ran several test hops, which I needed badly after so long a lay off. The next two days also passed along the same, but on Saturday, at about 10 o'clock, we were told an observation ship was flying near Mengzi, so we all took off, but all but four were told to return. McMillan, Shilling, Older and Haywood were the four who went to investigate. We were told to go to 20 angels over the field, but soon landed as we found out our four ships had intercepted three bombers. Shilling returned first stating he saw one go down for sure; soon after the rest returned and said two for sure and one probably. A little later the third was confirmed; so we hit 100% that time. That should vex the Japs to no end.

We heard over Tokyo radio that they had Mott in a hospital pretty badly burned up, but alright.

After the raid on Tak in Thailand, the 2nd Squadron down at Rangoon reported Moss missing, but he turned up several days later at Moulmein. Another piece of good luck.

The 1st Squadron finally got down to Hanoi for some pictures which turned out fairly well. They only had about 28 bombers and 15 fighters down there.

On Wednesday the 1st Squadron escorted 18 Chinese bombers (Russian SB-3) to presumably Hanoi, but because of overcast skies, went to Haiphong and bombed. They could not see their objective so could not get any results. All the fighters returned, but two bombers had some trouble and did not get back. The only opposition was some anti-aircraft fire.

A few alarms kept us in the air on several days, but a photo mission over Indo China, usually Hanoi, was the most flying any one put in. If it weren't for a test hop every other day or so, I'd be low on time and out of practice.

I had my first "Jing Bow" or Air Raid Alarm here at Kunming while on the ground away from the field. I had a day off and was writing a letter when I heard the siren and saw two red balls hoisted on the pole, which meant immediate danger. I took off with Tex Blaylock, our chief, who was at the dentist, into the hills about a mile from the hostel. As most of the hills are covered with mounds of grasses, it makes good bomb protection. They dig holes about four feet deep, large enough for one or two persons between the mounds and it affords the best protection next to a steel shelter. The only bad part of our hideout was that several anti-aircraft guns were located on top of the hills. As we were very near this hideout, we got situated and I could watch the multitudes streaming out of the city. The usual one way Burma road was packed with cars, trucks, rickshaws, carts and what not, taking up every inch of the road, and seemingly moving outward a few feet every little while, but surprisingly enough in fifteen minutes the road was clear along with the continuous blare of horns as everyone tried to out blow each other out of the way. The people on foot streamed past the traffic and many took refuge among our graveyard. There was room for plenty but plenty there were. To our relief, the alarm was false and the only planes we heard and saw were our own P 40's out on patrol.

We were still hearing of the good work the boys down in Rangoon were doing. Twelve of Sandell's 1st Squadron went down for assistance, arriving a little late for one raid, but getting one the following day. It seems the Japs are only sending over Army 96's and 97's – no model "0"s. Bombers are single engine 98's only once did they send over seven 97's and they lost all of those. They are also coming over in small formations at night, but one of the R.A.F.'s Hurricanes got two of those. Then they are supposed to have about 10 Hurricanes down there and expecting more. From the many fields in Burma, the R.A.F. are bombing Bangkok with Blenheims and Lockheed "Hudsons."

Today, the 30th, I got back a letter I mailed to Mary Jane Steckmort on September 4th at Toungoo; it went to N.Y. arriving the 24th, and as no forwarding address was left, it came back here!!! Twenty days there and four months back.

On Saturday, January 31, 1942, the residing pilots of the AVG at Kunming were presented with their wings from the Chinese Air Force. A representative of the Generalissimo presented them to us as we held our first dress formation since our being here. Colonel Chennault expressed his thanks for us.

February 1942

Ever so often in the Chinese army, they hold a "comforting day" which consists of speech making and presentation of gifts to bolster the morale of the troops. We had one on Monday, February 2, at which the commanding officer of the Chinese Air Force and the president of the China Aviation Association, along with other members of the association presented Colonel Chennault with a scroll and embroidered silk American Flag. To 10 of the pilots present were given an embroidered silk bed spread for their good work under fire. Only those who had victories confirmed were presented, which left me out as somehow or other my claim was not substantiated.

We had a surprise on Wednesday afternoon when the CNAC] landed and the Generalissimo and Madame Chang Kai-Shek alighted. They were here only about half an hour; looked over the field, talked with Colonel Chennault and left for Lashio. We didn't get introduced to either, but were with them. The British Ambassador to China along with several other high ranking Chinese officials were also aboard.

Robert and Crew Chief Frank Losonsky Photo courtesy Virginia S. Davis.

The past few weeks went by without any excitement here except for several mornings when some of the better Chinese pilots were checking out in the P-40's. Of seven, only one had difficulty and ground loped, doing considerable damage to the plane.

The 2nd Squadron men were dribbling back by planes, the Beechcraft and CNAC. Squadron Leader Sandell was killed down in Rangoon while testing a ship. The exact way is not known. I hit the jackpot one day when I received out eight pieces of mail, six being Christmas cards. Sunday, the 15th, while starting my day off, we were told to report to the field. We really thought there was something up. Upon reaching the ready shack we were told that there were 50 P-40's for us at Cairo, Egypt and that we were to ferry them here. Six of the fellows were to go the following day. McMillan, Smith, Greene, Older, Haywood, and Laughlin were the first fortunate six. They left by CNAC for Calcutta on Monday morning. I was put in charge of operation along with Engineering so had my hands full. Monday was also the wedding of Petach and Miss Foster, a long awaited event.

Wednesday will long be remembered by those members of the 3rd Squadron who scored victories down at Rangoon, for on that afternoon they were presented with medals from the Chinese Government for their bravery and good work. As several of them were on the ferry trip to Cairo, only six actually were present to receive their reward. Olson was given a 5th class medal for his fine work on the ground, handling the squadron in a magnificent manner. Duke Hedman received a 5th along with another five-point star medal for scoring five victories. The others were Dupouy, Read, Jernstedt, and Overend. They received 6th class with a small pair of gold wings with the number of stars representing the number of victories. As neither Hodges' nor my confirmations came thru till Friday next, we did not receive any thing at that time.

The following Sunday another six pilots of the 3rd Squadron took off for Cairo or points west to ferry back ships. As the Generalissimo and the Madame landed here on Saturday night and expected to stay about a week, we had to keep the more experienced pilots here for protection, just in case. For that reason, the logical ones to go for the ships had to remain here; instead Shilling, Bishop, Foshee, Cavanah, Adkins, and Raines left.

The 2nd Squadron men were coming in from Burma now in greater strength so the pilots were put on the alert with us while their mechanics worked on their planes.

Things were getting pretty hot down in Rangoon, the Japs had forced their way across Moulmein, the Salween River, and now were right east of Pezu, which is only about 50 miles from Rangoon. Almost everyone had evacuated Rangoon, including the R.A.F. and left only about 12 AVG planes and three R.A.F. The rest went up to Magwee where nothing was prepared for the AVG and the British were evacuating that. Looks like the AVG will soon have to evacuate Burma as they seem to be left holding the bag.

On Monday last, the 23rd, Olson, Jernstedt, Hedman and Reed went out on a photo mission over Indo China and the two elements got separated somehow. Olson and Jernstedt got back O.K., but Hedman and Reed shot forced landings on a river bed some place in the vicinity. They did a good job, Hedman damaging only a prop, but both able to take off with a gas supply. They had radio contact, but we could not locate their exact position, although the Chinese were supposedly to know their whereabouts. So far today, being Wednesday morning, they have not been located by us or nothing done to get them back. Olsen tried looking for them from the air but did not succeed in seeing anything.

Thursday afternoon, shortly after five, fellows came up from Rangoon to trade planes, in came our two prodigal sons – Duke and Reed. They got here about 2 o'clock. They had a fairly decent time of being lost, only about 80 miles from here. We later found out Olson had flown directly over them but did not see them.

Saturday, February 28th, was a momentous occasion for the AVG The Generalissimo, Madam and several high ranking Chinese officials gave a dinner for us at our hostel. I was picked as aide to General Chow, the chief of the Air Force. All members of the AVG were present in the auditorium for supper and entertainment. The Generalissimo said a few words of great praise of the AVG as well as did the Madam. Both people won over all the command with their pleasant personality and vibrant energy. They are both forceful persons and have their hearts in their work. The Generalissimo's speech was translated whereas the Madame spoke in very good English. Then Colonel Chennault acknowledged their offerings and accepted their good wishes. Among those present were eight Chinese ladies who acted as hostesses. One rendered several fine songs in English and Chinese. Finally a Chinese play was put on which was humorous and very picturesque with many beautiful costumes. It concerned a fisherman and a racket with the poor innocent fisherman's daughter giving the racketeers hell – all parts were played by young boys. The squeaking voice of the feminine character struck everyone's humor.

March 1942

The following day six of us were to escort the General's planes to Lashio, but I had a rough motor so did not go and Overend's prop went out. The four escorted for about a hundred miles and returned just before dark.

Monday, the original six of us went to Loiwing by way of the Auxiliary airfields, Tusung, Yunnanyi, Pao-shan, etc. We got there about noon and were taken to the CAMCO quarters about 10 miles from the airfield. The altitude is only 2400 feet so it was very warm there. CAMCO has a wonderful set up with about four hangars for plane repair, about six large bungalows for occupation and a beautiful club house upon a hill. The club house is rather large with rooms on either wings, private bath in each room, three large bay windows 10'x15' overlooking the valley. It is all beaver board with teak wood floor and woodwork. The furniture is modern overstuffed and they have a wonderful 24 record radio-phonograph. The food was super and everything too good to last.

On Tuesday I had to fly back to Kunming to deliver a message to Colonel Chennault, taking 1:15 there and 1:30 back. Jernstedt relayed the answer from Loiwing to Lashio. That night the Colonel came to Lashio on the CNAC to see the Generalissimo and on Wednesday morning four of us flew to Lashio at 7 a.m. and escorted the General, Colonel, and party back to Kunming. Took two hours cruising at 140.

On Thursday morning, the General and party left for Chungking amid ceremony with a parade of six planes which escorted them up about 80 miles. Another six of us were to take off for Magwee in the morning, but because of the excitement did not get off.

Our little trip to Magwee was held up till Tuesday morning when five of us left at 11:30. Hedman was leading, with Fish, Reed, and Overend, and myself. We ran into hazy weather near Lashio and by some miscalculation, Hedman thought he overshot Lashio so did a 180 and started back. Went back for about 15 minutes then flew S.W. for another ten and then did weaving back North; by then we knew we were lost. We hit a valley with a river, railroad and road which we flew down for almost 10 minutes. Duke thought he recognized it as Bhamo so flew 140 degrees to hit Loiwing, but we were wrong and came back to the valley. This time Reed, Overend, and Fish flew about 60 degrees and Duke and I flew 140 degrees again. When we had about 15 gals left, we headed back toward the valley once more for a forced landing. We were told over the radio we were at F-3; S.E. of Loiwing, but I did not have a grid, or even enough gas, it did not help me any. When we got back to the valley with about 5 gals of gas, Duke buzzed several fields and finally picked out a sand bank along the river. He overshot the first pass and as I was so low on gas, I landed next. I hit short and was rolling along nicely when I hit a mound and bounced up a foot or so. The landing gear horn sounded, but the wheels tested O.K. so I pulled off to a side and watched Duke land O.K. We got Pao-shan on the radio, telling them we two were O.K. but know nothing of the others. When we landed there were only two natives, but soon had a large group of Burmese, one who was an interpreter and told us where we were at – 80 miles on a direct line to Lashio from Kunming – all we had to do was follow the river or road in the valley to Lashio – several Burma Frontier Force soldiers took guard of the plane and a Mr. Lee, Chinese, of the Vernon Burma R.R., who soon arrived, took us to his station along the road to Kunlong about three miles away. I was wearing poor fitting boots and got a large blister on either heel – tough walking! He served us some coffee, cookies and can of fruit, while we waited for a car from Kunlong. Two trucks of Chinese soldiers also came as they thought we might be Japs, but several were placed on guard over the planes. Duke and I had a six mile ride over a typical Chinese-Burma road to Kunlong, arriving about 5 o'clock; we landed at 2:45.

Kunlong is a construction camp along the 413R, its main station with Mr. Change, a Chief Engineer. There were about 250 men, several college men from the U.S., Civil Engineers. There were also several Americans who were Malaria control workers. The only one there was a Mr. Wright of the Rockefeller Foundation. Spent quite some time listening to his exploits during the last 35 years. He was in 32 different countries on malaria control. We stayed in Mr. Chang's building; which consisted of one central main room and four adjoining bedrooms. Duke and I had one together. We tried getting the 24-F at Lashio to get us gas, but did not succeed that night at all. After supper, a very good one, we heard that two other planes had landed up the river at Ming Tung about 20 miles. We did not know who or anything regarding the fifth plane. The evening was spent discussing world problems with Mr. Chang, Wright, Mr. Liu, the company auditor, who was in the 1919 Washington Peace Conference, and Mr. Mar, Mr. Wright's assistant. The company doctor fixed up my blisters.

Did not sleep very well that night, but had a good breakfast next morning at 7. About 10 o'clock a plane buzzed over, too high for us to see who it was, but he flew over our planes and the others. We continued trying to get gas from Lashio; but nothing but promises. A little later heard two more 40's from Kunming to Lashio.

After a most refreshing shower about 5 o'clock, in walked the three lost flyers; Fish had landed about 30 miles up the river, and to keep from going over a cliff into a river, nosed over but did not get hurt. Reed and Overend landed together. Overend hit a soft spot and went on his back too. Reed hit a dyke and washed out his landing gear. They were about 20 miles up. These two were picked up by Dr. Hall, an American with the U.S. Public Health Mission, working with Mr. Wright. Fish traveled by boat and horse all night and met the other two the next morning. Reed and Overend contacted Paoshan and gave their details. Next morning the three took out guns, ammunition and radio form their planes. Except for the loss of our planes, we had a happy group together that evening.

The next morning two R.A.F. boys arrived with a YBR truck, with 16-20 gallon drums of gas. We all piled into cars and drove out to our planes and filled them up with gas. Coolies carried five drums on poles to the planes. Upon a further investigation, I saw I had sprung my landing gear and did not think it advisable to try to retract my wheels. Duke and I got off safely with our 2000 feet sandbank runway. It was very hazy and had a little difficulty finding Lashio, but landed O.K. My landing gear held up alright. We went to the CNAC hostel for sandwiches and received a note left by Olsen. Hedman was to go back by CNAC to Kunming, rest, get to Magwee by planes or car. I flew up to Loiwing in the afternoon and again made out O.K. with my landing gear down. Prescott came up with me (on instruments).

Dave Harris met us out at the field and took us to the clubhouse. I stayed in Dave's room for the night. Next morning I flew the plane to the runway next to the factory about 2500 feet long.

I found out that McGarry had flown over our planes to drop some food and messages and got lost; washing out another plane!!! Prescott took off for Lashio and Burgard and McGarry for Kunming.

Upon checking the plane more thoroughly we found that the bulkhead at landing gear section was cracked in two places so necessitated changing wings. This meant a lay off to the following Thursday. Friday was a day of rest.

Saturday, I took up a ship, the 100th assembled, for a check, but found out the prop was loose and caused vibration. Spent most of the day just loafing around. Saturday I checked the plane again and flew to Lashio, to check up on some supplies for the AVG The prop was changed so the plane flew O.K. Reed had flown Duke's ship to Magwee, Overend drove a truck there and Fish flew down Monday in the Beechcraft, because of a bad foot and stomach trouble came back to go back to Kunming. While at Lashio, I met Hennessey in the Beechcraft. He was lost two days on his way to Lashio from Kunming. They came up here on Monday and then went to Magwee. They returned Tuesday. Monday I went on a little excursion into the hills with a .22 hunting birds, but didn't hit anything. Didn't fly that day, but worked on an engine for the radio station, motor generator with Ciora.

Tuesday morning I ran the last check on the 100th, it was poor visibility so I did most of my flying buzzing everything in sight. The Beechcraft came in during the afternoon along with a convoy of the last gang from Rangoon, Fox, McClure, Overley, Harpold, and a couple others. Really had a gang here for dinner that evening.

Wednesday afternoon, Hennessey took off for Kunming and Mickelson took the P-40 there. Fish also was along. About 7 o'clock they all piled back! They had been out 3:10, getting almost to Yunnanyi, but because of bad weather, returned. They stayed overnight and left for Lashio, where Mickelson left the P-40, at about 2 o'clock Thursday afternoon. My ship was pushed out of the factory, but ran rough so could not fly. In the afternoon, DC-3 on CNAC landed with 18 passengers – among them General McGruether and General Naiden, several Colonels and General Maw. Quite a bunch of brass for one load. They all left Friday morning for Kunming. In the afternoon, I flew my ship from the factory to the field where they finished loading and hooking up the air speed. I did not have any [problem] taking off from the factory, but did not have any trouble. At about 3:30 I took for Lashio and Magwee, but when half way to Lashio my motor cut out and started running rough, I turned around and came back. We checked up and found out the gas was dirty, so they put new outside plugs in, cleaned the discharge nozzle. That afternoon Olson came up from Magwee. Next morning the weather was bad, so right after lunch we went to go back. He got off O.K., but my ship cut out on takeoff so I got about 200 feet and landed on the closest runway 60 degrees from the way I took off, making a 120 degree turn and landing, going over some railroad tracks, but not doing any damage. Olson got out ten miles and the weather closed on him, so he came back. After a short rain, it cleared a little so he took off again at 4 o'clock and got as far as Lashio where he stayed. I checked my plane again after they changed the inside plugs. It wasn't too good, but was alright.

Sunday morning I got up early to get a good start, but the weather was really closed in. I did get away about 2 o'clock and took it easy as the engine did not run smoothly. It was rather hazy at Magwee so I could not get a view of the field till I was right over it and to my surprise I saw the field was in ruins. The planes on the field were just charred messes, some of them still burning. The hangars were half up, no personnel was on the field. It sure looked bleak and deserted. Quickly I scanned the skies for any sight of enemy aircraft or a fight. To my good fortune there was no action above me, so I buzzed the field several times checking up on bomb craters on the runway. I found a good spot and landed. Olson and Reed were on the field checking up on the damage so they took me to their barracks in town. I found out they had a raid less than an hour ago and had no warning. About 60 bombers and 40 fighters came over and really cleaned up. There were no casualties that day, but on a raid the previous day, Johnny Fauth, a mechanic had his arm blown off and died. Swartz, Pilot, had his hand mangled, and Seiple, Mechanic, had a concussion; all three were caught running between trenches. That day, eight of our fellows got up, Jernstedt was hit in the windshield and got glass in his eye and face, but is O.K. Dupouy also had his windshield hit, but only got glass in his arm and shoulder. There was also an early morning raid on Sunday along with the afternoon, when nobody got off. The Japs really got us flat footed without any warning. I got gassed up and had a look around before I left. There were about 20 Blenheims which were all damaged beyond repair; most of them had bomb loads so they burned to a crisp. We had 12 P-40 of which about five burned, several were full of holes form strafing and four were able to fly up to Loiwing Monday. The Japs dropped mostly anti-personnel shrapnel bombs so did a lot of damage to planes. Luckily none of our personnel were hit. The RAF had already evacuated and our fellows were leading up. They left early Monday morning. That spelling the end of Magwee and probably Burma. I made out O.K. on my return trip to Loiwing, landing here about 6:40, just before dusk set in. A group of eight planes from Kunming were here, they were on their way down on strafing missions, there were two more at Lashio. Monday morning, four ships flew up from Magwee, Hodges, Prescott, Mass and Wolf. We sure were surprised to see four ships come up from that mess. In the afternoon, Neal and his gang took off for their strafing job. They landed at a field near Heho in Burma, refueled and left early the next morning for Sinkiang, Indo China. They split into two groups, Neal had six and Newkirk four. Neal hit the airfield at dawn and caught about 40 fighters lined up just perfect for a good strafing job. With about four passes, they got everyone. Later Newkirk came over but nothing was left for him so they strafed some troops and armored cars. One of the cars got Newkirk and he went right in. Another squadron leader lost to the AVG. Black Mac McGarry was hit by anti-aircraft fire, but flew for about 60 miles before his plane caught fire and he bailed out in no man's land between the two lines and about 30 miles east of the Sittang River. The other fellows tossed him a map and he took off for the woods.

That morning I also went to Pao-shan, 130 miles N.E. of Loiwing, to get a radio transmitter instruction book, so our boys could get our station going. I left without any breakfast and as soon as I got back, there was a Jing Bao, and as Neal's flight had returned and had not much ammunition left, we all took off to clear the field of planes. I went to Pao-shan again and stayed for several hours and returned here about 5 o'clock. That evening Olson and Dupouy came in with

Robert in China. Photo courtesy of the San Diego Air & Space Museum.

a car from Magwee, and started the incoming of the rest of the convoy which staggered in.

Wednesday we had a four ship alert here, Neal, Bond, Prescott, and myself, but nothing happened. Hodges returned from Kunming where he had gone Tuesday from the Jing Bao. In the afternoon, Neal left with eight others for Kunming, leaving us one good plane and four in repair.

Thursday, Olson went to Kunming and returned with seven other ships. Most of the mechanics came in and got settled in their barracks near the field. We moved into one of the bungalows below the club house and I lost my restful homestead "upstairs."

Friday the 27th, we had an eight ship alert and had one alarm at noon. But sighted nothing and only flew 45 minutes. The next few days we had patrols and alarms but except for one morning when Older and Greene ran into a lone observation ship, and Older got him on his first pass.

Wednesday, April 1st, Shilling brought a P-40E here, so we had our first look at our new ships. We thought they were pretty nice.

Nothing much happened the next week, except a few false alarms and one day Lashio was bombed twice, but we received the alarm too late to do anything. The following day Mandalay was bombed.

April 1942

The weather started closing in and we had several days of light rain. Sunday, April 5th, was Easter Sunday, so we had Easter Church Services in the club presided by a R.A.F. Chaplain. We were fortunate in having some moving pictures left here enroute to Kunming, and we saw the first Monday night, "Here Comes the Navy."

Also received about six Christmas cards, a letter and a telegram from Skid. More 40 E's have been coming thru and met a classmate of mine now on the PAA ferrying the ships.

Thursday was my day off, but spent the morning out in the hills due to an alarm, and then in the afternoon when we had another alarm, something told me it was the real thing. About 12 Model "O" fighters came over on a strafing job, but made only two passes on three ships which were left on the field, a Blenheim and two 40E's. Then eight of twelve ships we had up, they were all up over 25,000 feet, jumped the fighters and accounted for ten Japs, several of them right off the runways. None of our boys got hit but two hurry birds ran out of gas and had a forced landing. It was the first fight over Loiwing in several years and we were the victors. Seven 40E's and three 40's came in (Fri.) The next morning about 6 o'clock several of us still sleeping in were awakened by the sound of engines and within a few minutes hear the slow chattering of machine gun fire. From our room we could look toward the field and saw five fighters making passes at our field. Our alert pilots were half way to the field and several of the mechanics were in their ships, warming them up with five Japs came(sic) over on a dawn strafing job. The mechanics got out of the ships and hid safely so there were no casualties, but of 20 planes dispersed over the field, the Japs only damaged seven badly, but not beyond repair and about four which were only barely hit. None of our planes burned. As we did not have any planes in the air, the Japs had a circus and no opposition, but still did not score too great a victory. We carried out two reconnaissance missions over Toungoo area and also had another morning alarm. That afternoon at 2:45 we received an alarm and took off. Five of us got together at 25,000 feet and were cruising for almost a half hour when we were told there were planes over the field. We started down, the first two planes diving below a layer of clouds, then the second two, of which I was No. 2, saw planes above the base of the clouds. I pulled up sharply and got my sights on a lone Jap in a head on deflection shot. My sight was too dim so I used my tracers for aim, but did not get him in that pass. We then tangled up a bit, I getting in about three good bursts from all angles. On the last pass, we started head on. I opened fire and he turned to my left. I followed him still firing and then saw him turn over on his back, flames shot out from under his wing and he started down. I followed him a short distance and saw another plane to my right. It was another 40 so I pulled up and went into some clouds to clear myself. I flew over and under the clouds by could not see another plane in the sky. I climbed for more altitude and cruised mostly over the field. About five minutes later I saw a plane going south over the mountains and took off after him, but then saw another one below and behind which was closer so I turned after him. After a five minute chase I got close to him. He dived steeply, I followed, but as he started pulling out, I saw the Chinese star so it proved a wild goose chase. By then the scrap was over, so I landed, the third back, hardly got out of my plane when we got another alarm, but we took off into the hills and the alarm proved false. We counted the score, got four positive, three probables; the R.A.F. got two, but lost two ships; one pilot forced landed O.K. The other bailed out. Not one of our planes got a bullet in it.

Older and Hedman had a 100 mile dog fight with a Jap who proved to be a real pilot, but they finally bagged him.

Saturday morning we had(sic) up at dawn patrol, but nothing came over. It was my day off and had to spend the morning in the hills on a false alarm. That afternoon I wrote four letters! Hope they bring in returns. The 2nd Squadron which came down here from Kunming sent out two patrols of three ships each, 40E's over Toungoo area, but did not run into anything. We had a movie that night, "The Mad Empress."

Sunday, the 12th, I was spare pilot so got out a little late for the dawn patrol, but again nothing came over. Hill, Wright, and Croft were down over Toungoo and Tex Hill and Wright staffed the airport. Tex got three and Wright shot down an observation ship. Nothing else happened except perhaps that I checked out in a 40E that afternoon. I think it is a pretty good plane, but did not get a chance to put it thru its paces.

The next few days were filled by alarms, but no enemy ships ever came over. Some days we would have four alarms and never make any contacts. However, on Saturday, April 18th, the third alarm at about 11 o'clock proved to be rather interesting as far as I was concerned. We had a flight of six, led by Dupouy. I had the second element with Prescott on my wing and Haywood the 3rd element. At about 18,000 flying west over the field, I saw a twin engine, light colored plane with red circles on his wings. I tried calling Parker and then flew up close and wobbled my wings. He did not see me and the enemy plane was pulling away at about 60 degree angle to the north, 4,000 feet below, so I did a sharp wing over and started down. I dove behind and below, coming up at about 300 yards and started firing. My tracers showed I was firing low, so I brought the fire up till I saw it was going into the ship – the right engine started pouring smoke and I had to dive away to keep from running into him. By the time I got on him again, Prescott was on his tail, followed by Haywood. The ship was leaving a long trail of black smoke and diving down at over 350 m.p.h. about five miles away he finally did a sharp turn to his right, did a two turn spin and then dove into the ground with the right engine in flames. When he hit, a very large ball of flame rose 20 feet in the air and died out. I buzzed the spot but there was no wreckage left – it was all over the place – no part very large. We got together again and stayed up for another half hour before landing. Prescott and myself took credit for the one Jap observation ship (1/2 each!)

That afternoon, we discussed several missions we were asked to do and thought them too risky so started action against them. We had a meeting that night with Colonel Chennault, who was made a Brigadier General in the U.S. Air Corps. He gave us no satisfaction, so we signed a letter of resignation. 28 of us signed it. The next night, we had another meeting at which he told us he would not accept our resignations, but consider us as deserters if we left. He appealed to our patriotism, courage and everything else he could think of, but the desertion part seemed to change most of the fellows' minds. We decided to stick together and follow orders and see the thing out.

Monday, the 21st, Dupouy, Groh, Laughlin, and myself went down to patrol over Pyknic in the afternoon. All we did was dodge anti-aircraft fire which gave off black puffs of smoke about two feet in diameter and they would come pretty close too. Everything seemed hundred feet at the same level.(sic) We would twist and turn, dive and soar, never flying the same pattern for more than four or five seconds. We did not run into anything nor see anything on the ground, so we went back to Namsham to refuel and stay overnight for a return patrol the next morning. We landed at about four and at 4:30 saw an observation ship 10,000 feet above the field looking things over. As soon as he left, Laughlin and I took off just in case anything would come back to strafe. My oil temperature hit the peg and dropped down, so I had to land. Link stayed up. About 6:30 Older and Shield came in to pick off an observation ship that was in the habit of coming over in the morning.

The British had evacuated the place so there was nobody there but our own little gang and luckily two cooks who got something together for us.

Olson and Rogers worked on the planes all night and got them in shape for the next day.

We got up before dawn, had somewhat of a breakfast, got the planes warmed up. The canopy on my plane had blown off and could not be repaired so I was not going to go on the mission, but go back to Loiwing instead.

The three fellows took off at about 6:30 and got on their way. We pushed Shield's and Older's ships into the hangar and I went to take off.

The takeoff was normal, but the oil temperature started creeping up so I circled the field a few times and when the temperature hit the peg and the pressure dropped, I decided to come in. I landed way from the hangars, pulled off to a side to park the plane, but then thought it would be better if I put it in the hangar for the fellows to work on, so I started racing back down the runway. As I approached the taxi strip to the hangar, I started to turn when I saw white flashes and hear noises coming from the right side of my engine. My first thought was that my engine had caught fire.

(This should be the end of the diary, because by all rhyme and reasons, I should be dead and not writing any more – but will continue in the next book.)

--- DIARY PART TWO ---

After the flashes in the engines, they moved into the cockpit – I thought my guns were going off in the cockpit. The flashes blinded me, I felt sudden pangs in my legs, I heard a roar, I looked up and saw a plane sway low over my head, I knew I had been strafed. With the plane still moving very slowly I coolly unbuckled my safety belt, climbed out of the cockpit, felt my head set plug in jerk out of the socket, jumped on the ground, out of the way of the oncoming tail, and started hastily to take off my chute. The first three buckles came open easily, but the fourth stuck, as I played with it, I saw several things. First a small hole clean thru my thumb below the first joint, second a plane making a split S to come down and strafe and another formation of four planes flying overhead.

Luckily in not being killed and in getting out of the plane and the second in getting out about 20 feet from a covered dugout, which after I threw my chute off, I dove in head first, along with two Chinese soldiers. It was not till then that fright or pain overtook me. I could see blood coming out of my left shoe, so I took it off and saw a hole only through the top part of my sock. I took that off and saw a ragged wound. I could see the missile and tried forcing it out, but soon gave up. By then I felt other pains in my legs so pulled up my trousers and saw about four gun shots in each leg, all seemed to have stopped inside. I tore up several handkerchiefs I had and with the help of one Chinese soldier, tried making some sort of bandage to stop the bleeding.

All this time a continuous drum of machine gun bullets were splitting the air. My plane was on fire, the gas tanks giving off a dull roar, then gulping pants as it burned. The oxygen bottles gave way and sounded like a real high pressure force going off. Then the machine gun bullets started going off, first rapidly then intermittently, and soon the enemy planes left and only the flaming plane and shooting bullets broke the stillness of the morning. I tried to send one of the soldiers for the other fellows, but they came shortly. They were very happy to see me and though me a goner.

They put me in the back of a truck on a stretcher and took me to the hospital. Since the British had left there were no doctors, so Cross went to Loiwing and was very fortunate in getting Dr. Seagraves. We did not know this and Shield had started to drive me down there but we all came back. The doctor had two native nurses and at exactly 12 o'clock I went under chloroform. I came out at 3 o'clock, really cussing at the Japs. The doctor had left. Shield and Older left for Loiwing and Cross received orders to drive me to Lashio to be picked up by a plane.

I had a cast on my thumb and palm, bandage on my left ankle, calf and knee, and two on my right leg. I did not feel very bad. We left at 6 p.m. and drove till 10 when we got a flat and had to wait till morning to borrow another tire. We had a fairly rough ride of 240 miles to Lashio, getting there at almost 3 o'clock. They took me to the field, but the plane was late so they took me to the R.A.F. hospital in Lashio. There I met Dr. Klein from Toungoo who was a British officer now on his way up.

That night was a night of torture on a hard wooden bed, not sleeping or pain-killing powders.(sic)

The next morning they took some x-rays. We left by Beechcraft at about 1 o'clock for Loiwing with Dr. Richards who had come down to see me. I spent the night in one of the bungalows with Engle who was getting over the typhoid. Next afternoon doc took me to the hospital at Loiwing to take out some of the shrapnel they found with the x-ray and fluoroscope. They tried spinal anesthesia, but it wouldn't work, so they used ether. They used it twice as the fluoroscope after the first and found some more pieces. I came out at 8 o'clock and spent another torturous night on a hard wooden bed with no pain relief or sleeping pills. They picked out five pieces of shrapnel from the two legs, one from my right knee joint which might have proved fatal in the future.

Late that afternoon, they took me to the field, put aboard a DC-3 (CNAC) flew to Lashio and then to Kunming – got here about 9 o'clock and taken to a hospital where so far everything has been pretty good.

Dr. Sam Prino took charge and changed the dressing and also put a new cast on my hand.

The Jap mechanized spearhead took Namsham and went up and took Lashio. On several fighter sweeps the fellow ran into observation ships below Lashio. One day they did several strafing jobs on truck convoys. On one occasion, they ran into a formation of bombers, escorted by fighters going to Loiwing. They got about 12 fighters but the bombers went on and bombed the field at Loiwing.

The squadron moved to Mingshik and started evacuating Loiwing for Kunming as the Jap army was moving up. In several days everyone evacuated both Loiwing and Mangshi.

May 1942

On May 4th, the first squadron was at Pao-shan when bombers in two waves came over and bombed the city, killing Ben Foshee. Charley Bond took off, chased the bombers, got one, but when he came in to land, was jumped by fighters and his ship caught fire. He bailed out, but was burned on his face, shoulders and hands. He came to the hospital the next day. The Japs also came over Pao-shan on the 5th, but we had seven planes up and got about nine planes.
The next day we found out Peterson was turning back and could not take us on to Karachi, so we would have to wait for another ride.

That afternoon we looked up "Pappy" Greenelaw and we went to a jeweler in Old Delhi where I bought a diamond and emerald ring and bracelet to match. A really beautiful set! That afternoon, I went swimming at Hotel Cecil, where Pappy was staying with Edgar

Snow. Had a fine time, but almost overdid my exercise. McMillan got in that day so they went shopping and I met them at the hotel that afternoon. Spent the evening at Pappy's with Jernstedt who took Pappy into town with Acey-Deucy. Met "Mouse" Moore at the airport where he was control officer for that district. Another group of fellows or rather Jo Steward and McHenry got in the next day, spent the afternoon and evening with Joe and Mac.

We finally got off with Nowak as a pilot on a none-too-good ship. It was overloaded so could not go very high and had a rough and long slow trip. We got into Karochi about an hour late; in fact a ship that took off after us beat us in.

At Karachi we met some of the fellows who left Kunming before us and learned that some had gone on to Bombay to catch a boat home. There seemed very little chance of getting a plane out of here in the near future. I met Red Hall from Mitchel Field, so lived in his room at a cottage on the post. Belden was also stuck here awaiting a plane to Dingin.

Frank Schiel was missing, but turned up several days later at Yunnanyi. He had run out of gas and had a forced landing.

The Japs were now at the Salween River, 40 miles from Pao-shan and the fellows went down for several days on dive bombing and strafing missions routing the Japs into a retreat.

Crew Chief McAllister ran into trouble and was caught on the other side of the Salween. He took a roundabout course and after walking two days, got into Pao-shan and finally Kunming. Hastey also ran out of gas and had a forced landing, but finally hit Yunnanyi O.K.

Wednesday the 13th, Jones, Shield, Laughlin, Donovan, and Bishop, went down to Hanoi in E's and made a one pass bombing-strafing job. They got 15 for certain and probably 15 more. Donovan was shot and crashed near the field. The other fellows were raised a rank by the Generalissimo, Shield and Jones were made into Squadron Leaders.

The following day fate played a dirty trick. Jones was on the bombing range practicing dive bombing and dove too low and stalled on the pullout. He spun in from about 1500 feet. A rather unwanted ending for Jones.

The next few days several flights went down and strafed the Hanoi-Lake R.R. and got two trains – again fate came thru – Bishop was hit by AA over Lashio and when his ship caught fire, he bailed out. He was captured by the French, but was turned over to the Japs. They tried to ransom him from the French, but they would not cooperate.

Bob Little was the next to go. They were down on the Salween bombing artillery and bob got hit in the left wing by anti-aircraft fire. It just disintegrated as if his own bombs went off. He was pretty low so just spun in and burst into flames – a rather inglorious finish.

Made my debut in town by going to the movies one night and out to the field the following day. Sunday morning we had an alert due to Yunnanyi being bombed, but they did not come this way.

Sunday, May 31, the WASC gave us a lawn party in front of the Hostel. We had some delicious Chinese food and drank rice wine. Some of the fellows had a good amount so a good time was had by all.

June - July 1942

Monday I had my cast taken off and saw my crooked thumb. Was swollen a bit and could not move it hardly at all, but it looks O.K. May have a scar on each side where it went thru.

Not much happened for a while, had bad weather most of the time. The 1st and 2nd Squadrons could not go up to Chungking because of the weather.

They finally got me to go to work as operations officer on June 6th, and the next day the squadrons got away for Chungking. Also the following day we had reports of Japs coming up, but because of bad weather did not get here.

Wednesday night, June 10, about 10:30, a pilot of one of the DC-3's, Groh, along with Peret, the group engineering officer, came into the operations shack and started plotting a course to Hanoi. I tried my best to persuade them to call it off or postpone it, but they had their minds set on it. They took off at 12:20 with 800 gallons of gas and 3000 pounds of bombs. We traced their course to the border by the net but could not tell if they hit Hanoi or not. They said they dropped all their stuff on a city, but I think it was Haiphong or some other city, We never did get any confirmation from any news report. They got lost on their way back and hit way northeast of Kunming, but luckily enough we brought them in on the R.D.F. at about 7:30 next morning. I sure sweated them out.

Thursday afternoon I had a fatty tumor on my neck removed by Dr. Monyet, a Public Health doctor working with the group till the army comes in. He had quite a job removing it. I had a local so knew what was going on. It caused a little pain that night and today, but seems to be coming along O.K. Also heard today that the 1st Squadron bagged eight Japs near Kinelin.

Rested several days at the 1st Hostel before moving to the 2nd, when I took over Operations. Dr. Monyet took the stitches out about six days after the operation, so I was finished with that business.

Rains came and sort of held up my operations and the place got rather muddy.

Came the 27th, and the first detachment took off for home. I found out that I could get sick leave and go home earlier and perhaps avoid the rush, so Farrell and I went to the Mozir Gentry that evening. He told us to see him and the General the following morning, which we did and got an O.K. to leave. We did get away on a DC-3 that afternoon of the 28th at 2 p.m. The pilot was Peterson, a former T.W. boy, and did a very good job on instruments a good part of the way. We were up at 16,500 and I got a headache from lack of oxygen. We hit Dinjan with more rain about 5 o'clock. It was terribly muddy, but we were taken to the Officer's Barracks 15 miles away. The field looked very much like Toungoo except this had two finished runways. We stayed overnight in the upper floor of a tea drying warehouse on a plantation. The main building was full. I met Ham, a fellow student at Morton Junior College and class of '42 Flying School. Didn't think much of Dinjan at all and was glad to leave the next morning at 6 for Delhi. The first hour out we flew over the tree tops because of low ceiling, but finally made out O.K. I put in an hour as co-pilot. We arrived at Delhi about 1:30 at a very beautiful airport in a lovely city.

Delhi looks like a very well planned city before being built. Well laid out, plenty of trees and shrubbery and modern style buildings. The main attraction was the Government buildings and Viceroy's Palace. It was all of red brick, well styled architecture. Fountains and walks, shrubbery and trees made it a very pretty site.

The center of the circular is the Government buildings. On one side several miles is the airport and on the opposite side is the business circle. The center is a small park and the shops from(sic) around a circular drive around the park. The streets branch out from the park into residential sections. The homes are almost all yellow plaster finish, square, California style. A very beautiful sight form the air.

We stayed at the marina Hotel in town, having a double room with two beds in each. The hotel was used as the officer's quarters. Was very nice, including good food. We spent the first day looking the city over and did a little shopping. Had my first malted milk in a year that afternoon. In the evening we went to a pretty good theater. So spent some time sightseeing and going to show with him.

The city is very much like Rangoon, perhaps not as many newer buildings, but not so much of a native market place and a little cleaner and neater. They have several nice theaters of which I visited one.

Saturday, July 4, I celebrated at the officer's club in town, where I met Dave Wallace, old Pursuit Instructor from Langley Field and also Ray Boggs' old buddy from flying school, sister in-law who is one of 90 American nurses here. Windy Miller from Mitchel had her at the dance. Had a good time that night and slept with Wallace and Miller at their barracks, 51st Pursuit Group.

----- **END OF DIARY** -----

Coming Home

July 1942 – November 1942

In July 1942, the American Volunteer Group disbanded and the pilots and crew returned to the U.S. to rejoin the U.S. Army Air Corps and fight in World War II.

Robert flew home from his service in China by way of India, Africa and South America. After arriving in Milwaukee, Wisconsin, Robert boarded the train to Chicago and from the Chicago train station, made his way home via the "L".

Upon his arrival home the local newspapers began running almost daily accounts of his comings and goings and life overseas.

After an interview with the Chicago Daily Tribune it was written that "Robert recounts his experiences in a manner that is refreshingly modest and yet confident and alert. He is credited with knocking four Japanese planes out of the sky."22

The Berywn Life reported, "Bob displayed the modesty that marked his whole career ......strolling through the old familiar backyard of the Brouk residence, and surprising his mother – who was busy preparing a meal in the kitchen – with a quiet, 'Hello Mom.'"23

Patriotic spirit was high and Robert became Cicero's "hometown hero" because of his engagement with the Japanese in the skies over China.

The Berywn Life newspaper began planning a parade and ceremony to honor Robert which would be held on August 2, 1942. The newspaper ran articles almost daily in the weeks before "Bob Brouk Day," praising the heroic efforts of Robert, the Flying Tigers, and other local men serving in the Armed Forces in the war.

The July 22 issue of *The Berywn Life* stated, "As a member of the Flying Tigers, he received a rating of Flight Leader, a citation from General P.T. Mow, head of the Chinese Air Force, and a silk scarf from Madame Chiang Kai-shek for his bravery under fire."24

Robert quickly began making the rounds to various organizations, events, and radio programs. In late July, the Air Force held Cadet Rallies in Chicago to inform and inspire men to join the U.S. Air Force. Air Force sponsors were instructed to recruit 20,000 men from the Chicago area before the end of 1942. Robert attended one of these rallies with fellow Flying Tiger, Edwin Fobes. The men were honored at a luncheon at the Merchant's and Manufacturer's Club before they viewed a spectacular air show over the city. Chicago's Mayor Kelly said of Robert and Edwin, "These men have the key to the city and we mean that. They have felt enemy fire. They are not thinking of their lives, but of the country....."25 Later that week Robert spoke on a WMAQ radio program about the day's events.26

The Berywn Life's July 24 issue reported on the progress of the "Bob Brouk Day" plans. The Western Electric Hawthorne Works Plant approved the use of their Albright Memorial Field for the celebration ceremony. This was important in the history of the Western Electric Hawthorne Works Plant and Cicero because it was the first time in seven years that approval for a non-Western Electric event was given. The company reminded the planning committee "that the field is dedicated to the 61 employees who gave their lives for their country during the First World War."27 With this in mind, Western Electric Hawthorne Works felt using their field for the ceremony was in keeping with the patriotic spirit of the time in the country.

On July 27, Robert attended a reception in Chinatown with fellow Flying Tigers, Chaplain Paul Frillman and Sergeant Major Edwin Fobes. The *Chicago Herald-American* reported "Four thousand Chicago Chinese residents will give a tumultuous welcome to three of the famous "Flying Tigers….."28 After the reception he, along with Frillman and Fobes, were interviewed on the radio station WLS.29

Robert's radio interviews continued on July 30, when he spent an hour being interviewed on station WBBM during the Victory Matinee.30 His mother, Emily Brouk, was interviewed on August 6, on station WCFL during the Our American Service Stars hour.31

As the interviews continued to keep Robert in the spotlight, the "Bob Brouk Day" planning committee continued their plans for the celebration. They decided Robert and his parents would travel by car at the head of the parade route as military and civic leaders followed. No floats were allowed in the parade, however all Cicero clubs and organizations were invited to participate in the parade and ceremony.

Virignia Scharer 1942. Photo courtesy of Virginia S. Davis.

Some of the groups that participated included: Boy Scouts, a group Robert was very involved in as a teen; Girl Scouts; Morton High School Band; Local American Legion Posts; Bohemian Sokols; Cicero Fire and Police Departments; Chinese Boy Scout Drum and Bugle Corps; Cicero Post American Legion Drum and Bugle Corps; and other musical and civic groups.

Amid all this planning, Robert continued to visit various local clubs, businesses, and organizations. He spoke about his experience as a Flying Tiger. It was on one of these visits, to the Western Electric Hawthorne Works Plant that Robert met his future wife, Virginia (Ginny) Scharer. It is interesting to note that when

Robert was stationed in Burma with the Flying Tigers, he purchased a Chinese robe for the girl he would marry. Little did he know that within a few months of that purchase, he would meet that girl.

Virginia, an invoice typist, was the 1941 "Hello Charley" girl for Western Electric. "Hello Charley" became a tradition after a post card addressed to "Charley, Western Electric Hawthorne Works, Chicago, Ill.," was sent to the plant. It was intended for a man named Charles Drucker, but the sender could not remember Charles's last name. As the postcard circulated the plant searching for the proper owner, plant workers started calling each other "Charley Western" which became "Hello Charley" as a greeting.

Each year after the tradition began hundreds of women were nominated to be the year's "Hello Charley" girl. Elections were held in May and the "Hello Charley" girl and her court were crowned in June. Of course, promotional items followed -- including auto and luggage tags with the "Hello Charley" logo and the current "Hello Charley" Girl's photo, thus identifying Western Electric workers all over the world.[32]

Robert and Virginia met at the homecoming ceremony held by Western Electric Hawthorne Works Plant July 30, 1942. The event took place in the outdoor recreation area of the Plant where the employees caught a glimpse of the heroic ace. Virginia and another woman were asked to show him around the Plant and take him to lunch and make him feel at home.

Virginia described her first impressions of Robert. "He was so unassuming, kind and thoughtful. Therefore, I was flattered and excited when he said, 'Would you like to join me for a cup of chi after all this hullabaloo is over?' I joined him – we talked, then dated and you know the rest."[33]

As the month of July drew to a close, Robert spoke at a luncheon at Klas Restaurant to a group of about 80 Cicero Lions, Kiwanians and guests of service groups about his experiences in China. *The Berywn Life* described his apparel as "neatly clad khaki shorts and a pair of shoes," a uniform worn in China. *The Berywn Life* stated, "He described the Jap pilots as "methodical," stating that they lack initiative and cannot shoot straight." Robert went on to talk about the December 25, 1941, battle against the Japanese where the Flying Tigers fought against roughly 80 Jap bombers and 40 fighter planes while shooting down 26 of them without losing a man.[34]

Robert in uniform with his father Peter to his right seated next to his brother Harold before the parade. Photo courtesy Virginia S. Davis.

Hello "Ginny—
Best of Everything
Bob Brouk
"Flying Tigers"

Robert in the Bob Brouk Day Parade. Photo
courtesy Virginia S. Davis.

The month of July quickly ended, and "Bob Brouk Day" arrived on August 2. Thousands of local citizens lined the parade route in anticipation. The parade started at 2:00 p.m. and proceeded east on Cermak Road to the Western Electric Albright Memorial Field at Cermak Road and 50th Avenue. The parade line up was as follows: Division 1 – Military; Division II – Veterans; Division III – Sea Scouts, Boys Scouts, Girl Scouts; Division IV – Sign Painters Local Union No. 830; Division V – Civic; Division VI – Fraternal and Social.[35]

At 3:00 p.m., as initial vehicles in the parade lineup reached the Albright Memorial Field, a ceremony opened with the "Star Spangled Banner" sung by a schoolmate of Robert's, Keith Smejkal. The anthem was followed by a prayer given by Bob's former chaplain in China, Rev. Paul Frillman.

The prayer was followed by a speech by Mr. David Levinger, the Vice-President of Western Electric Hawthorne Works. Major Lloyd M. Showalter of the U.S. Army Air Corps followed and finally after many other speakers, Robert was introduced and interviewed. After Robert's speech, his parents were introduced before Robert presented Gold Stars to the families of Cicero's three known World War II Service fatalities. Following the presentation, a "parade in the sky" was held. Planes were flown from the Army Air Corps units, the Illinois Air Militia and the Civil Aeronautics Air Patrol.[36]

After "Bob Brouk Day," *The Berywn Life* continued to publish stories about Robert as he was honored by many local organizations. He attended a Lions Club luncheon in his honor on August 7 at Klas Restaurant. Before Robert left for China in 1941, the Lions gave him a luncheon at which *The Berywn Life* reported the Lions "filled him with a lot of raw meat, to prepare him for the fighting he was to do."[37] The Lions Club agreed the raw meat helped him fight the Japanese, so another platter was to be served to prepare Robert to re-enter the United States Army Air Corps and fight in World War II.

Robert participated in the Czech-American National Alliance fourth-annual Mobilization for Freedom parade on August 9. Participants watched a parade beginning at 26th Street and Karlov Avenue, and ending at 26th Street and Albany Avenue, before congregating in Pilsen Park for a War Bond Campaign. The gathering included not only Czech-Americans, but also local civic groups; federal, state, and local government officials; World War I Legionnaires; Sokol groups; and other patriotic organizations. Robert directed the war bond drive from the cockpit of an airplane placed in Pilsen Park for the event. He was assisted by women in Sokol uniforms for the duration of the afternoon.[38]

Robert at the Hawthorne Works Plant. Photo courtesy Hawthorne Works Museum.

Continuing his round of speaking engagements, Robert was the guest speaker at the Cardinal Council Knights of Columbus Meeting in Cicero on August 11. *The Berywn Life* reported "Brouk's visit to the council is in some respects a matter of reciprocation"[39] due to the fact a Knights of Columbus group participated in the "Bob Brouk Day" parade and festivities. Then on August 21, Robert was initiated into the Cicero Moose Lodge in what became known as the "Bob Brouk" initiation class.[40]

The September 1942 issue of the Western Electric Hawthorne Works internal newsletter, *The Microphone*, featured an article about Robert and another Hawthorne Boy, "Chuck" Laver. The article discussed not only Robert's appearance at a noon-hour program at the end of July at the Hawthorne Works Plant, but also "Bob Brouk Day" which was held August 2 at the Albright Memorial Field. It was written, "The crowd of Hawthorneans cheered the young pilot enthusiastically when he appeared here and told of several of his clashes with Jap planes."[41]

Robert continued making the rounds visiting organizations and appeared on radio programs into October. He participated in a radio program called, "Wings of the Army" on October 9 on WGN Radio. Robert was one of many Army and Air Force speakers to aid in the war's recruiting effort.[42]

Robert rejoined the Army Air Corps and *The Berywn Life* reported on October 12, 1942, that Robert was on his way to Washington, D.C., "in anticipation of orders which probably will transfer him to Orlando, Fla., as a flying instructor."[43]

The report was correct, and in October he was stationed in Orlando, Florida, at the newly formed Army Air Forces School of Applied Tactics (AAFSAT). Robert was promoted to the rank of Captain[44] and assigned to the 81st Pursuit Squadron, 50th Fighter Group, 10th Fighter Squadron.[45] Charles Bond, a fellow Flying Tiger from the 1st Squadron, served as the 81st Pursuit Squadron's Commander during that time.

One purpose of the AAFSAT was to train newly formed cadres in tactical combat flying techniques under simulated conditions. The cadres flew in and out of airfields with little infrastructure to prepare them for combat. Another purpose was to test and evaluate new tactics which could be used in any World War II combat theatre. Robert was made a Flight Instructor due to his training and combat experience with the Flying Tigers, shooting down Japanese planes and being credited with 3.5 "kills."[46] Robert soon began training pilots for the rigors of aerial combat.

While Robert went to Orlando, Virginia remained in Chicago. The two fell in love quickly at the end of July when they met, a whirlwind romance. "As I look back now, it almost seems like God said, 'Hurry up, do things fast. You only have a short time left on earth.'"[47]

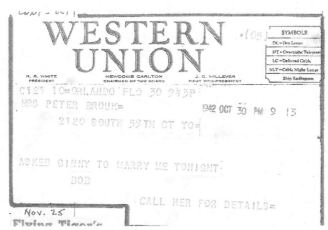

Telegram courtesy of Virginia S. Davis.

Robert proposed to Virginia on October 30, 1942, over the phone. He sent his parents a telegram announcing his proposal. Virginia spoke to her father about the proposal and he said, "Do you love him?" and after she answered yes, he said "All right, but remember it will be a permanent life style change."[48]

With Robert in Orlando on duty until shortly before their wedding, it was up to Virginia to obtain the marriage license. The Daily Times, Chicago, reported on November 25, "She went down to the city hall yesterday and obtained a marriage license for herself and her fiancé, Capt. Robert Brouk..."[49] The two were to be married three days later on November 28, 1942 at 8:00 p.m. at the First Congregational Church in Oak Park. Despite the time crunch, Virginia was able to put together a beautiful wedding party.

Robert and Virginia's wedding. Photo courtesy of Virginia S. Davis.

After the wedding the newlyweds drove to Orlando where Robert was stationed and began their new life together in a small house at

1209 E. Kaley. While Robert worked, Virginia set up the home they would share. The couple was young and in love with their whole lives ahead of them. Or so they thought.

The Final Flight

Life can turn on a dime and you never know what will happen next. On December 19, 1942, Virginia woke up excited because Robert was due home that morning. He had been training pilots in Tallahassee, Florida for three days. After breakfast, she drove to the airfield to await Robert's return.

Virginia recalled, "I left the house about 9:30 a.m. to pick up Bob who had been on maneuvers the past three days. He was a flight instructor and he and the student pilots were returning from southern Florida in close flying formation. I parked by the base hangars and sat on the hood of our car awaiting his arrival."

Upon arrival at the Orlando Air Base, Robert was the lead plane in a formation of six ships. What a magnificent sight! The planes rose and dove in formation as they practiced maneuvers. Eventually they would be sent overseas to whip the enemy.

The ships in Robert's formation, along with other formations, were simulating a strafing of the Orlando airfield. As the strafing simulation was being attempted, First Lieutenant Sidney O. Kane's plane, flying in the number two position, flew too close to Robert's plane as Robert began to pull up and turn left.

What happened next was inconceivable. Flying just a few hundred feet off the ground, Lt. Kane's wing tip touched Robert's right wing tip. This small action caused Robert's plane to immediately flip upside down, crash, and explode. What remained of his plane was almost unrecognizable as aircraft.

Virginia watched the entire event unfold from the hood of their car.

Witnesses reported Lt. Kane's plane flew on a short distance, gained some altitude and then turned and crashed into a field. He did not survive.

"I watched the planes pass overhead, then turn and prepare for a landing when all of a sudden two planes collided in mid-air and fell to the ground. Shocked, I sat there in silence and just stared until some people came and informed me that one of the planes was Bob's." Virginia recalled.[50]

Virginia was in such shock, her memories of the events after the crash Virginia hazy. It was too much for a 20 year old new bride to process. Moments before the crash she was excitedly anticipating her new husband's return and a day together. But that was not to be. Her blood pressure soared and she was put in bed and packed in ice to bring the pressure down.

The next thing Virginia remembered was that she phoned her in-laws to tell them Robert had died. Still in shock, she did as instructed by the military captain assigned to escort her home, packed a bag and departed for the train station. The rest was a blur.

After the Army Air Corps handled the packing of Robert and Virginia's belongings and shipped them to Chicago. The Chinese robe Robert gave her was not among the possessions returned. She has no idea what happened to it after his death.

The U.S. Army Air Force investigated the accident, Accident Number 43-12-19-12, dated December 19, 1942. The following witness descriptions and crash photos are taken from this Accident Report.[51]

Several Description of Accident and Witness Statements are included in the Accident Report 43-12-19-12. The first account was given by William J. Cummings, Jr. Maj. AC Aircraft Accident Officer, dated 24 December 1942.

On December 19, 1942 at approximately 1220 a P-40E Type airplane A.F. No. 41-24928, piloted by Lt. S.O. Kane, crashed and burned in the vicinity of Kissimmee, Fla after a mid-air collision with another aircraft. The crash proved fatal to the pilots of both airplanes.

It is found that Lt. Kane was flying in the number two position of a six ship flight which was acting as "top cover" for two other flights that were making a simulated "ground strafing" attack on the Kissimmee, Fla. Airfield. After the attack had been made by other flights the leader of the "top cover" flight gave orders by radio for his flight to execute a "number

*one" attack on the airfield. This type of an attack is executed
with individual airplanes flying in "trail" with approximately
100-125 yds. between airplanes.*

*It is further found that during the attack, the airplane
flown by Lt. Kane was entirely too close to the airplane leading and that the airplane flown by Lt. Kane struck the leaders airplane during a pull up after the attack. The leader's
airplane immediately went out of control and crashed and
burned. The airplane flown by Lt. Kane continued in a climb
for a short distance, lost the propeller and then crashed and
burned after what appeared to be an attempt by the pilot to
make a forced landing.*

*It is the opinion of the Aircraft Accident Board that, in
spite of previous orders and instructions, the pilot, Lt. Kane,
was not flying in the proper position for the type of formation
ordered and was directly responsible for the occurrence of the
accident.[52] (sic)*

*Robert's Crash Photograph. Courtesy of Army Air
Force Accident Report Microfilm.*

The second account was given by William Couldery, dated 19
December 1942.

*I was watching two planes as they dived and came across
Kissimmee Airport at an altitude of approximately 45 ft. The
two planes were flying one behind the other at an altitude*

*of 45 ft, when the rear plane tried to get ahead of the other
one and they collided wing tips. The plane that had been in
the rear turned over and dived to the ground within 30 yards
from where I was standing. The plane turned wing over wing
for approximately 50 ft. before the plane caught on fire,
bursting in half, part of the ship continued on for approximately 50 ft., burning all the while. The other plane started
gaining altitude and was up to about 200 ft. before it dropped
and hit the ground about a mile and a half from where I was
standing.*

*This happened at approximately 11:45 A.M. December
19, 1942, one quarter of a mile south of Kissimmee Airport.[53]
(sic)*

*Lt. Kane's Crash Photograph. Courtesy of Army Air
Force Accident Report Microfilm.*

Another account was given by Joseph P. Lemons, 1st Lt, Air
Corps, 10th Fighter Squadron.

*On December 19, 1942, about 12:10 o'clock, Captain
Brouk with a formation of six ships, of which I was flying
number four, made a strafing attack on Kissimmee Air Port.
The formation approached with Lt Kane flying very close to
Captain Brouk. I was about three hundred yards behind Lt
Kane directly in trail. As the two planes ahead pulled up to
clear the hangar one of them suddenly turned on its back and
crashed; then the other climbed up to about six hundred feet
and the propeller fell off. The second ship then apparently*

*assumed a normal glide toward a field almost directly ahead.
When the plane reached an altitude of about two hundred feet
the pilot made an extremely steep turn, toward a better field,
pulled his nose up in the turn and fell off on the left wing
and plunged straight into the ground. Both planes burst into
flames as they crashed. I did not see the two planes collide in
mid-air.*[54]*(sic)*

A fourth account was given by Walter J. Koraleski, Jr., 1st Lieut,
Air Corps, 10th Fighter Squadron stating,

*On December 19, 1942, 17 P-40E-1's of the 10th Fighter
Squadron took off at approximately 11:15 from Dale Mabry
Field, Tallahassee for the Orlando Air Base. There were three
flights of six, six and five ships. Captain Brouk in airplane
956 was leading our flight of six with Lieut. Kane in plane
928, his wing man and myself in number 3 position. We were
air support for the other two flights which were to attack Kissimmee.*

*When we came to Kissimmee the two flights made their
attack and left. Captain Brouk then gave us the order for
No. 1 attack and we peeled off from 4000 feet. The first attack was from Southwest to northeast. Captain Brouk then
pulled-up and turned for another attack at the hangar from
North to South. On making this last turn I noticed Lieut. Kane
was quite close to Captain Brouk, approximately one to two
ship lengths. After passing the hangar Captain Brouk pulled
up and started to turn to the left. Lieut. Kane, who was on
Captain Brouk's right wing turned also, and suddenly his
propeller hit the underside of Captain Brouk's ship. At this
time they were at an altitude of approximately 100 feet and I
was approximately 200 yards behind them. Pieces flew off at
the impact and then the two ships separated. Captain Brouk's
ship, which was still in its bank, did a sort of one half slow
roll as it went down and landed almost upside down. The ship
burned on impact with the ground and the flames shot along
the ground for what looked to be hundreds of feet.*

*Lieut. Kane's ship didn't seem to be damaged too much.
The prop was stopped and all three blades were bent back.
By this time I was approximately 100 yards behind him and
could see that his canopy was open and that meanwhile he
had pulled up to about 500 feet. Suddenly the prop fell off.
Lieut. Kane continued to glide straight ahead and seemed to*

have control of the plane. He continued south until passing the cement highway and now was heading toward a field that had either small trees or brush in it. To his left was a clear green field and when at about 200 feet he turned toward that field. He completed about 100 degrees of that turn when suddenly the ship dived for the ground and rolled almost on its back. It hit the ground and flames shot up immediately.

I called Captain Kiser on the radio and told him what had happened. He returned to Kissimmee and I led the remaining ships of our flight to Orlando and landed.[55] (sic)

The Family's Grief

Following the crash, Virginia quiet and withdrawn, accompanied Robert's remains, which were sent by rail from Florida to Chicago. Robert's body laid in state for two and a half days from December 22 – 24, 1942 at the Chrastka Funeral Home in Cicero, Illinois.

Remembering the kind, quiet, hero who had recently married Western Electric's sweetheart, thousands of people swarmed the funeral home and stood in line for hours to pay their respects to Cicero's Hometown Hero.

Virginia recalled standing for hours in the funeral home as people passed through. Quiet, strong, and detached, she accepted their condolences. It was improper to grieve or break down in front of all those people because she was on display for all to see. Because of her fame as a "Hello Charley" girl and being the widow of a famous Flying Tiger, Virginia was no longer Virginia Brouk. She would forever be remembered as The Tiger's Widow. Her fame, as a result, would be used by the newspapers and Army for years to come as part of the patriotic fervor.

In keeping with military tradition, a full military funeral service was held with Honor and Color Guards provided by soldiers from Fort Sheridan and local Veterans' organizations. These were many of the same organizations that participated in "Bob Brouk Day" just a few months earlier.[56]

During the funeral service, "Dr. Albert Buckner Coe, pastor of the First Congregational Church in Oak Park, delivered a brief eulogy in English after Otto Pergler had spoken for a short time in the Czech tongue."[57] Dr. Coe, who married Robert and Virginia just weeks before, spoke about the strength of Robert's character in life and death; how Robert loved freedom and did his part to fight for it; and how strong and courageous Robert was stating, "Captain Brouk was fearless in life, and we're sure, fearless in death."[58]

The Berywn Life reported on the services and funeral. The paper described the emotions of the young servicemen's wives and their parents, who attended the services, as deeply grieved; the emotions of the fathers as sober, yet understood the anger and sadness that Robert's father must have been feeling; and mothers whose hearts went out to Robert's mother and a whole community was in mourning for a heroic man lost so young.

These same parents who attended the wake and funeral were no doubt thinking about their boys fighting in Europe or the Pacific. Would their sons come home unharmed, unchanged? Or would they sleep forever in foreign soil among their brothers in arms? These thoughts cast more darkness on an already dark day.

Upon conclusion of the ceremony at the funeral home, Robert's casket was transported to Woodlawn Cemetery in Forest Park, Illinois. *The Berywn Life* reported it took three automobiles to transport the many floral arrangements sent to the funeral home for Robert; there were more than a dozen American and Veteran Flags as part of the funeral service; and six Army Air Corps officers served as pall bearers.[59]

Virginia and Robert's parents sat quietly near the grave site where the casket was placed and listened as Fort Sheridan post chaplain, Erling C. Grevstad officiated the graveside service. Following the eulogy, a wave of sadness descended upon the crowd as a soldier mournfully played Taps. Then the boom of the guns, as a salute was fired, woke them from their quiet reverie as they prepared to depart.

Robert was laid to rest in the Birchwood Section of the cemetery while his family silently grieved for the man who was a modest, heroic, honorable husband, son and brother.

Virginia described the whole funeral process as, "the most devastating of anything I had ever had to go thru. I passed out while watching them lower the casket into the ground. I was very young and completely unprepared for such a trauma. After all, I was still on my honeymoon."[60]

The following Tuesday, *The Berywn Life* reported the Berwyn city council adopted a resolution to be sent to the wife and parents of Robert. It said in part, "Our country is richer because of his bravery, and a world peace is nearer because of his labors."[61]

Robert's Distinguished Flying Cross. Author's photo.

Robert Is Remembered

In December 8, 1996 the Flying Tigers were awarded the Distinguished Flying Cross on, for extraordinary achievement while participating in combat as part of the American Volunteer Group in China.

I contacted the Flying Tiger Association and asked who would receive Robert's medal and citation. I explained I was one of the only family members left, as his parents and brother were deceased. I was fortunate and received Robert's award and its accompanying citation.

The Citation awarded stated,

The American Volunteer Group, the Flying Tigers, compiled an unparalleled combat record under extremely hazardous conditions. This volunteer unit conducted aggressive counter-air, air-defense, and close air support operations against a numerically superior enemy force occasionally 20 times larger. Members of the All Volunteer Group destroyed some 650 enemy aircraft while suffering minimal losses. Their extraordinary performance in the face of seemingly overwhelming odds was a major factor in defeating the enemy's invasion of South China. The professional competence, aerial skill, and devotion to duty displayed by Robert R. Brouk reflect great credit upon himself and the Armed Forces of the United States.[62]

Having this medal and citation brought me one step closer to knowing Robert. The fact still remained that no one knew where happened to Ginny and his story had not been told.

It seems someone wanted Robert's story told, for Robert's widow, Virginia, e-mailed me at the end of 2005. Apparently her grandson saw one of my posts about Robert on a Flying Tigers message board. We corresponded over several months, and Ginny shared some photographs, their love story, and Robert's war diary with me. She told me about her role in Robert's life and about what happened to her after his death.

Virginia and I lost touch for a while until early 2010 when I decided it was time to write Robert's story. I had enough information, his war diary, and with a little additional research, could tell his story. And the best part, I now knew what happened to Virginia after Robert's death.

Would you like to hear her remarkable story of life after death? Please look for the sequel to this story *The Tiger's Widow (to be released summer 2014.)*

6

The Tough 'Ombres!
James Privoznik

90th Infantry Division, 790th Ordnance and

90th Infantry Division, 358th Infantry

(1921 – 1945)

The Family Story

Each story in this book started with a family story that had been passed down. Or at the very least, pieces of a story. James Privoznik really had no story. He had been lost. My uncle showed me a photograph in an old scrapbook with a notation underneath that had his death date. At some point I ordered his Individual Deceased Personnel File (IDPF) because I wanted all the IDPFs for the servicemen in my family who died in service. I looked through it, added information to my family tree, and left it at alone, until Labor Day weekend 2012.

Genealogy research is a little about luck and timing. Some call it serendipity. Not everyone receives or recognizes such clear signs that it is time to research, but I did. That weekend, over the course of four days, I received an e-mail from a man named Mike Boehler in Luxembourg. Mike does Missing in Action research and had seen a blog post I had written about James. He asked if I needed any help researching his story.

The next day I received an email from a man named Norm Richards who lives near St. Louis, Missouri. He is an independent military researcher who pulls records at the National Personnel Records Center. You can find information about him on my website (http://jenniferholik.com.) He said he had some friends in Luxembourg who were interested in adopting James' grave. Their names were Norbert and Romaine. What is interesting is Norbert and Romaine knew Mike but Mike and Norm did not yet know each other. Norbert and Romaine and I connected on FaceBook and have been friends since.

Finally, I received a call from my cousin Jim, who is the nephew of James Privoznik. He said his father LeRoy was interested in getting a copy of James' IDPF and talking about James. Sadly we were not to get together until spring 2013, after LeRoy passed away.

If those contacts over a period of four days were not enough of a sign to start looking into James' military service, I do not know what is. Thus I started the long journey from phone calls, emails and an IDPF, to a story of a man who served his country. When his unit needed replacements, he was one of the men chosen to take up arms and fight on the front lines where he died in the Battle of the Bulge.

James' story has been the most difficult to write because of the intensity of the events surrounding his death. It is also the best example in this book of the resources available to tell a soldier's story when "all the records burned." Through his story I hope you understand the vast amount of information available if you look for it, or it finds you.

Civilian Conservation Corps

James Privoznik grew up in Chicago during the Depression. He was raised by his step-mother, Mae, after his father died when James was only eight years old. Times were tough for everyone and in 1932, when Franklin D. Roosevelt was elected President he called for a "New Deal" in America.

James Privoznik at Camp Lyman, 1939.
Photo courtesy Jim Privoznik.

The "New Deal" would create jobs across the country and help put young men to work. One of the first initiatives was to create the Emergency Conservation Work Act (ECW) which would bring young men together through the Army to work on the land to prevent soil erosion and declining timber resources. This Act became known as the Civilian Conservation Corps (CCC).[1]

CCC enrollees were paid $30 a month with almost all of that amount being sent home to the family. The men did have a little left for their use on tobacco, supplies, beer, or other sundries.

Upon induction, each enrollee was given a physical and vaccinations to ensure they were being shipped out to their camp as healthy as possible. The War Department also had strict hygiene standards at the camps to keep the men healthy.

James (left) on KP duty. Photo courtesy Jim Privoznik.

CCC pond construction. Photo courtesy Jim Privoznik.

Each camp provided employees with structured days, similar to Army soldiers. The day began with Reveille at 6:00 a.m. followed by breakfast and camp clean-up. Then the men jumped in trucks and headed out to their work project destination for the day unless they had kitchen duty. The men had three meals a day and ceremonies at 5:00 p.m. which involved flag lowering at the camp, announcements, and inspection. After dinner, the men were allowed to do as they wished and write letters, participate in sports or an educational program, or talk with their friends.

James applied to work for the CCC after he graduated high school in 1939. He was accepted and placed in Company 3692 which was stationed in Camp Lyman, Washington.[2] The Certificate of Selection stated James was best qualified for work as a machinist or draftsman, skills he learned in high school.[3]

In mid-July 1939, James was sent to the Discharge and Reception Center at Camp McCoy, Wisconsin. Camp McCoy had been an Army base for many years and utilized for many different purposes for the War Department. During the 1930s, it served as a Supply Base for the CCC and the Discharge and Reception Center. James spent July 16-19 at Camp McCoy going through induction, receiving training, clothing, and equipment. When his Company was ready, the men traveled from July 19 to 21 from Camp McCoy to Camp Lyman in Washington.[4]

James spent the remainder of 1939 working on various projects at Camp Lyman doing road construction, timber work or digging and building retaining ponds.

Hanging out at Camp Lyman. James 2nd from left on top row. Photo courtesy Jim Privoznik.

James' employment with the CCC ended in mid-December and he was transferred back to Camp McCoy to be discharged from the CCC and soon after he returned to Chicago to work in a mattress factory.

Chicago 1943

In Chicago in 1943, my family like others across the city was preparing to send their men off to war. Not only did my cousin Frank Winkler go into service late in the year, but so did three men from my Holik family; my grandpa, Joseph Holik, his brother Frank, and their sister's Mae's step-son, James Privoznik. Joseph, Frank, and Mae's parents were deceased and the siblings had each other and their growing families for support. The men in these families went off to fight leaving wives, sisters, and children on the home front.

Frank Holik was inducted into the Army and was stationed stateside due to a vision issue. He was 28 years old and married but did not yet have children. Joseph Holik joined the Naval Armed Guard and was sent off to fight. He was 37 years old and left behind a wife and three young boys, ages 12, 10, and 8.

James Privoznik was born July 30, 1921 in Chicago, Illinois to James George Privoznik and Christina Kurtz.[5] James' mother died in 1928. Mae's husband, James' father, died in 1933. At 22 years of age, James had only Mae and his brother LeRoy left in his immediate family. James tried several times to enter the service with his friends in each different branch. The family lore was that no branch would take him because of a heart murmur. Finally in early 1943, the Army accepted him.

Based on the information provided by the family, military records, and research into the life of an Ordnance Soldier during World War II, the following is what I believe James may have experienced in his military life. This story is told in his voice.

James, Mae, and LeRoy Privoznik, 1938 Chicago. Photo courtesy Jim Privoznik.

James Privoznik – Army Life

I officially entered the Army on February 10, 1943 and by February 17 was on my way to Camp Butner in North Carolina.[6] I was placed into the 126th Medium Maintenance (MM) Ordnance Company, part of the 66th Ordnance Battalion. The 126th was activated at Camp Butner on August 27, 1942.[7] Here I received basic training and additional training in ordnance. My job as an Ordnance Soldier, defined by the Army was "Designs, procures, issues and maintains weapons, motor vehicles, and ammunition."[8]

Barracks at Camp Butner in North Carolina. Photo courtesy Camp Butner Society.

Camp Butner, named after Major General Henry Wolfe Butner, a Surry County native who died in 1937, opened August 5, 1942.[9] The Camp was the training ground primarily for the 78th Infantry Division which trained soldiers for the European Theater. It also served as the training ground for the 126th MM Ordnance Company.

The camp was over 40,000 acres large and served as a training base for infantry, artillery, and engineering elements. Here we learned about basic military drill, gas attacks, and how to bridge and cross rivers. The camp consisted of wooden barracks for the men, a hospital, swimming pools, churches, and theaters. It also held a rifle and artillery ranges, barracks for the men, and support services.[10] Camp Butner was also a Prisoner of War compound for Germans and Italians.

The Ordnance Department supplied and maintained all weapons small and large, anti-aircraft artillery guns, and the ammunition for all types of equipment. It was also responsible for bombs and bomb fuses. Ordnance soldiers were trained to do two main jobs. First, even though we were often behind the front lines, we needed to know how to protect ourselves and our unit through the use of firearms and ordnance. Second, to maintain, protect, recover, repair, and distribute equipment, vehicles, arms, and ordnance to the troops. I was first trained in Medium Maintenance. In a combat zone, we would be farther behind the lines than a Light Maintenance Organization. Yet when I was transferred into the 90th Division 790th Ordnance, I was placed into Light Maintenance. The difference between Medium Maintenance and Light Maintenance was the amount of work and specific work we did as an Ordnance Soldier. In Medium Maintenance we trained on every piece of possible equipment we could encounter. When we were transferred to Light Maintenance, we were given more specific jobs closer to the infantry so we could more easily and quickly recover, repair, and reissue weapons and vehicles.

> The Ordnance Companies handled "approximately 1,800 major items and more than 60,000 principal components."[11] These items and components were things like ordnance we issued to troops and equipment to fix vehicles and armaments.

Training consisted of a great deal of physical fitness to ensure we were strong. We practiced loading and unloading vehicles in all types of weather. We had to be strong under any circumstance even though we would not be on the front lines with a rifle. This strength ensured we could do our jobs under calm conditions or combat.

We received *The Ordnance Soldier's Guide* as part of our training. This book outlined everything we needed to know to get through training. We covered basic topics on insignia, tables of order, care and cleaning of equipment, sanitation, first aid and possible diseases we might contract in training and overseas.

Then we moved into more war-related topics. We spent a lot of time learning how to care for and fire a rifle and care for our equipment. This would be important when we were sent into battle. The many types of ordnance were discussed and we were shown how to use and store these items. There were sessions on chemical warfare, how to protect ourselves from an attack, and what to do in case of a chemical attack. Our instructors usually tried to keep the classes lively as some topics were very dull.

We learned how to distinguish Allied vehicles and aircraft from enemy vehicles and aircraft. In this part of our training we learned how each type of vehicle functioned, how to maintain it, and in some cases, drive.

We learned how to dig foxholes and build field fortifications. Knowing how to dig a foxhole would come in handy when I transferred to the infantry. We were taught map reading because we had to know where we were moving, how the terrain was laid out, and where the various units would be located during battle.

Sometimes our job included rigging and hauling equipment. We learned to tie various types of knots, how to build pulleys and hoisting devices and move heavy items using these devices. Demolition was also covered so we could destroy equipment that we had to abandon.

Part of our training included how to kill a Jap or German with our bare hands. Diagrams were printed in our book that explained all the points on a man where you could inflict damage. Many diagrams were shown teaching how to use leverage, strength, balance, and momentum to throw off the enemy. We hoped we would not have to use this training. As part of enemy training, we learned to build and dismantle booby traps and other firing devices.

There was a lot of equipment we learned how to maintain and repair throughout the training which included artillery. We had to learn about each component, how it functioned, and how to repair it. Beyond the vehicles and arms, we learned how to cite and repair instruments like aiming circles, range finders, binoculars, telescopes, quadrants, and mortar sites.

The Ordnance Company had access to many trucks which hauled our equipment. We were essentially a traveling machine shop using several trucks. We had the Artillery Repair Truck, Automotive Repair Truck, Electrical Repair Truck, Instrument Repair Truck, machine Shop Truck, Small Arms Repair Truck, and a Welding Truck. Within each truck were toolboxes of equipment and supplies.

Between April 25, 1943 and June 19, 1943, the 66th Ordnance Battalion was transferred to Tennessee for Maneuvers.[12] The Tennessee Maneuvers were a type of war games through which we were trained for combat and our military job. I was technically a member of the Ordnance Department but also trained as an infantryman during basic training and maneuvers.

Tennessee Maneuvers spring-summer 1943.
Photo courtesy Jim Privoznik.

We spent eight weeks in Tennessee working through "Problems." The units during this time period were broken into Red and Blue teams which specific missions as part of each "problem." There were Umpires who graded the three components and the team as a whole on how well they performed each war game.

These problems were the various war games designed to help us learn to move quickly, change course, attack, adjust, and compensate when things were not going as planned. Each "problem" was designed to see how well the Staff component, Combat Component, and Support components worked together. The "problems" had a mission, restrictions for both teams, a list of the troops involved, and other missions that would be encountered as the week progressed.

The Staff received orders for the week and had to inform the Combat and Support components of the initial plan of attack or defense. Throughout the week, information would come down the pipeline indicating we had lost men, equipment, the attack or defense plans had changed or any combination of the three. It was also possible we were now being infiltrated by "enemy" troops.

As an Ordnance Soldier, my job was to continue securing, maintaining, issuing, retrieving, fixing equipment, and providing material and maintenance support to the Combat Soldiers. There were times when we were told to take up our rifles and be prepared for an attack or to defend our perimeter. Just because we were behind the lines did not mean we were always out of harm's way.

The entire point of the war games was to train us for the quick moving, ever changing war that we were about to be thrown into overseas. Each of us, regardless of our specific job, needed to completely understand how to work with all the other components in a time when everything could change in an instant. It was an intense eight weeks but we were all the better trained in the end.

The Problems presented to the units were defined by a Type. This might be "Meeting engagement, aggressive action by a large force and the withdrawal of a small force."[13] In some problems, a situation would follow that might define bridges or roads that had been destroyed or provide reconnaissance information. Then the specific mission of the Blue and Red teams would be defined.

In some problems, additional plans would be noted and restrictions for each team were presented. This might have been described as certain roads or bridges being off-limits during the attack or mission.

From Training to War

James in uniform on right. Photo courtesy of Jim Privoznik.

On February 9, 1944, I was transferred from Camp Butner to the NYPE-RP or New York Port of Embarkation Replacement Pool at Camp Kilmer in New Jersey.[14] Camp Kilmer served as a large Replacement Depot on the east coast. The Camp was similar to a sprawling city and we enjoyed a lot of entertainment while we were stationed there. The Camp sat on over 1,500 acres and held 1,120 buildings.[15] There were barracks buildings, chapels, movie theaters, libraries, a gym, dining halls, a hospital, post office, and post exchanges. There were sports teams and games played; we had USO entertainment, dances, movies, and a post band and orchestra. The Army treated us well before we were shipped overseas.

I was in the hospital for a period of time and was released back to service in Camp Kilmer on February 15, 1944.[16] A few days later I was given eight days of furlough to get my affairs in order. We would be shipping overseas soon.[17] [18] After furlough, our training continued.

On March 21, 1944, I was transferred from the Replacement Pool to the 790th Ordnance Light Maintenance Company in the 90th Division.[19] Two days later on March 23, 1944, at Staten Island, New York I boarded the *M.S. John Erickson* destined for overseas. We were not told where we were going, but our final destination was Liverpool, England.[20] Unfortunately, the ship had engine trouble and after a day at sea, we returned to the dock. For three days we sat on the ship waiting for repairs to be completed so our journey could begin. Once we set sail again, we had no contact with the enemy or any further maintenance issues.

When we arrived in England on April 8, we boarded a train and later transferred to trucks to reach our destination in Kidderminster, England, south of Liverpool. This is where the company was stationed while we were in England.

We knew an invasion of some sort was being planned but no one knew when or where. Secrets about the invasion and upcoming events were kept close to those in charge. We were tense and scared yet apprehensively confident and ready to go. We prepared for an unknown date with destiny. There were rumors circulating and questions being asked. Where were we going? Will this fight ever end? Will we make it out alive?

For weeks our ordnance company waterproofed vehicles and artillery in preparation for the invasion. We practiced loading and unloading vehicles. We installed gun mounts and checked and distributed artillery pieces. Our men also built litter racks for the medical battalion. 48 of these were constructed which further enforced the reality of invasion.[21] And we asked ourselves again, would we make it out alive?

The Normandy Campaign

The 90th division was ordered to participate in the invasion. The time had come, the word was given, and on June 4, 1944[22] we anxiously boarded a Liberty Ship at Cardiff, Wales in preparation for the invasion. The tension in the atmosphere heightened as the time neared for combat. Prayers were said, letters written home, and the greatest armada ever assembled in history prepared to set sail.

On June 6, our Allied forces deployed the airborne infantrymen, sent gliders and dropped numerous boxes of supplies over northern France for our use. Men stormed the beaches after daybreak and began ferociously fighting their way off the wet, bloody sands up the cliffs or toward the roads and hedgerows of France.

The 790th Ordnance Company spent four long days waiting on the ship as the invasion took place. Our Company was not needed until the beaches were secure. The atmosphere on board was filled with excitement, queasiness, tension, anticipation, and young men's robust confidence that we will win this war.

On June 8, our men departed the ship at Utah Beach at 1400 hours (2:00 p.m.) amidst artillery fire from both sides. The sound was thunderous and the smell of smoke, blood, and death surrounded us. Ordnance men not driving vehicles off the Landing Ship Tank (LSTs) waded through the waters carrying equipment over their heads. As dusk approached, the LSTs carrying vehicles was able to move close enough to disembark the additional men and vehicles.

The 90th Division boarded the ships, the *Susan B. Anthony*, the *Excelsior*, the *Explorer*, and the *Beinville*. The *Susan B. Anthony* struck a mine off Utah Beach and sank with no loss of life.[23] With the sinking, many supplies were lost unless they were being carried by the soldiers. This caused a disruption in the planned attack that was to take place after the men moved off the beach inland. Weapons and equipment had to be salvaged from other soldiers, beach hospitals, and the supply dumps. Although there was a lack of supplies and parts, the ingenuity and resourcefulness of the Ordnance Company got the job done. The Ordnance men also captured German equipment and mortars, refurbished them to be used by our troops. The 790th Ordnance History talked about capturing this equipment as a way to, "spew forth death on their original makers."[24]

It is important to note that personal effects of the officers and enlisted men were carried separately into France. These were turned over to the Personnel Section of the 90th Division on June 19th when that group entered France.[25]

The beach was a mass of confusion and death. Rain poured down from dark sobbing skies. Bodies, equipment, ammunition, and vehicles were everywhere. It took our men a little while to maneuver our vehicles through the maze of destruction. Once we accomplished this, it was then time to de-waterproof the vehicles brought ashore, re-issue arms and ammunition, and repair damaged weapons from our unit. Surprisingly our Ordnance Company lost not one man in our part of the invasion.

The Company took over abandoned German vehicles and put them into service. These vehicles were used to help move the 90th Division troops and supplies off the beach to their destinations. As we moved forward we were able to secure food, clothing, arms, and other supplies from German dumps which had been abandoned. This helped us clothe, feed, and re-arm our men who were on the *Susan B. Anthony* and made it to the beach wet and without gear.

Our Company arrived by motor convoy at our bivouac, or camping area, area near Ecoqueneauville, France about 1900 hours (7:00 p.m.) on June 8.[26] When we arrived we were told to camouflage the vehicles and dig in! We dug as fast as we could as the German planes swooped down from the heavens unleashing bombs around us. The noise was deafening.

From the time we landed in France, our jobs varied little. The Armament Platoon was constantly salvaging, repairing, and reissuing equipment and artillery for which they did not always have spare parts. The Automotive Section was repairing vehicles and building medical litter racks. The Supply Platoon was locating supply dumps, breaking down boxes of supplies to issue to our troops. All the Ordnance men worked with as much creativity as we could muster to repair into perfect working order all the arms, equipment, and vehicles with whatever supplies we were able to gain access. When our Sections were not engaged in work, we were moving from place to place to keep up with the troop movement. Our stays in each bivouac area ranged from one day to up to 13 days when the supplies were running low.

On June 8 we camped near Ecoqueneauville and remained there until June 16 when we moved nine miles to Fresville.[27] On the 19th, the Ordnance dispatched four 2 ½ ton trucks to the front lines carrying troops.[28] June 23, we moved again, five miles to Chef du Pont.[29] It was around this time that our Ordnance patrol located a supply dump near a swamp. This meant new equipment and supplies for our guys which enabled us to do our jobs with greater ease.

July 6 we were on the move again just a few miles up the road to Deuzeville-la-Bastille.[30] Two days later we departed by motor convoy another five miles to Ponte-le-Abbe.[31] July 10th was an incredible day for us because a mobile shower was made available. We had our first shower since landing on Utah Beach over a month before.[32] Can you imagine not showering for over a month? That was not something I thought about when I joined the Army!

July 21 saw us depart by motor convoy again four and a half miles to St. Jores.[33] Even though we were not on the front line, we were always following the troops and within artillery distance. We had to deal with "Bed-check Charlies" (what we called the German planes that flew overhead each night.) This was never enjoyable because we were constantly diving into foxholes. Thankfully by July 24, 1944, the Normandy Campaign was over and we were off to secure Northern France.

The Battle of Northern France

July 28, we moved again to Gorges, France and the next day 10 miles by motor convoy to Periers, France.[34] By the end of July through the month of August, we were constantly on the move, staying no more than two days in each bivouac area. On August 3 we moved again 43 miles to St. Osvin. As we approached Avranches, we got a taste of what our boys on the front lines dealt with every minute. We were attacked by enemy planes flying cross-wise to our convoy. The planes found our slow moving convoy and took aim as men dove from the trucks into ditches. Some would say we dove into our helmets like a snail. Men were doubled up as small as they could make themselves as the bullets flew. The Quartermaster vehicles behind us were hit and there were casualties. Thankfully the Ordnance Company suffered no damage or loss of men. When the attack was over, the convoy continued moving.[35]

Throughout August we moved from an area near Landivy,[36] approximately 50 miles to Le Mans, France.[37] In Le Mans, the 90th closed up the Falaise Gap and wiped out the German Seventh Army. It was a great victory for the 90th Division. Around Chambois, the Ordnance men were able to watch from a distance, the fighting of our infantry and artillery. It was a site to behold as our men decimated the German fighting units. At times there were cease fires so the German troops could surrender.[38]

From there we moved to Ballon a distance of 17 miles[39] and later departed for Chaillous, moving a distance of 20 miles.[40] August 27 was another travel day, this time 23 miles to Nangis, France.[41] August 30 we traveled 39 miles to Chenay, France.[42] In Chenay we were only a couple of miles from Rheims, France. Here we were housed in palatial houses and once again, offered a hot shower.

This was the second time we were able to bathe and clean up since landing in France on June 8. It felt really good to have a shower, shave, and fresh clothes. That really improved morale and we felt human again. We were also able to rest and take a momentary break from the war. There was hot food to eat, mail call, and church services in the town. All of these things increased our spirit and will to continue fighting.

The Rhineland and Ardennes

September arrived and on the 6th we traveled 101 miles to Etain, France.[43] On September 10, we were located near Lixieres, 1 mile North of Verdun after having traveled 11 miles. I was promoted from Private to Private First Class on that date.[44] On September 12, we traveled 14 miles to Fontoy.[45] Two days later we moved another 11 miles to Briey.[46]

The Rhineland Campaign had started and the 90th Division was to be a part of this push. Unfortunately, it was slow moving as the rains came and the mud rose. For much of September we were pummeled by rain. The mud was so thick and sticky that it was almost impenetrable. We were forever pushing and pulling vehicles down the road. Repair and maintenance of equipment was difficult but we still the job got done. Finally, we were to move again and traveled six miles to Giraumont, France on September 26. Here we stayed in an iron mine where we were dry. Some of the Company was stationed indoors while the rest slept outdoors. The French miners running the mine allowed us access to the showers and gave us tours of the mine and their equipment. It was quite an education and we were thankful for their kindness. We remained in Giraumont until the end of October.[47]

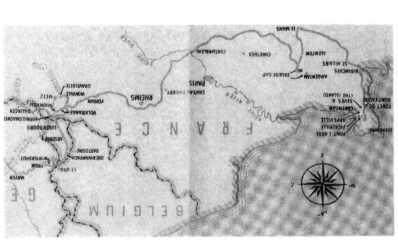

The 90th Division, 358th Infantry's trek across Europe. Photo credit: Peragimus We Accomplish.

The division was later given a Commendation for their outstanding work in the months of September and October, 1944. It stated,

HEADQUARTERS

90th DIVISION ARTILLERY
APO 90, U.S.A.

SUBJECT: Commendation

7 March 1945

TO: Commanding Officer, 790th Ordnance Light Maintenance Company, APO 90, U.S. Army. (Thru Channels).

>*During the period September and October 1944 when the 90th Division was in position before fortress Metz there was a chronic shortage of artillery ammunition. In order to give proper artillery support to the division, in its various efforts we called upon your organization to secure for us captured weapons and ammunition. The results of the effort and risk of the mend and officers of your organization are clearly written among the outstanding successes of the division.*

>*The officers and men of your artillery section searched over many miles of France locating weapons that could be conditioned for use. The untiring efforts and outstanding technical ability quickly made available almost an entire battalion of captured material and we are cognizant of the risks involved in their testing of these weapons.*

>*The work of your ammunition section in locating and hauling ammunition; of experimenting and testing, made available to us some 50,000 rounds which were fired from the captured material.*

>*The often unheralded efforts of such energetic and capable officers and men extending their efforts far beyond the call of ordinary duty is the foundation of success of our division.*

>*S/ Ernest A. Bixby, Brigadier General U.S. Army, Commanding.*[48]

Fall arrived in Northern Europe and the rains came, a constant, steady rain which turned the landscape into liquid mud.[49] We continued to slog through it just behind the troops. The weather was turning colder but our fighting men were becoming tougher. November 3 saw us moving 19 miles to Piennes, France.[50] On November 9, we departed by motor convoy again 24 ½ miles to Hettange Grande, France.[51] November 18 we departed from Hettange Grande, crossed the Moselle River and proceeded to a bivouac area near Thionville, France.[52] Near Thionville we set up shop in an abandoned gas factory. We had luxuries such as protection from the weather, lights, a cement floor on which to work, and plenty of space to spread out. During this time, the Recovery Section of our Company was assigned to establish a Collecting Point near Basse Yutz. The Recovery Section then began scouting through heavily mined areas to recover both American and German ammunition, equipment, and vehicles. Not everything could be collected and brought to the Collecting Point because of the mines. Some of the equipment and vehicles had to be demolished.[53] Once the ammunition, equipment and vehicles were procured, they were brought to our bivouac area for repair, testing, and issue to the troops. This is how we spent the end of November.

On December 5, we moved to the vicinity of Veckring, France roughly 13 miles from our current station and remained here until December 23.[54] It was during our time in this area that the Company was housed near Bouzonville. On December 14, we encountered a rough night when the Germans attacked and everyone ran for the air raid shelter in the building. The shelling continued throughout the night and at 0230 (2:30 a.m.) our building was hit. The Company experienced its first battle death as the rear of the building was hit by shells, shook, and exploded. Debris flew everywhere and Pfc. Hedgepeth was killed. A few of our members suffered cuts and bruises and several officers had to be dug out of the rubble amidst the roar and rumble of shells hitting all around us. No one slept that night as we were on pins and needles waiting to see what else would happen.[55] Just four days later, my MOS or job, was changed within the Company to rigger.[56]

December 1944 experienced one of the worst winters in history in Luxembourg. By mid-December, a high pressure system had moved into Europe from the Atlantic causing some thawing and fog. The weather quickly changed when a front from Russia moved in just before Christmas, causing blizzards, ice, and chilling winds to blow across the land.[58]

The Battle of the Bulge

Heavy fighting had been oc-
curring in the Ardennes for two
weeks between the Germans
and our forces. The generals
met and discussed tactics and it
was decided that Patton's Third
Army which included the 90th
Division, would be committed
to fight the Nazi's at the Bulge.

The weather in Northern
Europe went from cold and
rainy to frigid and snowy.
Heavy snow fell, temperatures
dropped below zero, roads
became impassible, and biting
winds hit us as we moved. The
Army did not provide adequate
winter clothing and we wore

Fighting the blizzard.. Photo credit: Peragimus We Accomplish.

our Army green camouflage uniforms rather than winter white camouflage. Our boots were also inadequate and our feet were in constant danger of freezing.

Within days of the snow, the elevated lands in France, Germany,
and Luxembourg were frozen and roads were nearly impassable. We
struggled to find rock or wood or anything that might help us clear
the roads and provide some traction. It was slow going from place to
place during this time.

On December 23, we moved to Elzange, France about eight miles
from Veckring.[59] Four days later, on December 27, I was transferred
into the 90th Divisions, 358th Infantry Regiment with no refresher
training in combat skills. I left the Ordnance unit stationed at Elzange
and proceeded to meet the 358th. I joined the 358th Infantry Regiment, Company F, at Wehingen, Germany, on the 29th of December.[60] Once in the 358th we were sent out on patrol to gather information and capture German prisoners when possible. Our job was to
keep the Germans from advancing any further into the Ardennes.

General Patton issued a Christmas Greeting on prayer cards at
Christmas. Patton asked everyone to pray for good weather, for the
rains to cease and for victory to be theirs. In part his prayer said,
"call upon Thee that named with power we may advance from

victory to victory and crush the oppression and wickedness of our enemies..."[61]

Patton had been short on fighting men due to lack of replacements throughout the fall. This was a source of great frustration for him. He felt if he had the men, he could have done a much faster job of driving the Germans back to Germany and out of the Bulge area. He began pulling men from the rear echelons to serve as replacements. By December 20, 1944, he again ordered replacements be provided from the rear. This time he wanted to completely fill the ranks of the 90th Division.[57]

January 1, 1945, we moved into the front lines and changed places with Company E of the 358th Infantry near Scheuerwald, Germany. We were under heavy mortar fire the entire day although we sustained no casualties.[62] The weather conditions in Belgium and Luxembourg in early January 1945 were miserable. On January 3 the temperature hovered around zero degrees Fahrenheit. As the snow fell it reduced visibility to roughly 50 yards.[63] The ground was frozen at least six inches down making foxhole digging nearly impossible. We were so frozen we had trouble firing our guns. Some men rode on the hood of the jeeps to stay warm. Due to the low visibility, the larger weapons and tanks were virtually useless.

For days, sleet, snow, and then blizzard conditions with wet and heavy snow pummeled the area. Visibility was terrible and movement was slow and even more dangerous.

Imagine being frozen, physically and mentally exhausted, while constantly on the move from location to location in biting winds and knee-deep snow as we fought the enemy. Our vehicles and tanks slid off the road into ditches as our men attempted to scale a hill or mountain. Some vehicles and tanks were irretrievable as they slid down steep slopes. Our rifles wouldn't fire because of the cold. It was hell. There was nothing we could do to change the circumstances. At times the snow was waist-deep and we had trouble moving.

We were lucky to have a cold breakfast before moving on to the next location. At night we dug foxholes in the snow next to the tanks

On January 4 the Associated Press ran an article in the *Chicago Daily Tribune* which said, "a snow and sleet storm which turned the fighting in these mountains and forests into a white hell."[64]

which offered some protection from the enemy and elements. Every town we moved through had been hit at least once. There was almost no shelter anywhere to give us a break from the weather. We attempted a shivering sleep while we remained soaked and frozen.[65]

Near Berle, Luxembourg. Photo courtesy Norbert Morbé.

Between January 1 and 5, the 357th, 358th, and 359th Infantry Regiments prepared for an attack to the "confluence of the Saar and Moselle Rivers, so we stayed put and waited in the cold."[66] However, on January 5, the Division received a message from Corps stating "Be prepared for movement."[67] The plans the Division was crafting were put aside as we prepared to move again. On January 6, 1945, we moved by truck to Waldwisse, France.[68] January 7 we moved again by motor convoy about 35 miles to Nagam, Luxembourg. We were behind the lines and saw no enemy contact on our trip. It was cold and snowed the entire day as our convoy tried not to slide of the icy roads.[69]

The 90th Division's mission was to cut off enemy penetration Southeast of Bastogne and reinforce units already there fighting. The original plan was to assemble behind the 35th Division and 26th Divisions on January 9th. Attack would come from the 90th Division through the 26th Division. But plans were changed and the 90th Division commander received permission to directly attack the enemy.[70]

The 358th Infantry Regiment moved with the Division roughly 50 miles to the Bigonville-Rambrouch-Hustert-Noerdange vicinity in hellish weather. Here we were put on reserve and housed.[71] And again, there was no shelter for us because the towns we marched through had been destroyed at least three times before we arrived to push the German armies out.

We spent weeks on the frozen ground next to our tanks and trucks at night with only a blanket to shield us from the elements. We freeze. There is no warmth here. We went from rain and ankle deep mud for weeks to a frozen wasteland within days. Patton prayed for a break in the weather. He got it and then hell froze over.

Finally, on January 11, 1945, we were commanded to assemble behind the 357th Infantry at Bavigne and move toward Bras, Belgium to attack.[72]

With our identification blacked out on our uniforms, we fought with all our strength through heavy snows, frigid temperatures, and piercing winds. You could say in January we were engaged in a two enemy war – the weather and the Germans. We pushed the Germans back.....back .....and closed the Bastogne Pocket of the Bulge as we marched through Sonlez, Doncoles, and arrived in Bras, Belgium, on January 11, 1945.[73]

I am lost.

Will anyone find me or will I be undiscovered until the spring thaw?

On a very cold and dark, overcast day in January as our unit trudged along on snow packed roads contemplating the bitter wind-swept white landscape. We moved toward the enemy with as much silence as we could muster. On this day, January 11, 1945, I was killed by a high explosive shell near Bras, Belgium.[74]

The Living Must Go On

Mae was notified of James' death by the War Department after January 27, 1945.[75] On March 8, 1945, *The Chicago Daily Tribune* reported his name in the list of casualties.[76] This made his death even more real than it already was. There was his name in black and white in the newspaper.

James was buried originally in the U.S. Military Cemetery in Hamm, Luxembourg.[77] This cemetery was created by the 609th Quartermaster Grave Registration Company (QMGRC) on December 29, 1944 as a temporary burial ground.[78] It initially served to inter those who fought in the Ardennes area. Many soldiers who fought in the Battle of the Bulge were buried here. The cemetery site selected sat in a forest glade near a community, railroad facilities, and good roads.

Initially, a Third Army service detachment was sent to construct temporary buildings, clear roads and begin interring the Soldier Dead. This detachment built a garage, office, x-ray and morgue building, an ornamental gate, and sentry box at the entrance of the cemetery. The Army used prisoner of war labor troops to dig the cemetery plots and handle the burials. At the time all of this was happening, the Germans were still fighting the Third Army in the area and occasionally work would cease due to shelling. Once the shelling stopped, work would resume on the cemetery buildings, processing of the dead, and interments.

As the war dead were being buried, their personal effects were shipped to the Quartermaster Effects Depot in Kansas City, Missouri. In the Effects Depot, personal effects were cleaned of debris and blood. Items were checked and sent to the families with a letter. James' mother Mae did not receive any of James' effects after his death and initial burial.

In April Mae sent the War Department a letter asking about James' personal effects. She wrote,

> *4/19/45*
>
> *Dear Sir –*
>
> *Will you please send me my son's personal effects.*
>
> *P.F.C. James F. Privoznik – 36640529*
> *Co F 358 Infantry. A.P.O. #90*
>
> *Killed in action January-11-1945*
>
> *Yours Truly*
> *Mrs. Mary Privoznik*
> *3124 So Ridgeway Ave, Chicago, 23, Ill*[79]

Mae received a response from the Quartermaster General on May 14, 1945. The letter read,

Privoznik, James F.
S.N. 36 640 429

14 May 1945

Mrs. Mary Privoznik
3124 South Ridgeway Avenue
Chicago, Illinois

Dear Mrs. Privoznik:

Reference is made to your inquiry regarding the personal effects of Private First Class James F. Privoznik.

A copy of your letter has been forwarded to the Effects Quartermaster, Army Effects Bureau, Kansas City Quartermaster Depot, 601 Hardesty Avenue, Kansas City 1, Missouri, for reply to you. That office has jurisdiction over the disposal of their personal effects of our deceased military personnel outside the United States. However, considerable time is often necessary to process these personal belongings back to this country due to lack of shipping space and the great amount of work involved.

I extend to you my sincere sympathy in your loss.

FOR THE QUARTERMASTER GENERAL:

Sincerely Yours,

C.C. Pierce
Captain, QMC Assistant[80]

By April 1, 1945, the 609th QMGRC had been transferred and the 612th QMGRC under Captain Roundtree had been assigned to the Cemetery.[81] The Third Army had moved beyond the area and any remains that were being collected as they marched east were being brought to back to Hamm. The U.S. did not bury their dead in temporary cemeteries on German soil.

The 612th QMGRC was not on duty long and by the end of the month had been transferred out. The 3045th QMGRC Detachment B had moved in and was focusing on the beautification of the grounds. The Army planned to have Memorial Day services at each military cemetery so graves had to be leveled, walkways had to be built and maintained, crosses had to be painted or touched up, and a flag pole had to be built. This detachment had less than a month to prepare.

Memorial Day services were held at the Luxembourg Cemetery on May 30, 1945 amidst a crowd of people and visiting dignitaries.[82] The program, according to the History of the Luxembourg Cemetery was,

Prelude (Band Music)
Call to Worship
Reading of Gospel
Memorial Address
Wreath Ceremony
Firing of Volleys
Taps and Silver Taps
National Hymns (American and French)
Benediction
Postlude (Band Music)[83]

The ceremony was a moving tribute to all our war dead.

By late spring, Mae had still not received any of James' personal effects. She did receive a letter dated May 24, 1945 from the Quartermaster's Office. It read,

Dear Mrs. Privoznik:

Your inquiry directed to Washington, D.C. has been referred to the Army Effects Bureau for reply in connection with the personal effects of your son, Private First Class James F. Privoznik.

I am sorry to report that we have not yet received any of your son's property. There is enclosed an information circular which will give you some idea of the time which may elapse before personal effects arrive here from overseas.

You will note from Paragraph 3 of the circular that this Bureau needs certain information in order to make disposition of the property. You may furnish the necessary information at this time, if you wish, so that your son's effects may be forwarded promptly upon receipt here.

For your convenience, there is enclosed a self-addressed envelope which needs no postage.

*I wish to express my sincere regret of the circumstances
prompting this correspondence.*

Yours very truly,

Harry Niemiec
2nd Lt. Q.M.C.
Chief, Correspondence Branch[84]

On August 22, 1945, the surviving men of Company "F", 358th
Infantry Regiment, held a Memorial Service in Vohenstrauss, Germany in honor of all their fallen comrades. The program consisted of:

The playing of the National Anthem
An invocation
Scripture reading of 2 Corinthians 5:1-9
Words by Chaplain James L. Neighbours
A solo of "Sleep, Comrades Sleep" by S/SGT Richard A.
    Loring
An unveiling of the memorial
Words by 1st Lt. Paul A. Lutar
Following this was a prayer
The men sang "My Country, 'Tis of Thee"
Taps was played

Decoration Day [85]

Sleep, comrades, sleep and rest
  On this Field of the Grounded Arms,
Where foes no more molest,
  Nor sentry's shot alarms!

Ye have slept on the ground before,
  And started to your feet
At the cannon's sudden roar,
  Or the drum's redoubling beat.

But in this camp of Death
  No sound your slumber breaks;
Here is no fevered breath,
  No wound that bleeds and aches.

All is repose and peace,
  Untrampled lies the sod;

The shouts of battle cease,
  It is the Truce of God!

Rest, comrades, rest and sleep!
  The thoughts of men shall be
As sentinels to keep
  Your rest from danger free.

Your silent tents of green
  We deck with fragrant flowers;
Yours has the suffering been,
  The memory shall be ours.

The words from 2 Corinthians 5:1-9 were, "For we know that if the earthly tent we live in is destroyed, we have a building from God, an eternal house in heaven, not built by human hands. 2 Meanwhile we groan, longing to be clothed instead with our heavenly dwelling, 3 because when we are clothed, we will not be found naked. 4 For while we are in this tent, we groan and are burdened, because we do not wish to be unclothed but to be clothed instead with our heavenly dwelling, so that what is mortal may be swallowed up by life. 5 Now the one who has fashioned us for this very purpose is God, who has given us the Spirit as a deposit, guaranteeing what is to come.

6 Therefore we are always confident and know that as long as we are at home in the body we are away from the Lord. 7 For we live by faith, not by sight. 8 We are confident, I say, and would prefer to be away from the body and at home with the Lord. 9 So we make it our goal to please him, whether we are at home in the body or away from it."[86]

MEMORIAL SERVICE

COMPANY "F", 358TH. INFANTRY
VOHENSTRAUSS, GERMANY
22 AUGUST 1945

Memorial Service Program. Photo courtesy 90th Division Association Archives.

ORDER OF SERVICE

THE NATIONAL ANTHEM   141

INVOCATION

SCRIPTURE READING   2 Cor. 5:1—9

WORDS   CHAPLAIN JAMES L. NEIGHBOURS

SOLO "SLEEP, COMRADES SLEEP" S/SGT RICHARD A. LORING

UNVEILING OF MEMORIAL, AND WORDS 1ST. LT. PAUL A. LUTAR

PRAYER

MY COUNTRY, 'TIS OF THEE

TAPS

IN MEMORY OF

Robert E. Laurence	2nd Lt.	Parley L. Draper	Pvt.
George L. Salazar	2nd. Lt.	Michael J. Duncan	Pvt.
George Adams	Pvt.	James W. Ewing	Pfc.
David I. Autrey	Sgt.	Paul F. Fergerson	Pvt.
Joseph C. Baker	Pvt.	Manuel P. Ferriera	S/Sgt.
Robert P. Baker	Pvt.	James J. Fick	S/Sgt.
Howard F. Jr. Batchlor	Pvt.	Ed Fleckenstein	Pfc.
Winford P. Bennett	Pvt.	Willis F. Follstaedt	Pfc.
Leonard J. Betts	Pfc.	Earl E. Freel	Pvt.
Henry J. Bloomquist	Pvt.	Leon J. Jr. Frugoli	Pfc.
James L. Broderick	Pvt.	Richard A. Fuller	Pvt.
Millard Bryant	Sgt.	Virgil E. Garner	Pfc.
Benjamin S. Bujanowski	Pvt.	Robert R. Garrett	Pfc.
Lee E. Burt	Pvt.	Cleon E. Glines	Sgt.
John E. Chaney	Pvt.	Valentin H. Gonzalez	Pfc.
Throton D. Chisholm	Pfc.	Richard J. Graue	Pfc.
Jonnie J. Gulak	S/Sgt.	Ruben O. Henson	Pvt.
Leonard A. Dembowski	Pfc.	Kenneth D. Huffmann	Pvt.
Buford E. Denny	Pfc.	William H. Hulsizer	Sgt.
Jr., Walter C. Dietrich	Pfc.	Denver B. Isaacs	Pfc.
Nicholas Di Filippe	Pfc.	Clifford H. Jack	Pvt.
James L. Donnelly	Pfc.	Theodore Jackmann	Pfc.

Joseph F. Jaromin	Pfc.	Martin E. Phillis	Pfc.
James L. Joyce	Pvt.	Frank H. Pineda	Pfc.
Edward G. Keith	Pfc.	Edward J. Piotrowski	Pfc.
Ralph W. Kelly	Pfc.	James F. Privoznik	Pfc.
Frederick E. Kenyon	Pvt.	Daniel J. Reboczi	Pvt.
Charles H. King	T/Sgt.	Hector F. Reyes	Cpl.
Morton Kirshner	Pfc.	Walter Reyna	Pfc.
Raymond F. Knox	Pvt.	Matthew G. Reynolds	S/Sgt.
Vernon L. Kregar	Pfc.	Luther B. Rhodes	Pvt.
John J. Kubicek	T/Sgt.	Harry F. Rishel	Sgt.
John C. Lapinski	Pfc.	Paul Ritchie	Pvt.
Harold P. Lebens	S/Sgt.	Noah L. Robinson	S/Sgt.
Howard T. Lewis	Pfc.	John L. Ruibal	Sgt.
Bjorn S. Lindboe	Pvt.	Melvin R. Saksvig	Cpl.
Samuel F. Linn	Pfc.	Victor Schaefer	Pfc.
Stanley B. Lorenz	Pvt.	Clavin E. Scharrer	Pvt.
Leonard G. Magnus	Pfc.	Lester C. Schlueter	S/Sgt.
Edwin J. Mahler	Pfc.	Wilbur Simmons	Pfc.
Jack T. Maline	Sgt.	Ossie F. Snellings	Pvt.
Chon C. Martinez	Pvt.	Russell N. Snow	Pfc.
Rocco Marzigliano	Pvt.	Michael J. Sepko	Pvt.
John R. Maurer	Pfc.	Alfred R. Steen	Pfc.
Dale L. Maxwell	Pfc.	Buel Stephenson	Pfc.
William F. Merriman	S/Sgt.	Robert H. Strube	Pvt.
Eugene Messersmith	S/Sgt.	James Toogood	Pfc.
David M. Miller	Pfc.	Robert J. H. Tooley	Pvt.
Albert V. Mills	Pvt.	Doyne D. Travillian	Pvt.
Everett F. Minor	Pvt.	Floyd E. Turner	Sgt.
Armin O. Moeller	Pvt.	Louis Uphoff	Pvt.
Walter H. Mollenhauer	Pvt.	George A. Upshall	Pvt.
Jessie L. Moore	Pfc.	Paul Jr. Varela	Pvt.
Stoner B. Moore	S/Sgt.	Ignacio G. Vasquez	Pfc.
James E. Moriarty	Pfc.	Alfredo M. Villarreal	Pvt.
Souren D. Movessian	Pvt.	Floyd E. Wagner	Pfc.
Frank E. Mutter	Pvt.	William P. Waldrop	Pfc.
George W. Nelson	Sgt.	Donald A. Walker	Pfc.
Ples L. New	S/Sgt.	Jay B. Walston	Pvt.
James R. Newman	Pvt.	Walter J. Waskiewicz	Pvt.
Robert S. Oberst	Pfc.	Lloyd J. Wells	Pvt.
Paul W. Owens,	Pfc.	Arnold L. West	Pvt.
Stanley R. Oleski	Pfc.	Thomas White	Pfc.
Hyman H. Oxman	Pfc.	Cecil C. Wood	Pfc.
Adam P. Pacyna	Pvt.	Ernest F. Wood	Pvt.
Rufus E. Palmer	Pvt.	Edward G. Wyatt	T/Sgt.
Jack W. Pears	Pfc	Joe O. Ybarbo	Pfc.

While the men were honoring the memories of their fallen comrades and celebrating life, Mae was still waiting at home for any notice about personal effects the Army received for James. Mae sent another letter on December 7, 1945 to the Quartermaster requesting an update about James' personal effects. I imagine Mae was frustrated by not receiving them after so long. She wrote letter after letter inquiring. The government was not in a position to inform the families about the circumstances surrounding their loved one's death. So many questions went unanswered.

> *No 396327 [shipment claim]*
> *Dec-7-1945*
>
> *Dear Sir:*
>
> *It will be 11 months December-11-1945- that my son P.F.C. James F. Privoznik was killed in Luxembourg and I am still waiting for his personal effects. Will you kindly answer my letter if you received anything.*
>
> *Gratefully yours*
> *Mrs. Mary Privoznik*
> *3124 So Ridgeway Ave*
> *Chicago 23 Ill.*
>
> *Killed in action January-11-1945*
>
> *For personal effects of my son James F. Privoznik*
>
> *Single*
>
> *Mother – Mrs. Mary Privoznik – father is dead*
> *3124 So Ridgeway Ave Chicago 23 Ill*[87]

Mae received a response from the Quartermaster on December 18, 1945. That letter read,

> *Dear Mrs. Privoznik:*
>
> *This refers to your recent inquiry regarding the personal effects of your son, Private First Class James F. Privoznik.*
>
> *I am sorry to report that the Army Effects Bureau has not yet received any of his property. It is reasonable to assume, however, that his belonging ultimately will reach here, as all*

War Department agencies have instructions to forward the personal effects of military personnel to this Bureau for disposition. Transportation delays generally are encountered in delivery of effects, and considerable time should be allowed for the return of property from overseas.

Promptly upon receipt here of any of your son's belongings, disposal action will be taken.

Yours very truly,

Harry Niemiec
2nd Lt., QMC
Chief, Correspondence Branch[88]

In 1946 the Hamm cemetery had 28 plots which held 8,412 soldiers. United States labor troops and German prisoners of war were brought in to help expand and build the cemetery. These troops and POWs built a chapel, office and visitor's lounge on the grounds. It was about this time that the Graves Registration Service took over development and the running of the cemetery and began to redesign the cemetery to its current layout. Mr. R. Warren Davis was made Superintendent of the Cemetery as the Army continued to move Officers and Enlisted men out of Europe toward home.[89]

Hamm Cemetery (then Luxembourg Cemetery) 1945. Photo courtesy American Battle Monuments Commission.

As the cemetery development continued, a grave adoption program was started. The Superintendent noted in his history of the cemetery that while this program may have served a purpose, few asked to adopt the graves of Unknown Soldiers, or those of the Jewish or Protestant faiths. The surrounding communities were primarily Catholic which may have accounted for the lack of adoption of graves of non-Catholic faith.

General George Patton, commander of the Third Army, was buried in the Hamm Cemetery after he died in an accident after Vitory in Europe Day. His grave was moved from the original location to the west end of the grounds. The reason for the move was visitors wanted to see the General's grave and be photographed next to it. The number of people that came through the cemetery daily to see this particular grave made it difficult to keep the grass and area surrounding his grave and those resting next to him in good shape. So the decision was made to move his grave and surround it with bushes and a chain. Visitors could stand in front of it without disturbing the area of his grave or those near him.

In 1946, the Army began notifying families of the location of their deceased soldiers. The families were given the option to have their soldier disinterred and repatriated or permanently buried in an American Battle Monuments Commission Cemetery overseas. On September 26, 1946, Mae was sent a letter from the Quartermaster General indicating where James was buried in Luxembourg and asked what her wishes were in regards to his final interment. By this time he had been buried over a year and a half.

26 September 1946

Mrs. Mary Privoznik
3124 South Ridgeway Avenue
Chicago, Illinois

Dear Mrs. Privoznik:

The War Department is most desirous that you be furnished information regarding the burial location of your son, the late Private First Class James F. Privoznik, A.S.N. 36 640 529.

The records of this office disclose that his remains are interred in the U.S. Military Cemetery Hamm, plot L, row 11, grave 265. You may be assured that the identification and interment have been accomplished with fitting dignity and solemnity.

This cemetery is located two and one half miles east of the city of Luxembourg, and is under the constant care and supervision of United States Military Personnel.

The War Department has now been authorized to comply, at Government expense, with the feasible wishes of the next of kin regarding final interment, here or abroad, of the remains of your loved one. At a later date, this office will, without any action on your part, provide the next of kind with full information and solicit his detailed desires.

Please accept my sincere sympathy in your great loss.

Sincerely yours,

T. B. Larkin
Major General
The Quartermaster General[90]

Mae now knew where James was buried but still had not received his effects. She waited and waited and yet nothing ever came. Then in 1947 she sent another letter requesting James' effects.

Dear Sir   *396327*

It was 2 years January-11-1947[5] that my son P.F.C. James F. Privoznik was killed in action in Luxembourg and I think that by this time you must have received his personal belongings. Please let me hear from you as soon as possible.

Mrs. Mary Privoznik
3124 So Ridgeway Ave
Chicago 23-Ill[91]

Mae received a response which stated,

28 January 1947

Mrs. Mary Privoznik
3124 South Ridgeway Avenue
Chicago 23, Illinois

Dear Mrs. Privoznik:

This acknowledges your recent letter regarding the

personal effects of your son, Private First Class James. F. Privoznik.

I regret that no property of Private Privoznik has been received here to date. A search of the personal effects records of the European Theater Area now at this Bureau, has failed to reveal any information concerning your son's effects.

As it is our desire to be of all possible assistance in this matter, I have sent a tracer today to determine whether any of your son's property was recovered.

Promptly upon receipt of this information, you will be notified.

Yours very truly,

L. Rumfield
1st Lt. QMC
Asst Effects Quartermaster[92]

Mae received a follow-up letter just weeks later.

19 February 1947

Mrs. Mary Privoznik
3124 South Ridgeway Avenue
Chicago 23, Illinois

Dear Mrs. Privoznik:

This refers to Army Effects Bureau letter dated 28 January 1947 advising tracer action was being instituted in an endeavor to locate the personal effects of your son, Private First Class James F. Privoznik.

A reply to our tracer has been received but revealed no information and due to the lapse of time since he was reported a casualty; it is unlikely that any of his personal property was recovered.

I wish to assure you that should any property belonging to your son be unexpectedly received at this Bureau at a later date, prompt disposition will be made.

Yours very truly,

L. H. Blank
Administrative Assistant[93]

By the summer of 1947 the Quartermaster General was preparing to disinter remains of our Soldier Dead. The Quartermaster General sent Mae a letter which explained she had the option to have James' remains repatriated or buried in a permanent American Military Cemetery overseas. The letter stated,

31 July 1947

Pfc. James F. Privoznik, 36 640 529
Plot L, Row 11, Grave 265,
United States Military Cemetery
Hamm, Luxembourg

Mrs. Mary Privoznik
3124 South Ridgeway Avenue
Chicago, Illinois

Dear Mrs. Privoznik:

The people of the United States, through the Congress have authorized the disinterment and final burial of the heroic dead of World War II. The Quartermaster General of the Army has been entrusted with this sacred responsibility to the honored dead. The records of the War Department indicate that you may be the nearest relative of the above-named deceased, who gave his life in the service of his country.

The enclosed pamphlets, "Disposition of World War II Armed Forces Dead," and "American Cemeteries," explain the disposition, options and services made available to you by your Government. If you are the next of kin according to the line of kinship as set forth in the enclosed pamphlet, "Disposition of World War II Armed Forces Dead," you are invited to express your wishes as to the disposition of the remains of the deceased by completing Part I of the enclosed form "Request for Disposition of Remains." Should you desire to relinquish your rights to the next in line of kinship, please complete Part II of the enclosed form. If you are not the next of kin, please complete Part III of the enclosed form.

If you should elect Option 2, it is advised that no funeral arrangements or other personal arrangements be made until you are further notified by this office.

Will you please complete the enclosed form, "Request for Disposition of Remains" and mail in the enclosed self-addressed envelope, which requires no postage, within 30 days after its receipt by you? Its prompt return will avoid unnecessary delays.

Sincerely,

Thomas B. Larkin
Major General
The Quartermaster General[94]

Mae responded she wished for James to remain buried overseas.

Beginning in March of 1948, the cemetery was closed to visitors and shielded from view so exhumations could begin. The Army built a large hangar in the east meadow of the cemetery. This served as the location where exhumed remains were taken and the final identification was conducted before they were prepared for casketing. All remains were exhumed, re-identified and placed in caskets.

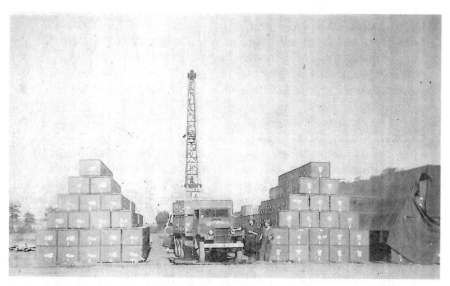

Caskets in shipping cases awaiting return to the U.S. in Luxembourg. Photo courtesy of the American Battle Monuments Commission.

The casketed remains were loaded on a narrow-gauge railway constructed on the grounds to transport the remains to a "rented field in Hamm for storage under tarpaulins."[95] Eventually the soldiers to be repatriated were sent to the port of Antwerp to be loaded onto funeral ships and brought home to the U.S. The rest of the caskets were stored until the grounds could be leveled and arc burial trenches dug. The arc allowed the caskets to be laid in such a way that when the grass had been planted and marble crosses put in place, that the cemetery would have a uniform look. The crosses would be lined up in such a way that no matter where you looked, you would always see a straight line.

Under Directive number 6020 06129, the permission for James to be disinterred was given on March 15, 1948. James was disinterred May 24, 1948 and Captain Charles L. Walls verified his identification. His remains were described as,

"Advanced decomposition. R/Fibula fractured. Face shattered as well as base of skull and R/Radius and Ulna, Pelvic Girdle fractured. Proximal end right Femur, Distal end right Fibula, Left Scapula missing. Proximal 2/3 left humerus except head missing. All ribs and vertebrae fractured."[96]

What this means is that all of James' ribs and vertebrae were fractured. His face and base of his skull were shattered. He was missing his right leg. His left scapula was missing. The lower part of his left humerus or from the bicep area of the arm down was missing.

James was buried in a uniform and his remains were prepared and placed in a new casket box on May 25, 1948. On December 15, 1948, James was reburied in Plot E, Row 15, Grave 76. To his right lies K.J. Reinecke. serial no. 36284708. To his left lies G.R. Yasher, serial no. 32233046. The Cemetery Superintendent noted in his history the following about burials during this time.

"Just prior to lowering, each remains received the interment rites of an appropriate clergyman. Curé Jaques Schmit of Hamm, Pastor Nicolas Housse of Luxembourg, and various Jewish Chaplains performed these services. The flag used in each case was mailed to the N.O.K. [Next of Kin.]

It is to be noted for all time that the remains were so carefully controlled during the entire period that an error in identification or in the location of any headstone is

*unthinkable. No visiting N.O.K. need ever entertain the
slightest doubt in this regard."*[97]

The flag with gold stars that was placed on James' casket during
reburial was sent to his mother, Mae, on December 23, 1948.[98] A
final letter was sent by the Quartermaster General in March of 1949
providing Mae with the exact location of James' grave.

11 March 1949

*Mrs. Mary Privoznik
3124 South Ridgeway Avenue, Chicago, Illinois*

*Pfc James F. Privoznik, ASN 36 640 529
Plot E, Row 15, Grave 76
Headstone: Cross
Hamm (Luxembourg) U.S. Military Cemetery*

Dear Mrs. Privoznik:

*This is to inform you that the remains of your loved one
have been permanently interred, as recorded above, side by
side with comrades who also gave their lives for their country. Customary military funeral services were conducted over
the grave at the time of burial.*

*After the Department of the Army has completed all final
interments, the cemetery will be transferred, as authorized
by the Congress, to the care and supervision of the American
Battle Monuments Commission. The Commission also will
have the responsibility for permanent construction and beautification of the cemetery, including erection of the permanent
headstone. The headstone will be inscribed with the name
exactly as recorded above, the rank or rating where appropriate, organization, State, and date of death. Any inquiries
relative to the type of headstone or the spelling of the name
to be inscribed thereon, should be addressed to the American
Battle Monuments Commission, Washington 25, D.C. Your
letter should include the full name, rank, serial number, grave
location, and name of the cemetery.*

*While interments are in process, the cemetery will not be
open to visitors. You may rest assured that this final interment
was conducted with fitting dignity and solemnity and that the*

grave-site will be carefully and conscientiously maintained in perpetuity by the United States Government.

> *Sincerely yours,*
> *Thomas B. Larkin*
> *Major General*
> The Quartermaster General[99]

This letter also specified that the cemetery would be placed into the authority of the American Battle Monuments Commission once all reburials were finished. The cemetery was renamed Luxembourg Cemetery. It went on to state the cemetery would be closed until all reburials were completed and that James' burial was done with "fitting dignity and solemnity" and that his grave would be properly cared for by the United States Government forever.

The Luxembourg American Cemetery was transferred from the control of the Graves Registration Service to the American Battle Monuments Commission in December 1949. Then on March 20, 1951, a treaty was signed granting the United States perpetual right to use the 50.5 acres of land on which the cemetery rested. The Luxembourg American Cemetery was officially dedicated on July 4, 1960 and since that time many distinguished visitors and family members have passed through its gates.

James is Remembered

James was awarded the Purple Heart and based on General Order 623 of the 90th Division Headquarters, James was awarded, posthumously, the Bronze Arrowhead Service Award on August 16, 1945.[100] The Bronze Arrowhead Service Award was given to those who participated in an initial assault landing.

The General Order stated,

Award of the Bronze Service Arrowhead

Under the provisions of Section 1, Circular 465, War Department, 9 December 1944 as amended, and letter, Headquarters, United States Forces European Theater, file AG 200.6, subject: Individual Service Award of Bronze Service Arrowhead, 9 May 1945, the following officers and enlisted men who were or are now members of the units indicated below on June 6, 7, 8, and 9 1944 are awarded the Bronze Service Arrowhead.[101]

Throughout the year at the Luxembourg Cemetery, many ceremonies were held honoring the heroic dead. November 1, 1945, All Saints Day in Luxembourg, saw the arrival of the Luxembourg Guards, French and Belgian Legions and members of the nearby communities. A wreath-laying ceremony was held to honor those sleeping in that foreign soil and flowers were laid on the graves. [102] This is only one example of the many holidays, Saints Days, and special days the people of Luxembourg visit the cemetery to honor the dead. Those traditions started in 1945 after the first Soldier Dead were interred, continue today.

A Personal Journey[103]

Written by Patricia Holik

We first visited Luxembourg Cemetery in the fall of 2009. At that time, we were not aware that my husband's cousin was buried there. When we returned home, our daughter informed us that my husband's cousin James was in Luxembourg Cemetery. James had left instructions with his family, that should he be killed, he wanted to be buried where he fell. His family honored his request, we made a promise to ourselves to return, and we embarked on our second visit to Luxembourg.

Yes, General George Patton is also buried in Luxembourg Cemetery. He is buried at the front of the cemetery, still leading his troops. But he wasn't our focus on this trip. We walked out through the rows of crosses blazing white in the sunlight until we found James' gravesite. After visiting so many WWI and WWII cemeteries, to finally come upon the grave of someone who belonged to our family was gut wrenching. We stayed at the grave for a while just trying to process

Thomas Holik, author's father by James' grave in Luxembourg. Photo courtesy Patricia Holik.

all our thoughts upon seeing James at rest. I left my husband there to give him some privacy, and as is my habit when visiting the cemeteries, I wandered around touching the crosses and Stars of David and said a word of thanks to each soldier at rest.

My husband then walked to the Visitor Center and told them why we were there. One of the staff got a bucket of sand and took my husband back out to the gravesite and pressed the sand into the words on the cross. Then he took photos of the grave and of my husband kneeling next to it. They processed the photo and gave us a copy of it to take home. We were also told we could order a large lithograph and a CD with the photos on it. This service is free to family members at the American Battle Monuments Cemeteries. Promise kept.

Remembered by Those in Luxembourg

On the anniversary of James' death in 2012, Norbert Morbé and Romaine Fraiture visited the Luxembourg Cemetery. They placed flowers on James' grave for me and took photographs. When I received the photos I was surprised. The day James was killed, it was bitterly cold and there was deep snow on the ground. The day Norbert and Romaine visited James' grave it was cold and there was some snow on the ground.

Norbert and Romaine did adopt James' grave. This means they will help care for it, share his story, and place flowers on special days like the anniversary of his death, Memorial Day, Veterans Day, and at Christmas.

These two special people have become part of my family because of their love of the 90th and their devotion to James. The Privoznik family and I are deeply appreciative of their love and support of the men who fought and died during the war.

Norbert Morbé in Luxembourg Cemetery, January 11, 2013. Photo courtesy Norbert Morbé.

The End of the Story

As I finished writing James' story, I realized there was a greater purpose to the process of telling his story. What began as a way to remember a great man in my family took the route of digging deeper than I was able to with my other stories. James' records, bread crumbs of clues, family stories, and unmarked photographs that seemed to appear out of nowhere, proved that you can fully research and write a soldier's story. While the service records did burn in the fire in 1973, there are many other resources available to researchers if they look and have some patience.

James' story also taught me that much is written about the pilots, artillery, tank, and infantrymen but little is written about those who supported these fighting men. This story has also become an example of what can be learned and taught about the men behind the lines. Men who also put their lives in danger as they scoured mined fields for supply dumps and leftover ammunition and equipment as the Germans departed an area. Without these men working together with the fighting units, the war could not have been fought and won. Their stories deserve to be told so their memories live on.

7

Caring for The Fallen

The Men of the Graves Registration Service

The American Battle Monuments Commission

Upon conclusion of both World Wars, the U.S. government began bringing home the soldiers who survived and handling the final disposition of those who did not. Due to high numbers of Soldier Dead buried overseas, the government had to make a decision about their remains. Ultimately, it was decided the government would establish permanent American Military Cemeteries overseas. Families had the choice to leave their soldier buried overseas in a military cemetery or repatriated. The government paid the bill for both options.

> Soldier Dead is a term used by the military to describe those valiant men and women who gave the ultimate sacrifice during military service. This term will be used throughout this chapter to refer to our honored war dead.

After World War II, for the families who chose to leave their Soldier Dead overseas, and for the unknown soldiers, re-interment in permanent American Military Cemeteries took place after all the dead who needed to be repatriated were returned home. The 209 temporary cemeteries across Europe, North Africa, and the Pacific were condensed to 14 cemeteries in foreign countries.[1]

The American Battle Monuments Commission (ABMC) oversees the cemeteries which hold our American military dead around the world. ABMC was established in 1923 by Congress to honor our Great War dead.[2] These cemeteries were granted in perpetuity to our government and remain tax free. Burial in these cemeteries was not just of our male G.I.'s but also Red Cross workers, USO entertainers, and others seen as military personnel during World War I and II.

Memorial Day Fly Over at Luxembourg Cemetery. Photo courtesy American Battle Monuments Commission.

Remember the Glory of Their Spirit, The Normandy American Cemetery [6]

The Normandy American Cemetery and Resource Center was not merely a stop on our itinerary of WWII sites, but the place where I hoped to find answers to a 65 year old family mystery involving my cousin who served in the 29th and was killed in June 1944, four years before I was born. As we visited the US Military Cemeteries in Belgium and France, I asked questions and received bits of information. Searching the museums also helped answer questions. But the breakthrough came on a rainy day in October when I walked up to the desk of the Normandy American Cemetery Resource Center and handed my cousin's information to a young man there. He in turn gave me the name of a man in Maryland who served as the historian for the 29th Infantry Division. We had traveled all the way to France to find the person with the information we needed, right here in the United States. And our questions were answered.

The Normandy American Cemetery is a place of quiet beauty, sitting atop a cliff overlooking Omaha Beach. As we stepped out of the Resource Center, the sun came out and we felt as if the men at rest there were welcoming us. The serenity of the cemetery, the chapel, the monument to the fallen young men, were heartwrenching. But nothing compared with the sight of the rows upon rows of white crosses and Stars of David indicating the final resting place of those who made the ultimate sacrifice for our freedom. Every American visiting Europe should make an effort to visit one of the American Battle Monument Cemeteries or Memorials. It is a truly humbling experience.

The cemeteries were laid out to be green, expansive, beautiful, and full of peace. Each headstone is made of marble in the shape of a cross or Star of David, depending on the religion of the soldier. Visitor's centers were erected which depict battles fought nearby. Memorials were built listing the names of the missing and to honor all who fought and died.

The cemeteries are groomed and cared for by AMBC staff and decorated with flags and flowers for ceremonies throughout the year. The ABMC offers photography services for families who wish to have a photograph of their Soldier Dead's grave and the cemetery. They also offer floral services if you wish to have flowers placed on a soldier's grave.

To fully appreciate how these cemeteries came into existence and honor those buried beneath the foreign soil, we must discuss the men who helped build the cemeteries. Who were they? What kind of job did they have during and after the wars? How did they care for our most honored dead? And how did they shape the cemeteries we visit today?

These men were from the Quartermaster Graves Registration Service. What follows is not an exhaustive history of this unit because many books have been written on the subject. The purpose is to provide an overview to help put each soldier's life and death into greater context.

Graves Registration Service History

The Graves Registration Service (GRS) has a long history dating back to 1862 when Congress gave the President authorization to create permanent American military cemeteries. This act gave the President the ability to seek and purchase land for these cemeteries.[3] In 1867 Congress gave the Quartermaster General in the U.S. Army the responsibility to establish military cemeteries, handle burials, keep records, and handle ongoing maintenance of these cemeteries.[4] The Quartermaster handled the burials of our soldiers from the Civil War, Spanish-American War and World War I.

During World War I, the number of dead was in approximately 77,000, scattered over many battlefields and buried within 2,400 cemeteries in England and Europe.[5] Eventually roughly ¾ of these Soldier Dead were either repatriated to the U.S. or interred in one of the eight permanent military cemeteries in England or Europe. When World War I ended, the Graves Registration Service worked to consolidate these cemeteries and recover remains buried in enemy lands.

When the U.S. entered World War II, one thing the Army was determined to do was not established thousands of small cemeteries. Instead, they planned to establish several cemeteries near the fighting and bring Soldier Dead to these cemeteries. Collection points were established so the combat units could assist in the collection and identification of the deceased. The GRS men found if identification could take place near the battlefield with information from the combat unit there was a higher chance of positively identifying the deceased. When the unit had moved on and no one was available to help identify the dead, many were brought to the collection points and cemeteries as unknowns.

The Job

When we think of a cemetery in the U.S. or one of the ABMC cemeteries, we picture a beautiful, expansive, quiet, peaceful, rolling green, lush, and clean cemetery. Just as we are conditioned to think of our World War II veterans as older men and women, we are conditioned to see military cemeteries as beautiful. This was not always the case.

As the U.S. prepared for war, the men of the Graves Registration Service was trained and prepared to go with the troops and handle the casualties. GRS workers were responsible for locating suitable cemetery sites overseas. Once selected after examining the terrain, soil quality, and distance to enemy lines, they began plotting the cemetery. Maps were drawn, processing tents were set up and the men assigned tasks. Local civilian workers were called in to help dig graves and bury the dead.

The job of a Graves Registration Service man was not glamorous. Nor was it discussed and publicized very often. As unsung heroes, these men worked tirelessly to care for the remains of not only our U.S. Soldier Dead but also enemy dead. Within practically every U.S. established cemetery, there was a section for German dead. Our GRS men worked to identify every casualty they buried. This was not always possible. When information was gathered about the unidentified soldiers, it was placed in a canister or bottle and buried in the grave.

Both U.S. and enemy dead were buried in these temporary cemeteries. Why? It was important to bury all the dead for several reasons. The primary reason was health concerns. Decomposing bodies out in the open would spread disease and lower troop morale. It was better the troops did not encounter the remains of their comrades, lest the fear and panic they already felt increase, making them unable to do their job effectively.

Collecting Soldier Dead during the Battle of the Bulge, January 1945. National Archives (111-SC-199094-A)

There was also the respect for the fallen and families back home. Our men and women made the ultimate sacrifice for their country. They deserved respect from those who cared for them after death since their families could not.

Also, soldiers were buried for forensic reasons. Information was gathered to not only identify them but also on how they were killed. Furthermore, GRS buried for political reasons which showed both allies and enemies we have a heart, are human and care for others with compassion.

The GRS in World War II was not only responsible for collecting, identifying, and burying the Soldier Dead, but also handling personal effects. The men had a system by which they worked on the stripping line to handle personal effects which would be returned to the owner's family.

There are many people who make up the Quartermaster Graves Registration (QMGR) Unit. The individuals who primarily handled the Soldier Dead are described here. The description which follows is not meant to be an exhaustive look at the make-up of the QMGR Unit, but to give you an idea of some components. An in-depth examination can be found in the *Department of the Army Field Manual 10-29* and *Department of the Army Field Manual 10-63* (see bibliography.) GRS personnel duties varied by person. Each was trained for a specific job during and after basic training.

GRS Platoon Headquarters

Platoon Leader

The Platoon Leader's duties varied depending on whether or not the platoon was part of the company at the time of operation. Overall the Platoon Leader selected a cemetery site and was responsible for training, discipline, supplies, and transportation. When the platoon was part of the company, other miscellaneous duties were assigned.[7]

Platoon Sergeant

The Platoon Sergeant assisted the Platoon Leader in his duties.[8]

Surveyor

The Surveyor supervised the layout of the cemeteries. He usually trained a team to work with him to clear a space for use.[9]

Other Positions

The Liaison Agent served as a replacement for the Platoon Leader at various meetings. A Supply Specialist requisitioned and maintained stock for the unit. And a Light Truck Driver was the messenger for the Platoon and had miscellaneous duties as assigned.[10]

GRS Collection and Evacuation Section

Section Chief

The Section Chief was the supervisor of all the GRS specialists. In certain situations when the combat troops are unable to help evacuate the Soldier Dead, the Section Chief assumes this responsibility.[11]

Graves Registration Specialists

Graves Registration Specialists were specifically trained in receiving Soldier Dead, identification procedures, record keeping, effects collection and distribution, and burial. These men worked with Assistant Graves Registration Specialists who had many of the same tasks.[12]

Graves Registration Clerk

The duties of the Graves Registration Clerk were to prepare all the reports on the Soldier Dead which became part of the Individual Deceased Personnel File (IDPF) and were sent to Headquarters in weekly reports.[13]

Still Photographer

A Still Photographer was used in cases where remains could not be identified. The photographer took photographs of the face and torso, tattoos, other identifying markings on the body and fingers in case prints could be identified.[14]

Technical Operations Personnel

Graves Registration Chief

The Graves Registration Chief supervised the Technical Operations Personnel under his command. He also oversaw four platoons and planned personnel jobs and in some cases, the cemeteries.[15]

Identification Chief

The Identification Chief worked with the Graves Registration Chief to supervise all the teams who worked with the Soldier Dead. He ensured the effects were transferred appropriately, records were completed, and as often as possible, each soldier was identified. He was also responsible for, "taking of fingerprints, preparation of tooth charts, ...and recording of accurate physical descriptions on appropriate forms."[16]

Draftsman

The Draftsman planned the cemetery layout and plotted it on a map.[17]

Fluoroscope Operator

The Fluoroscope Operator had an important job within the Technical Operations Personnel group. He was responsible for scanning the body to identify the location of identification tags which may have become embedded in the body. He also looked for possible foreign bodies such as shrapnel, unexploded devices, and other objects. When needed, the Fluoroscope Operator ran a chemical laboratory.[18]

Carpenter

The Carpenter handled all the usual carpentry duties within a GRS unit including creating crosses for the grave markers, building fences around the cemeteries, constructing signs to direct Collection Units and others to the GRS collecting points or cemeteries, and other miscellaneous duties as required.[19]

A GRS worker paints crosses. Photo courtesy of the American Battle Monument Commission.

Obstacles after D-Day

As well-prepared and trained as GRS men were, nothing could have prepared them for the onslaught of dead which would appear when the Allies invaded the beaches of Normandy on June 6, 1944.

The GRS men participating in the Normandy Invasion were underprepared for the number of soldiers who would be killed during the invasion. Improvising along the way, these GRS men established ways to track both the identification of Soldier Dead and their belongings. It was not, however, a perfect system. Not only were the dead brought to each collecting station, but the GRS men were given maps and coordinates of temporary graves or downed planes and gliders which needed to be cleared.

Colonel Elbert E. Legg, a GRS Sergeant in the 603rd Quarter-master Graves Registration Company, stated they used parachutes as a burial shroud since they had landed without mattress covers.[20] The number of dead arriving daily, even before the cemetery could be marked out, exceeded their supplies and manpower. Until more manpower was brought in, the bare minimum was done in tracking personal effects. At one point, Colonel Legg was required to move to a new sector due to heavy enemy fighting. He tied up the personal effects bags in a parachute and hid it in a hedgerow until he could return to the area.[21]

We must always keep in mind when discussing any facet of war, the men did the best they could at the time with the resources and knowledge they had. It was war. War is hell, full of chaos and confusion. Bullets flew and guns boomed which made it difficult for the GRS men to do their jobs perfectly when they received each new dead soldier.

Establishing Temporary Cemeteries

Before a cemetery could be established and Soldier Dead collected and buried, sites had to be examined. GRS men looked for good terrain, sites close to main roads, and with natural protection in the form of trees or hedges. These trees or hedges would grow over time and offer more privacy to the cemetery grounds. They also checked soil conditions, evaluated drainage, looked for potential mines, and the destruction which surrounded the potential cemetery area. In some cases, GRS men looked for areas near combat zones where they knew heavy fighting would occur. This made it somewhat easier to transport and collect the Soldier Dead.

When a cemetery was laid out there were certain guidelines to be followed.[22] These included:

- Graves were to be at least five feet in depth.
- When soldiers were interred, the head of each should face the same direction.
- A marker was to be placed at the head of each grave.
- Graves were to be numbered consecutively.
- If a trench burial system had to be implemented, the same procedure for laying out Soldier Dead was followed.
- Graves should align horizontally and vertically with other graves.

- A cemetery map should be drawn for indicating north. Separate plans should be drawn for each cemetery or burial plot if it is a trench burial.

Hamm temporary cemetery 19457. Photo courtesy of the American Battle Monuments Commission.

A bivoac site, or camping area, was selected near the cemetery site which provided shelter from the weather, water, good drainage, and was free of disease. When possible, GRS men selected towns which provided undamaged homes, hospitals, schools, and other buildings to house the men.

In some cases, the dead would not be buried in temporary cemeteries, but temporary graves on the battlefield. The combat units were instructed to create a burial duty of at least two soldiers to bury the dead as quickly as possible. Due to combat conditions, there was not time to fill out paperwork or pull identification tags or personal effects. The Soldier Dead were buried and some marker was placed at their grave and notes written to indicate where the remains were located. The GRS men would later sweep the battlefields and disinter these hastily buried men.[23]

The Collection Point - Remains Recovery Process

A Collection Point was established on a main road and was the location the Soldier Dead were brought by units in combat or by GRS men. Collection Points contained an administrative tent, examination tent, examination area, and a screen to shelter passing troops from the view of their dead comrades.

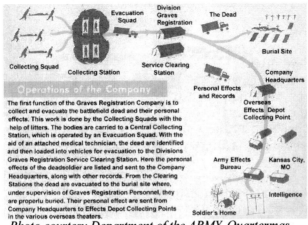

The first function of the Graves Registration Company is to collect and evacuate the battlefield dead and their personal effects. This work is done by the Collecting Squads with the help of litters. The bodies are carried to a Central Collecting Station, which is operated by an Evacuation Squad. With the aid of an attached medical technician, the dead are identified and then loaded into vehicles for evacuation to the Divisions Graves Registration Service Clearing Station. Here the personal effects of the deadsoldier are listed and sent to the Company Headquarters, along with other records. From the Clearing Stations the dead are evacuated to the burial site where, under supervision of Graves Registration Personnel, they are properlu buried. Their personal effect are sent from Company Headquarters to Effects Depot Collecting Points in the various overseas theaters.

Photo courtesy Department of the ARMY, Quartermasters Corps, Graves Registration Service.

The GRS men at Collection Points identified when possible, collected personal effects, and transported the Soldier Dead to the nearest American cemetery for burial. When they arrived at a cemetery, GRS workers again checked identification, effects, and rechecked records before temporary burial occurred.

GRS claimed the remains of a soldier from a unit, along the road side or battle ground. Men worked in the mud, rain, deep snow, jungles and on beaches in their recovery efforts. During December and January 1945 when the Battle of the Bulge raged, the weather was bitter cold and snow packed the ground for weeks. This made the job of grave digging and handling the dead ever more difficult.[25] These men also crossed back and forth over enemy lines putting their own lives in danger.

The recovery process meant to collect both complete bodies and scattered remains. Consider the soldier who received a gunshot wound to the head. That most likely constituted a complete body or set of remains. Now, think about the men hit by shells. These bodies would have been in all sorts of condition and may have been scattered around the area in which they were killed. GRS could not always attend to the dead immediately after they were killed so these men encountered all stages of decomposition.

What They Carried

A common question families would ask when they received word their Soldier was dead was, "Where are his personal effects?" Families wanted every piece of their soldier they could get both as a way to remember them and grieve for them.

First, it is important to note that all usable clothing, shoes and equipment were stripped off and sent to the Quartermaster Supply Depots to be reused. What families were not told is the soldiers carried very little of what was theirs on their person. The Army issued their clothing, bags, and equipment. They did wear identification tags and may have carried wallets, rings, insignia, letters, photos, and money; but little else was theirs.

GRS worker bagging personal effects. Photo courtesy of the American Battle Monument Commission.

What happened to the things they carried? The enemy may have picked items off the dead. The soldier may have sold or given away watches and such. Friends may have taken an item off their dead buddy for safekeeping. Or it may have been destroyed when the soldier was killed.[26] There were other reasons personal effects may have been missing. Duffle bags were usually on a truck or ship and not always near the troops. In cases where the truck or ship was bombed or hit a mine and blew up, the personal effects were likely lost.

Effects collected were bagged and sent to the Effects Bureau in Kansas City, Missouri. Here effects were cleaned of blood and grime. It was then determined if the effect should be returned to the family. In some cases, things were not sent to the family.

For instance, if letters from a girlfriend were found on a soldier and he was married, based on the service records, those letters would have been destroyed. If an item was destroyed or badly damaged as a result of the cause of death, those items were described to the family in a letter. The family was then given the choice as to whether or not they wanted the item.

GRS worker logging personal effects. Photo courtesy of the American Battle Monuments Commission.

Most families were happy to receive anything from their soldier and sent letters to the Quartermaster thanking them for sending the effects. In other cases, the Quartermaster received letters from family members accusing them of being thieves and the lowest men on earth for "stealing" money or other items from their Soldier Dead. The government did not educate the public about the chaos overseas or the work of the GRS men and the conditions under which they worked. Combine this with the pain and grief of a family member and anger and hate was directed at the only place they could think of, the Quartermaster General in the Effects Bureau.

Identification Process

When a soldier's remains, either U.S. or German, were recovered, every attempt at identification took place.

The procedure for processing remains and identification began at the stripping line where troops initially removed explosives and equipment. Another soldier would take these items to a nearby ammo and equipment area so they could be inventoried and reissued.

The next step was when medical sergeants came in with a clerk. The sergeants cut pockets and other pieces of clothing in order to locate identification tags and remove personal effects. Typically these men worked without gloves in destroyed and decomposed remains. Identification tags were sought as part of this process even when the remains were in bad condition.

To identify a Soldier Dead, identification tags were sought first. If those could not be recovered then a soldier's comrades were consulted if they were available, to help identify the soldier. Rings, insignia, pay records, letters and photographs that may have been carried were also used in the process. In some cases, dental records and laundry marks were used.

Upon first issue of clothing in the Army, a soldier would put a laundry mark in his clothing to show that it was his. This mark was the first letter of his surname plus the last four digits of his serial number. However, when serving on the front lines, when a soldier entered a wash-up station, he may or may not have had his duffle bag with his clothing available. In those cases, the men stripped, left their clothing, went into the wash station on one end, came out the other and were given new clothes. It was the hope that the clothes were the size they needed but this was not always the case. Because clothes were reissued over and over, there may have been several different laundry marks which would have made it very difficult to positively identify the Soldier Dead.

Positive Identification

When a Soldier Dead was identified, a mattress cover which was used as a shroud, was prepared for him by painting his name, rank, and serial number on it. Then his remains were arranged and closed in the shroud. One identification tag was inserted into deceased's mouth before he was placed in a grave. The other identification tag was attached to the cross on the grave. Next paperwork would be sent to the War Department in order to notify the next of kin. The bags of personal effects were shipped to Kansas City, MO.

Painting the name and serial number on a mattress cover. Photo courtesy American Battle Monuments Commission.

Unknown Identification

Not all Soldier Dead were identified because of the condition of the body when it was received by the GRS. Other factors included advanced decomposition and none of the soldier's comrades being available to help identify him.

To assist in identification, a still photographer was brought in to photograph the face, torso and other identifying marks on the body when the remains were in a condition this would be helpful. Photos were also taken of the fingers and hands in case prints could not be obtained. A fluoroscope was used to see if the identification tags were embedded in the body or if other foreign matter resided there.

When all available identification options were exhausted and remains could not be identified, they were assigned an X number since there was no serial number by which to identify them. This X number was placed on reports. Duplicate reports were created for the unknown soldiers. When possible, fingerprints of all 10 fingers were taken and put into the Report of Death.[27] Unknown remains were placed into a mattress cover and X number was painted on the bag. The personal effects were shipped to Kansas City, MO.

Two metallic tags with the X number were made and then one was inserted into deceased's mouth and the other was attached to the cross on the grave. The duplicate copy of records was placed in a bottle and buried with Soldier Dead. This allowed for possible identification at a later time when the remains were disinterred.

In cases where bodies were mangled or adhered together due to a plane crash or other disaster, if the GRS men were unable to disentangle the remains, a group burial would have been conducted. In these cases most were unidentified because the remains were destroyed beyond recognition.[28]

Individual Deceased Personnel File (IDPF)

An Individual Deceased Personnel File (IDPF) was created for every Soldier Dead upon receipt of remains by the GRS. Each form within the file contained, if the soldier was identified, the name, rank, serial number, and in many cases the next of kin information. While every file is somewhat different, it generally contained the following forms.

Report of Burial

A Report of Burial contained the soldier's name, serial number, rank, date of death, place of death, and a copy of his identification tag which was stamped onto the form using an addressograph machine. The report also contained the grave location of the soldier along with the man buried on either side of him, to help with identification purposes. At the time the report was created, if the emergency contact and religion information was available the information was also added to the report. A list of personal effects was to be included if any were found on the body.

An addressograph machine used the medical or death form, ribbon or carbon paper, and the identification tag.[29] The tag was placed on the machine with the ribbon and form over it. A trigger lever was pushed to close the top of the device to adhere pressure to the inserted items. The identification tag was then copied to the designated form. This alleviated many potential errors in identification of medical records and death and burial records.

If Deceased Was Unidentified

If the deceased was unable to be identified then a form which allowed for fingerprinting and dental records was used and inserted into the Soldier Dead file. This form contained space to list a physical description and information on personal effects or other things which might help identify the deceased.

Battle Casualty Report

The Battle Casualty Report had the usual service information in addition to the date of casualty, which could have been designated as Missing in Action (MIA) or Killed in Action (KIA), name of the next of kin and relationship to the deceased as well as the date notified of the casualty.

Report of Death

The Report of Death was a form for the Adjutant General's Office which listed the deceased's usual information, branch of service, date of birth and death, date of active entry in service, where he was killed, emergency contact and beneficiary information. There was a section at the bottom of the form which allowed for additional information about the deceased. Usually some statement about when the evidence of death was received by the war department was included in this section.

In some instances, there were duplicate or almost duplicate copies of this form in a file. In the case of James Privoznik, a second report was made a month after the first indicating a change in pay status. He had been made a Combat Infantryman per General Order #6, Headquarters, 358th Infantry. He was in the infantry the last 14 days of his life. Prior to that he was within the same division, the 90th, but was in the 790th Ordnance Group.

Summary Court Martial Form

The Summary Court Martial form was not a court martial for a soldier who had caused a problem, but a court which convened to handle financial effects of a soldier. This court established whether or not there were debts to be paid before money found on a Soldier Dead was forwarded to the next of kin.

Inventory of Effects

The Inventory of Effects form described the items collected to be sent to the family. It was broken out by package number in case there were multiple packages to send to a next of kin. These were accompanied by a letter to the family regarding the remains. There was a duplicate letter sent which had to be signed by the next of kin acknowledging the receipt of effects.

A GRS worker inventories effects. Photo courtesy of the American Battle Monument Commission.

Disposal of Pay Records

The Disposal of Pay Records was not a form, but a memo to the Adjutant General forwarding pay records. This memo contained the soldier's name, serial number and rank. In some cases it also listed the job the soldier performed.

Letters from the Quartermaster General

Letters from the Quartermaster General fill these files because they contain responses to letters written by family members regarding their loved one. The Quartermaster also sent informational circulars on the distribution of personal effects and the disposition of remains.

Request for Disposition of Remains

The Request for Disposition of Remains form was sent to the next of kin to complete so the government would know what to do with the remains of the Soldier Dead. The choices were:

- To be interred at a Permanent American Military Cemetery Overseas.
- To be returned to the United States or any possession or territory thereof for interment by next of kin in a private cemetery.
- To be returned to [insert foreign country] the homeland of the deceased for interment by next of kin.
- To be returned to the United States for final interment in a National Cemetery.[30]

Disinterment Directive

The Disinterment Directive form contained the basic identifying information on the Soldier Dead: Name, rank, serial number, date of death, cemetery name and location of grave, name and address of next of kin, condition of remains, date disinterred and remains prepared.

Receipt of Remains

The Receipt of Remains was used for Soldier Dead repatriated, not buried in overseas cemeteries. This form was signed by the next of kin or funeral home receiving the remains when they arrived in the hometown.

Inspection Checklist

The Inspection Checklist form was used before a shipping case containing a soldier's casket was removed from the ship and train. If there was any damage to the case or casket, it would be repaired before the remains were shipped to the family.

Certificate

The Certificate form was the request for reimbursement of interment expenses and transportation expenses born by the family of the Soldier Dead. The expenses were reimbursed by the U.S. Government.

Miscellaneous

Most IDPFs contain letters from family members to the Quartermaster asking questions about personal effects or the location of their soldier. In many cases these letters are handwritten, not typed, so researchers get a copy of their ancestor's handwriting.

Records Created by the Graves Registration

Service

The GRS created records which were occassionally included in a soldier's IDPF. These included the following forms.[31]

Collecting Point Register

The Collecting Point Register was created at a collection site and was not a standard form. It included name, rank, serial number, evacuation number and other pieces of information relevant to the death and location of the remains.

Certificate of Identity

The Certificate of Identity was Form DD 565 which was signed by the person identifying the remains in the field. It may have been a comrade in arms or anyone who could present evidence as to the identity of the Soldier Dead.

Report of Recovery of Unknown

The Report of Recovery of Unknown contained information regarding the unknown Soldier Dead, where he was recovered, the condition of the remains, and anything that might identify him in the future.

Grave Plot Chart

The Grave Plot Chart was a standard form DD 568 created for every plot in a cemetery. Names and grave numbers of all deceased were listed here.

Historical File

The file was a register of interments and additional records held by the GRS to identify both cemetery burials and isolated burials.

Burial Overseas

Each temporary cemetery had different policies, but ceremonies were held to honor the dead daily or as often as a military chaplain could be spared. In Margraten, Holland, burial services were held daily by the military chaplain sent from headquarters. The company of GRS men at Margraten performed their own small ceremony with the village priest after the official one to honor the dead they had buried that day. Upon conclusion of the ceremony, a firing squad shot their volleys, Taps was played and the flag was lowered from the flag pole with great reverence.[32]

Notification of Family

The family was notified of Missing in Action and Killed in Action statuses within a couple of months of the event. When the family was notified, they were done so through the War Department. The War Department then published lists of the Missing in Action or Killed in Action or Prisoner of War soldiers and their next of kin in the newspapers. Usually the next of kin's address was included in these lists. These notices appeared as soon as a month after the status changes but could take three months or more before the names would appear in the paper.

What was not usually explained to the family was exactly how their soldier died. They were not told about the condition of the body at death or upon locating the remains. The family was not told if there were personal effects on the body. This made it difficult for the family who not only was grieving for their soldier but could not understand why no effects were coming back.

Final Disposition of Remains after the War

After the war ended, the U.S. government began working with overseas officials to secure the authorization to use ports, disinter remains in private cemeteries, and authorization to use rail and waterways to transport remains to major sea ports.[33] Once this was in place, the government was able to contact families of the Soldier Dead to inquire about their wishes for the final burial of their Soldier Dead.

There were four major areas of concentration during the repatriation process. These were: to locate isolated graves and identify the remains buried within these graves; condense the cemeteries into as few as possible across Europe and Asia; and return Soldier Dead to the U.S. if requested by the family.[34]

GRS went in search of unfound remains and began disinterring remains from temporary cemeteries in enemy lands. Every effort was made to find all MIA and those killed in action.

The government began notifying families of the location of their Soldier Dead beginning in late 1946 and continued for several years afterward. Depending on when the soldier died, it is possible he had been buried overseas two or more years before the family was notified of the location.

The GRS men stationed overseas after the war ended had the duty to now disinter and prepare our country's Soldier Dead for final burial at home or overseas. Civilians in the areas where the temporary cemeteries had been built were hired to help with disinterment. What they uncovered were remains in all states of decomposition. Disinfectants were used to help mask the odor but did little good.

At Margraten, the procedure was to take disinterred remains to the morgue where "all clothing and flesh were removed, then burned"before the remaining skeleton was cleaned and sterilized for final placement in the hermetically sealed casket.[35] During the entire disinterment process, identities were checked, double checked and triple checked before they were finally laid to rest in their caskets and boxed for shipping. It was a job few would want to do, but the GRS men carried it out with great dignity and decorum for the soldiers who gave the ultimate sacrifice.

Luxembourg reburial Honor Guard holds a service for each Soldier's permanent interment. Photo courtesy of the American Battle Monument Commission.

Repatriation

Shortly after, the government gave the families the option to have the remains disinterred at government expense and returned to a U.S. cemetery for burial. The other option was reburial in a permanent American cemetery overseas. The disinterment and repatriation process took several years after the war ended, partly due to a shortage of materials for cases for the caskets and a shortage of metal for the caskets themselves.

One of the first shipments to Europe took place in May 1947, when the Liberty Ship *Joseph V. Connolly* was sent to deliver steel coffins. The coffins were "made of steel with bronze finish" and "were seamless, a cover set on a rubber gasket is sealed with thirty-two lugs."[36] These coffins were placed into a wooden shipping case after the Soldier Dead was placed inside and the lid sealed. The shipping cases had the name, rank, and serial number of the soldier inscribed on the case. The shipping cases were stored in warehouses when possible, or stacked in fields and covered with tarps until they were ready for transport by rail or water to the ports. Upon transport to the ports, each shipping case was covered with an American Flag. The flag remained on the case until it was delivered to a home or funeral home in the U.S.

Once the Soldier Dead were returned to the U.S., they were sent to one of fifty receiving stations set up in to receive the casketed remains. The caskets were transported to these receiving stations on converted Army and Navy train cars which held 66 shipping cases per car. Each funeral train held an honor guard which traveled with the Soldier Dead.[37]

The soldiers who remained behind at the request of their families, or who were unknowns, were interred permanently in a permanent American Military Cemetery which became part of the American Battle Monuments Commission. For those who remained, burial services were held for each Soldier Dead at the permanent cemetery. Burial flags were then sent to the next-of-kin.

Adopting Graves Overseas

After the war ended, people all across Europe who lived near American Military Cemeteries came out to pay their respects to the men who had liberated their countries. The people were so proud of these men who gave their lives that they began adopting graves. Communities near the cemeteries then formed organizations to handle grave adoptions and assist with ceremonies at the cemeteries. The practice of adopting graves continues today.

This story was written by Martijn van Haren, a resident of Holland.

Since I was a young boy I have been very interested in the Army and in WWII. My father was in the Army and my grandparents always told me stories about WWII. I guess that is how it started. I also collected items from the Army when I was young and did not realize that some of the items were from WWII. My grandfather gave me his gasmask that was given to Dutch citizens during WWII and he also had some ammunition for my collection. At that age I dressed up as a soldier a lot and played war games outside in the streets with my friends.

My grandparents witnessed the war. My grandmother saw the heavy bombardment here in Holland in Rotterdam. She survived the famous hunger winter by eating flower bulbs. Her older brother was in the Dutch army and found a way to escape and ended up in England to join the famous Prinses Irene Brigade. He landed in Normandy in August 1944 and fought in Belgium and Holland again for our freedom. He survived the war and died 13 years ago. The other younger brother was too young to be in the army and witnessed an execution of several citizens by the Germans. This was a revenge for an attack on German soldiers by the Dutch resistance.

When I became a little older, around 14 to 16 years old, I wasn't that involved in collecting stuff anymore. My interests changed a bit and I sold a part of the collection (except the items that my grandfather and my father had given me).

When I was 18 or 19 years old, I joined the Dutch army. After basic training I became a member of the 154th Battery Field Artillery. I had a great time but after 2.5 years I realized that the Dutch Army wasn't what I expected. I left the army at that time. I miss the Army every day and there are a lot of occasions that I regret leaving.

In 2004 I was 28 years old and more interested in WWII again. My interest surged because Band of Brothers was on TV and I had the opportunity to meet several US and British veterans of WWII who liberated my hometown. I was very excited and it felt really special. After meeting those men who were really down to earth, I was looking for a way to thank them. I didn't just wanted to say "thank you", I wanted to do more.

I found out about an adoption programme at the U.S. cemeteries in Europe. I contacted the adoption organisation in Holland at the U.S. cemetery Margraten and I applied for two graves. I remember receiving the certificates saying that I adopted the graves. I was over the moon. Again, it felt so special and I could not wait to visit the graves.

The first two graves that I adopted are Private Ralph J. Carter from Illinois and Private First Class Joseph Fernandez from New York. I remember when I visited the graves for the first time I had a pit in my stomach and I cried because it felt like visiting family.

Martijn with the first grave he adopted.
Private Ralph J. Carter. Photo courtesy
of Martijn van Haren

I spent hours at the gravesites "talking" to the two graves. From that day I knew I wanted to adopt more graves.

I applied for three more graves and after receiving those certificates and visiting the graves I decided to create a website about the graves. I thought it was a great way to remember the soldiers and make sure that they will never be forgotten.

My website is: WWW.FAC-ESBEYONDTHEGRAVES.COM

I realized I needed more information about the soldiers and requested their IDPF's. I decided to write to newspapers and libraries in the state and counties in which the soldiers had lived.

Doing that helped me a lot as I found new friends and they were very helpful. I was able to gain a lot of information, obituaries, and pictures of my adopted soldiers.

The Chicago Sun Times newspaper was interested in my request for information on Private Carter. The newspaper ran a piece about my search for information on Private Carter with a story about the adoption programme. To my luck a niece responded to the article and we became friends. She gave me more information and pictures about Private Carter. I was able to use that on my website. I was over the moon especially because I found out that Private Carter got married right before he went overseas. This was new information to his niece and other family members, so for me that was the cream on the cake.

I applied for more graves at Margraten, but the adoption programme had become so popular in Holland that more than 8,000 graves were adopted. Today there is a waiting list.

I contacted two other American cemeteries in Belgium, Henri-Chapelle and Ardennes. I found out that the adoption programme wasn't as popular in Belgium as it was in Holland. There were many graves still available for adoption. I requested five graves at each cemetery and later applied for five more at each cemetery adopting 25 graves in total at three different U.S. cemeteries. Since I adopted the 25 graves I found 17 families and met several members of these families.

The adoption programme and my search for information gained me invitation to the 65th WWII *USS Indianapolis* reunion in Indiana in 2010. Twenty-six survivors of the USS Indianapolis tragedy were in attendance. It was a great honour for me because I was asked to be a guest speaker. I also was contacted to be interviewed on Stardust Radio in New York. I had to wake up in the middle of the night but it was another great honour for me.

Through this process of adopting graves, I picked up my Army collection again. I sold several items to change it into a WWII collection and since that day I have several mannequins with original uniforms in my attic. I have six glass cabinets filled with original personal items, medical items, medals, pins, tobacco, and other items all from WWII. I love to sit near the collection and ask myself: what if these items could speak? I placed some pictures of my collection on my website.

My website in never finished because I hope to find new information about each soldier that I adopted. I also hope to find relatives to tell them that their uncle, brother, father or friend is in good hands and will never be forgotten. I visit the graves at least twice a year and I place roses at each grave. I think it is the least I can do back for the sacrifice those men gave so much for us.

Because of my commitment to these Soldier Dead, in 2012, I was asked to be a volunteer at the U.S. Cemetery Ardennes in Belgium each Memorial Day. I love being of service and bringing families to the graves of their loved ones.

I am still in contact with several family members of my adoption graves and I enjoy every minute of it. They all feel like my family.

Repatriation of War Dead Today

Today there are many government and private organizations looking for our country's war dead from World War I to the present day. The U.S. government needs your help if you have a family member who was Missing in Action or unrecoverable during any war. You can help by submitting DNA samples for use in identification efforts as remains are recovered.

To learn more, visit the Army's Past Conflict Repatriations Branch PCRB website. https://www.hrc.army.mil/TAGD/Past%20 Conflict%20Repatriations%20Branch%20PCRB%20Mission%20 Statement

8

Lost

Lost. Four letters.

Lost. One little word.

Lost. A powerful word that evokes many images.

As our men stood on that foreign shore so many years ago and contemplated life and death, love and loss, do you think they wondered if anyone would tell their stories? Do you wonder if they thought anyone would care? Do you think they worried that if they died, their story would be lost forever?

Writing this book was something I felt I had to do so the stories of my ancestors who never returned from battle would be preserved. Not lost in time. Digging deep into the research and writing is not an easy thing. It becomes very emotional at times when we try to put ourselves in their shoes. I believe we must endure the pain and sadness and tell our soldier stories.

I hope the stories and history provided in this book touched you and gave you a deeper understanding of what our men endured during World War I and World War II. Each soldier deserves our respect and deserves to be remembered, especially those who were unable to return and tell their stories.

We must never forget their sacrifice. We thank them for their service.

Notes

The Doughboy Notes

1. Ancestry.com, New York Passenger Lists, 1820-1957 (Name: Ancestry.com Operations, Inc.; Location: Provo, UT, USA; Date: 2010;), Year: 1880; Arrival: New York , United States; Microfilm serial: M237; Microfilm roll: M237_430; Line: 9; List number: 1243.

2. Illinois, Cook County, marriage license number 49003 (1880), Joseph Kokoska, Majdalena Priban: Cook County Clerk's Office, Chicago, Illinois.

3. Ancestry.com, 1900 United States Federal Census (Provo, UT, USA, Ancestry.com Operations Inc, 2004), www.ancestry.com, Database online. Year: 1900; Census Place: Chicago Ward 10, Cook, Illinois; Roll: T623_255; Page: 23B; Enumeration District: 269. Record for Joseph Kokoska.

4. Ancestry.com, World War I Draft Registration Cards, 1917-1918, record for Michael Kokoska, no. 105.

5. Ancestry.com, 1900 United States Federal Census, database record for Joseph Kokoska.

6. Ancestry.com, 1910 United States Federal Census (Provo, UT, USA, The Generations Network, Inc., 2006), www.ancestry.com, Database online. Year: 1910; Census Place: Chicago Ward 12, Cook, Illinois; Roll: T624_253; Page: 3B; Enumeration District: 583; Image: 380. Record for Michael Kokoska.

7. Ancestry.com, World War I Draft Registration Cards, 1917-1918 (Online publication - Provo, UT, USA: The Generations Network, Inc., 2005.Original data - United States, Selective Service System. World War I Selective Service System Draft Registration Cards, 1917-1918. Washington, D.C.: National Archives and Records Admin), Ancestry.com, http://www.Ancestry.com, Registration Location: Cook County, Illinois; Roll: 1493541; Draft Board: 26.. Name: Michael Kokoska; Birth Date: 28 Sep 1891; Birth Place: Residence Date: Residence Place: Chicago, Cook, Illinois. http://search.ancestry.com/cgi-bin/sse.dll?db=ww1draft&h=771956&ti=0&indiv=try.

8. Ancestry.com, World War I Draft Registration Cards, 1917-1918, database record for Michael Kokoska.

9. Michael Kokoska entry, World War I Bonus Files; Temporary Boards for Projects Record Group 503.000; Adjutant General records. Illinois State Archives, Springfield.

10. Muster Roll of 32nd Division, for December 1917; Orders, Muster Rolls, and Returns of Regular Army and Volunteer Forces, 1890-1917; Records of the Adju-

tant General's Office, 1780s-1917, Record Group 94; National Archives, Washington, D.C

11. Muster Roll of 32nd Division, for March/April 1918; Orders, Muster Rolls, and Returns of Regular Army and Volunteer Forces, 1890-1917; Records of the Adjutant General's Office, 1780s-1917, Record Group 94; National Archives, Washington, D.C

12. A Staff Correspondent 1917. Camp grant prepares to greet first of new army September 3. *Chicago Daily Tribune (1872-1922)*, Aug 12, 1917. http://search.proquest.com/docview/174256697?accountid=38403 (accessed November 12, 2012).

13. A Staff Correspondent 1917. Camp grant prepares to greet first of new army September 3. *Chicago Daily Tribune (1872-1922)*, Aug 12, 1917. http://search.proquest.com/docview/174256697?accountid=38403 (accessed November 12, 2012).

14. A Staff Correspondent 1917. Camp grant prepares to greet first of new army September 3. *Chicago Daily Tribune (1872-1922)*, Aug 12, 1917. http://search.proquest.com/docview/174256697?accountid=38403 (accessed November 12, 2012).

15. Joint War History Commissions of Michigan and Wisconsin. *The 32nd Division in the World War 1917-1919*, 33

16. Joint War History Commissions of Michigan and Wisconsin. *The 32nd Division in the World War 1917-1919*, 35

17. Center of Military History. *Order of Battle of the United States Land Forces in the World War*, vol. 2, *American Expeditionary Forces: Divisions* (1937. Reprint, Washington: U.S. G.P.O., 1931-1949), 181.

18. Michael Kokoska (France) to "Dear Sister" [Chicago, Illinois], letter, 12 Apr 1918; privately held by Jennifer Holik [Address for private use,] Woodridge, Illinois, 2013.

19. Center of Military History. *Order of Battle of the United States Land Forces in the World War*, vol. 2, *American Expeditionary Forces: Divisions* (1937. Reprint, Washington: U.S. G.P.O., 1931-1949), 181.

20. Joint War History Commissions of Michigan and Wisconsin. *The 32nd Division in the World War 1917-1919*, 41

21. Michael Kokoska Western Union Telegram dated August 10, 1918, *World War I Bonus Files*; Temporary Boards for Projects Record Group 503.000; Adjutant General records. Illinois State Archives, Springfield.

22. Memo on cause of death of Michael Kokoska, serial no. 275180, 21 Feb. 1919; General Records 92.8.1; Records of the Quartermaster General's Office, Record Group 92; National Archives, Washington, D.C,

23. Letter to Chief of Graves Registration Bureau, 17 Dec. 1919; General Records 92.8.1; Records of the Quartermaster General's Office, Record Group 92; National Archives, Washington, D.C,

24. Letter to Joseph Kokoska from Office of the Quartermaster General, 19 Jan 1920; General Records 92.8.1; Records of the Quartermaster General's Office, Record Group 92; National Archives, Washington, D.C,

25. Letter to the Office of the Quartermaster General, 7 June 1920; General Records 92.8.1; Records of the Quartermaster General's Office, Record Group 92; National Archives, Washington. D.C,

26. Letter to the Office of the Quartermaster General, 21 Oct 1920; General Records 92.8.1; Records of the Quartermaster General's Office, Record Group 92; National Archives, Washington, D.C,

27. Letter to the Office of the Quartermaster General, 15 Feb 1921; General Records 92.8.1; Records of the Quartermaster General's Office, Record Group 92; National Archives, Washington, D.C,

28. Letter from the Office of the Quartermaster General, 28 Feb 1921; General Records 92.8.1; Records of the Quartermaster General's Office, Record Group 92; National Archives, Washington, D.C,

29. Letter to the Office of the Quartermaster General, 3 Mar 1921; General Records 92.8.1; Records of the Quartermaster General's Office, Record Group 92; National Archives, Washington, D.C,

30. Letter from the Office of the Quartermaster General, 11 Mar 1921; General Records 92.8.1; Records of the Quartermaster General's Office, Record Group 92; National Archives, Washington, D.C,

31. Telegram to Joseph Kokoska regarding return of remains, 13 May 1921; General Records 92.8.1; Records of the Quartermaster General's Office, Record Group 92; National Archives, Washington, D.C,

32. Telegram from Joseph Kokoska to Graves Registration Service dated 13-14 May 1921; *World War I Burial File*; Military Textual Reference Branch, National Archives, College Park, MD.

33. "Pvt. Michael Kokoska," undated clipping, ca. May 27, 1921; Holik Family Papers, privately held by Jennifer Holik, [Address for private use,] Woodridge,

Illinois, 2013. Received a copy from Charles Kokaska, a nephew of Michael Kokoska.

34. "The Weather," *Chicago Daily Tribune (1872-1922);* May 29, 1921; digital images, ProQuest Historical Newspapers; Chicago Tribune (1849-1989), pg. 1.

The Replacement Notes

1. Bohemian National Cemetery (Chicago, Cook County, Illinois), Frank J. Winkler marker, section 23 lot 244; personally read, 2013.

2. 1940 census, Cook County, Illinois, population schedule, ED 103-1505, pg. 9A, family 190, Frank Winkler; digital image, Ancestry.com (http://ancestry.com : accessed 31 August 2013); citing NARA microfilm publication T627.

3. 2,047 To Close High School Careers. Chicago Daily Tribune (1923-1963), January 25, 1942. http://search.proquest.com/hnpchicagotribune/docview/176596024/1 403A17A35659959F4F/2?accountid=38403 (accessed August 27, 2013).

4. Report of Death Dated 30 Aug 1944 - Individual Deceased Personnel File Frank J. Winkler, Serial No. 36695605; Records of the Quartermaster General's Office, Record Group 92; National Archives, Washington D.C.

5. Electronic Army Serial Number Merged File, ca. 1938 - 1946 (Enlistment Records); database on-line, Record Group 64; National Archives and Records Administration.

6. Service Numbers (united States Armed Forces), Wikipedia, digital encyclopedia (http://en.wikipedia.org/wiki/Service_number_%28United_States_armed_forces%29 : accessed 31 Aug 2013.)

7. Balkoski, Joseph. Beyond the Beachhead. (Mechanicsburg, PA: Stackpole Books, 1999,) 222.

8. Battle Casualty Report dated July 24, 1944 - Individual Deceased Personnel File Frank J. Winkler, Serial No. 36695605; Records of the Quartermaster General's Office, Record Group 92; National Archives, Washington D.C.

9. Company Morning Report dated 4 Jul 1944, 29th Infantry 115th Regt, Co G, Records of U.S. Army Operational, Tactical, and Support Organizations (World War II and Thereafter), Record Group 338.

10. Report of Death Dated 30 Aug 1944 - Individual Deceased Personnel File Frank J. Winkler, Serial No. 36695605; Records of the Quartermaster General's Office, Record Group 92; National Archives, Washington D.C.

11. Army reports 1,820 soldiers dead in action. 1944. Chicago Daily Tribune (1923-1963), Nov 03, 1944. http://search.proquest.com/docview/177017728?accou ntid=38403 (accessed January 10, 2013).

12. Report of Burial Dated 2 Jul 1944 - Individual Deceased Personnel File Frank J. Winkler, Serial No. 36695605; Records of the Quartermaster General's Office, Record Group 92; National Archives, Washington D.C.

13. Letter from Frank Winkler to Army dated 19 Nov 1944 - Individual Deceased Personnel File Frank J. Winkler, Serial No. 36695605; Records of the Quartermaster General's Office, Record Group 92; National Archives, Washington D.C.

14. Report of Burial dated 2 Jul 1944 - Individual Deceased Personnel File Frank J. Winkler, Serial No. 36695605; Records of the Quartermaster General's Office, Record Group 92; National Archives, Washington D.C.

15. Letter from Quartermaster General dated 2 Dec 1946 to Frank Winkler - Individual Deceased Personnel File Frank J. Winkler, Serial No. 36695605; Records of the Quartermaster General's Office, Record Group 92; National Archives, Washington D.C.

16. Disinterment Directive dated October 15, 1947 - Individual Deceased Personnel File Frank J. Winkler, Serial No. 36695605; Records of the Quartermaster General's Office, Record Group 92; National Archives, Washington D.C.

17. Change in Instructions by Next-of-Kin dated 31 Mar 1948 - Individual Deceased Personnel File Frank J. Winkler, Serial No. 36695605; Records of the Quartermaster General's Office, Record Group 92; National Archives, Washington D.C.

18. U.S., Headstone Applications for Military Veterans, 1925-1963, digital image, Ancestry.com (http://ancestry.com : accessed 31 August 2013); citing application for Frank J. Winkler application dated 14 Jul 1948.

The Tiger Notes

1. "New York Passenger Lists, Roll T715_99: 1820-1957." Database Ancestry. com. (http://www.ancestry.com : accessed 5 May 2010), entry for Peter Brouk, age 11, arrived New York, New York, 1900 [Noordland].

2. Florida Office of Vital Statistics, death certificate 23196 (1942), Robert R. Brouk; Bureau of Vital Records, Tallahassee.

3. "Social Security Death Index." Database Ancestry.com (http://www.ancestry. com : accessed 25 September 2010), entry for Harold Brouk, 1983, SS no. 336-18- 0271.

4. City of Chicago, Illinois, probate case files, no. 43P 1805, Robert R. Brouk (1943), Petition for Letters of Administration, 12 March 1943; Circuit Clerk's Office, Chicago.

5. "1910 United States Federal Census Roll T624_254 : 1910." Database Ancestry.com. (http://www.ancestry.com : accessed 3 September 2010), entry for Peter Brouk, Chicago, Illinois.

6. "Richard Kauffman Heads Cicero Business Group," Chicago Daily Tribune (Chicago), 8 March 1931, p. H5; digital images, ProQuest (http://www.proquest. umi.com : accessed 3 June 2010), Historical Newspaper Collection.

7. "J. Sterling Morton Year Book 1935." Database Ancestry.com. (http://www. ancestry.com : accessed 1 May 2010), entry for Robert Brouk, Cicero, Illinois.

8. Karen Halla, Cicero, Illinois. [(E-address for private use),] to Jennifer Holik, email, 10 May 2010, "Re: Historical Society of Cicero," Robert Brouk Correspondence File, Robert Brouk Book Research Files; privately held by Jennifer Holik [(E-address) & street address for private use,] Woodridge, Illinois.

9. Chemistry Club column and photograph, in Pioneer Yearbook, ca. 1936, p. 66; Held by Morton Junior College Library, [3801 S. Central Avenue,] Cicero, Illinois, 1936.

10. "Wrestlers Have Largest Squad For Many Years," (Cicero) Morton Collegian, 6 November 1936, p. 4, col. 4.

11. "Cicero Chapter of Builders to Induct Leaders," Chicago Daily Tribune (Chicago), 21 June 1936, p. W7; digital images, ProQuest (http://www.proquest.umi. com : accessed 3 June 2010), Historical Newspaper Collection.

12. Wrestling Club, column and photograph, in Pioneer Yearbook. ca. 1937, p. 66;. Held by Morton Junior College Library, [3801 S. Central Avenue,] Cicero, Illinois, 1937.

13. "Class Prophecy," (Cicero) Morton Collegian, 28 May 1937, p. 2, col. 4.

14. Robert Brouk sophomore photograph, in Pioneer Yearbook, ca. 1937, pg 91; Held by Morton Junior College Library, [3801 S. Central Avenue,] Cicero, Illinois, 1937.

15. "Untitled," (Berwyn) Berwyn Life, 11 November 1942, p. 1, cols. 4-5.

16. "1940 United States Federal Census." Database Ancestry.com. (http://www.ancestry.com : accessed 10 October 2012), ED 15-20, p. 22A, line 37, entry for Robert R Brouk, Randolph Field, Bexar Texas.

17. "Nine Young Chicagoans Receive Commissions as Lieutenants in Army Air Corps Reserve :Fifth Recent Class. " Chicago Daily Tribune (Chicago), 31 August 1940, p. 6; digital images, ProQuest (http://www.proquest.umi.com : accessed 3 June 2010), Historical Newspaper Collection.

18. "Tiger Diary," (Chicago) Herald-American, 26 July 1942, p. 1.

19. Schultz, Duane. The Maverick War, p. 110.

20. Bond, Charles, and Terry Anderson. A Flying Tiger's Diary, p. 39.

21. Chennault, Anna. Chennault and the Flying Tigers, pg. 98.

22. "Cicero to Honor Own Flying Tiger: Day of Tribute to all Fighters is Next Sunday." Chicago Daily Tribune (Chicago), 26 July 1942, p. W1; digital images, ProQuest (http://www.proquest.umi.com : accessed 3 June 2010), Historical Newspaper Collection.

23. "Bob Brouk Air Crash Victim," (Berwyn) Berwyn Life, 20 December 1942, p. 1, col. 5.

24. "Committee Works on Plans for Brouk Day Celebration," (Berwyn) Berwyn Life, 22 July 1942, p. 1, col. 2.

25. "Sees Permanent U.S. Air Force of Two Million Men," Chicago Daily Tribune (Chicago), 23 July 1942, p. 6; digital images, ProQuest (http://www.proquest.umi.com : accessed 13 October 2010), Historical Newspaper Collection.

26. "Complete Radio Programs and Highlights for Today," Chicago Daily Tribune (Chicago), 22 July 1942, p. 12; digital images, ProQuest (http://www.proquest.umi.com : accessed 13 October 2010), Historical Newspaper Collection.

27. "Further Fete Plans Honoring Flying Tiger," (Berwyn) Berwyn Life, 24 July 1942, p. 1, col. 2.

28. "Chinese to Honor 'Flying Tigers'," Chicago Herald American, 26 July 1942, p. 16, col. 3.

29. "Complete Radio Programs and Highlights for Today," Chicago Daily Tribune (Chicago), 27 July 1942, p. 10; digital images, ProQuest (http://www.proquest.umi.com : accessed 13 October 2010), Historical Newspaper Collection.

30. "Complete Radio Programs and Highlights for Today," Chicago Daily Tribune (Chicago), 30 July 1942, p. 8; digital images, ProQuest (http://www.proquest.umi.com : accessed 13 October 2010), Historical Newspaper Collection.

31. "Complete Radio Programs and Highlights for Today," Chicago Daily Tribune (Chicago), 6 August 1942, p. 12; digital images, ProQuest (http://www.proquest.umi.com : accessed 13 October 2010), Historical Newspaper Collection.

32. Hawthorne Works Museum, Hello Charley 1963, pamphlet (Cicero, IL. : 1963), inside panel 2.

33. Virginia S. Davis (Phoenix, Arizona) to "Dear Jen", letter, 1 February 2006; information on Robert Brouk; Robert Brouk Correspondence File; Robert Brouk Book Research Files; privately held by Jennifer Holik, [address held for private use] Woodridge, Illinois, 2006.

34. "Tells How 'Tigers' Shot Down Japs," (Berwyn) Berwyn Life, 31 July 1942, p.13, col. 2.

35. "It's Bob Brouk Day Today," (Berwyn) Berwyn Life, 2 August 1942, p. 1, col. 5.

36. "Huge Turnout Predicted for Brouk Fete Sunday," (Berwyn) Berwyn Life, 31 July 1942, p. 3, col. 1.

37. "Flying Tiger Will Invade Lions Den, (Berwyn) Berwyn Life, 7 August 1942, p. 5, col. 1.

38. "Czechs to Renew Their Pledge to Free Way of Life," Chicago Daily Tribune (Chicago), 9 August 1942, p. W5; digital images, ProQuest (http://www.proquest.umi.com : accessed 13 October 2010), Historical Newspaper Collection.

39. "Bob Brouk will Join Moose Lodge," (Berwyn) Berwyn Life, 9 August 1942, p. 1, col. 7.

40. "Bob Brouk will Join Moose Lodge," (Berwyn) Berwyn Life, 9 August 1942.

41. "Flying Tiger Gives Vivid Account of His China Air Fights," The Microphone 18 (September 1942) : 5.

42. "Radio Stars Join in Show to Aid Air Recruiting, Chicago Daily Tribune (Chicago), 9 October 1942, p. 22; digital images, ProQuest (http://www.proquest.umi.com : accessed 13 October 2010), Historical Newspaper Collection.

43. "Capt. Bob Brouk," (Berwyn) Berwyn Life, 14 October 1942, p. 10, col. 7.

44. War Department Report of Death 29 December 1942; Individual Deceased Personnel File; Military Textual Reference Branch, National Archives, College Park, MD.

45. Compiled Army Air Force Accident Report, Robert R. Brouk, Captain, 50th Fighter Group, 10th Fighter Squadron, Records of the Army Air Force, p. 20.

46. Jo Neal, President AVG-FTA, [(E-address for private use),] to Jennifer Holik, email, 13October 2010, "Robert Brouk," Robert Brouk Correspondence File, Robert Brouk Book Research Files; privately held by Jennifer Holik [(E-address) & street address for private use,] Woodridge, Illinois.

47. Virginia S. Davis to "Dear Jen," 1 February 2006.

48. Virginia S. Davis (Brouk), "Memoir 1918 – 2010" (MS, Phoenix, Arizona, 2010), p. 139; privately held by Virginia S. Davis, [Address for private use,] Phoenix, Arizona, 2010.

49. "Flying Tiger's bride-to-be gets license," (Chicago) The Daily Times, Chicago, 25 December 1942, p. 20, col. 3.

50. Virginia S. Davis (Scharer), "Memoir 1918 – 2010," 145.

51. Compiled Army Air Force Accident Report, Robert R. Brouk, p. 19.

52. Compiled Army Air Force Accident Report, Robert R. Brouk, page 4.

53. Ibid, page 10.

54. Ibid, page 12.

55. Ibid, page 24.

56. "Brouk Rites are Thursday," (Berwyn) Berwyn Life, 22 December 1942, p. 1, col. 6.

57. "Thousands see Brouk Rites," (Berwyn) Berwyn Life, 27 December 1942, p. 1, col. 6.

58. "Thousands see Brouk Rites," p. 1, col. 6.

59. "Paying Final Tribute to Captain Brouk," (Berwyn) Berwyn Life, 29 December 1942, p. 1.

60. Virginia S. Davis (Scharer), "Memoir 1918 – 2010," 146-147.

61. "Thousands see Brouk Rites," (Berwyn) Berwyn Life, 27 December 1942, p. 1, col. 6.

62. Robert R. Brouk Distinguished Flying Cross Medal and Citation; privately held by Jennifer Holik-Urban, [Address for private use] Woodridge, Illinois.

Tough 'Ombres Notes

1. CCC Legacy, Brief History, online article (http://ccclegacy.org/CCC_Brief_History.html : accessed 28 Feb 2014.)

2. 16 July 1939, CCC Certificate of Selection; Civilian Conservation Corps Enrollee Records, Record Group 35; National Personnel Records Center, St. Louis, MO.

3. 16 July 1939, CCC Enrollee Cumulative Record; Civilian Conservation Corps Enrollee Records, Record Group 35; National Personnel Records Center, St. Louis, MO.

4. 19 July 1939, CCC Individual Record of Service; Civilian Conservation Corps Enrollee Records, Record Group 35; National Personnel Records Center, St. Louis, MO.

5. Ancestry.com, Cook County, Illinois Birth Index, 1916-1935 (Online publication - Provo, UT, USA: The Generations Network, Inc., 2008.Original data - Cook County Clerk, comp. Cook County Clerk Genealogy Records. Cook County Clerk's Office, Chicago, IL: Cook County Clerk, 2008.Original data: Cook County Clerk, comp.), Ancestry.com, http://www.Ancestry.com, Birth date: 30 Jul 1921 Birth place: Cook County, IL. http://search.ancestry.com/cgi-bin/sse.dll?db=cookcountybirths&h=2218881&ti=0&indiv=try&gss=pt.

6. 9 Feb 1943, Station: Camp Butner, North Carolina, Organization:126th MM Ordnance; Company Morning Reports Adjutant General's Office 1917-, Record Group 407; National Archives and Records Administration, Washington, D.C.

7. "66th Ordnance/Maintenance Battalion – History," website Military.com (http://www.military.com/HomePage/UnitPageHistory/1,13506,106874|100096,00.html : accessed 30 December 2013.)

8. U.S. Army The Ordnance Replacement Training Center. The Ordnance Soldier's Guide. Aberdeen Proving Ground: undated, p. 10.

9. Stradling, Richard, "History buffs, soldiers plan museum for Camp Butner," Newsobserver.com, 30 November 2013, online archives (http://www.newsobserver.com/2013/11/30/3416989/history-buffs-soldiers-plan-museum.html : accessed 24 December 2013) para 10.

10. http://www.butnernc.org/pages/ButnerHeritage.html Town of Butner website accessed 15 Sept 2013.

11. Barnes, G. M. Weapons of World War II. Birmingham: Palladium Press, 2013, 3.

12. McMillan, Woody. In The Presence of Soldiers. Nashville: Horton Heights Press, 2010, 443. This is an excellent resource outlining the problems each group that moved through the Tennessee Maneuvers experienced in 1942, 1943, and 1944. The author shows the progression of changes based on experience and wartime data. He also provides a full appendix of every unit that participated and their full problems.

13. McMillan, Woody. In The Presence of Soldiers. Nashville: Horton Heights Press, 2010, 446.

14. Extract Special Orders No. 37 dated 9 Feb 1944; Adjutant General's Office 1917-, Record Group 407; National Archives and Records Administration, Washington, D.C. and 15 Feb 1944, Station: Camp Kilmer, New Jersey, Organization: NYPE-RP Cp. Kilmer Br. (Casuals); Company Morning Reports Adjutant General's Office 1917-, Record Group 407; National Archives and Records Administration, Washington, D.C.

15. "History Camp Kilmer," website Rutgers Makerspace Association, (http://makerspace.rutgers.edu/content/history-camp-kilmer : accessed 30 December 2013.)

16. 15 Feb 1944, Station: Camp Kilmer, New Jersey, Organization: NYPE-RP Cp. Kilmer Br. (Casuals); Company Morning Reports Adjutant General's Office 1917-, Record Group 407; National Archives and Records Administration, Washington, D.C.

17. 23 Feb 1944, Station: Camp Kilmer, New Jersey, Organization: NYPE-RP Cp. Kilmer Br. (Casuals); Company Morning Reports Adjutant General's Office 1917-, Record Group 407; National Archives and Records Administration, Washington, D.C.

18. 2 Mar 1944, Station: Camp Kilmer, New Jersey, Organization: NYPE-RP Cp. Kilmer Br. (Casuals); Company Morning Reports Adjutant General's Office 1917-, Record Group 407; National Archives and Records Administration, Washington, D.C.

19. 21 Mar 1944, Station: Camp Kilmer, New Jersey, Organization: NYPE-RP Cp. Kilmer Br. (Casuals); Company Morning Reports Adjutant General's Office 1917-, Record Group 407; National Archives and Records Administration, Washington, D.C.

20. 790th Ordinance Light Maintenance Company, 90th Division Association (http://www.90thdivisionassoc.org/90thDivisionFolders/mervinbooks/790/790Ord/790O01.htm), 7. and United States Army. Peragimus

"We Accomplish," A brief history of the 358th Infantry. (Washington, D.C. Undated,) 9.

21. 790th Ordinance Light Maintenance Company, 90th Division Association (http://www.90thdivisionassoc.org/90thDivisionFolders/mervinbooks/790/790Ord/790O01.htm), 6.

22. 790th Ordinance Light Maintenance Company, *90th Division Association* (http://www.90thdivisionassoc.org/90thDivisionFolders/mervinbooks/790/790Ord/790O01.htm), 8.

23. 90th Division History, *90th Division Association* (http://www.90thdivisionassoc.org/90thDivisionFolders/90thhistorybook/histbkmainframe.htm), 5.

24. 790th Ordinance Light Maintenance Company, *90th Division Association* (http://www.90thdivisionassoc.org/90thDivisionFolders/mervinbooks/790/790Ord/790O01.htm), 4.

25. After Action Report 90th Division January 1945, *90th Division Association* (http://www.90thdivisionassoc.org/afteractionreports/PDF/Jun-44.pdf), 7.

26. 8 June 1944, Station: On board ship, Organization: 790th Ord Co; Company Morning Reports Adjutant General's Office 1917-, Record Group 407; National Archives and Records Administration, Washington, D.C.; 16 June 1944, Station: Fresville, France, Organization: 790th Ord Co; Company Morning Reports Adjutant General's Office 1917-, Record Group 407; National Archives and Records Administration, Washington, D.C.

27. 16 June 1944, Station: Fresville, France, Organization: 790th Ord Co; Company Morning Reports Adjutant General's Office 1917-, Record Group 407; National Archives and Records Administration, Washington, D.C.

28. 19 June 1944, Station: Fresville, France, Organization: 790th Ord Co; Company Morning Reports Adjutant General's Office 1917-, Record Group 407; National Archives and Records Administration, Washington, D.C.

29. 23 June 1944, Station: Chef du Pont, France, Organization: 790th Ord Co; Company Morning Reports Adjutant General's Office 1917-, Record Group 407; National Archives and Records Administration, Washington, D.C.

30. 6 July 1944, Station: Deuzeville-la-Bastille, France, Organization: 790th Ord Co; Company Morning Reports Adjutant General's Office 1917-, Record Group 407; National Archives and Records Administration, Washington, D.C.

31. 8 July 1944, Station: Ponte-le-Abbe, Organization: 790th Ord Co; Company Morning Reports Adjutant General's Office 1917-, Record Group 407; National Archives and Records Administration, Washington, D.C.

32. 790th Ordinance Light Maintenance Company, *90th Division Association* (http://www.90thdivisionassoc.org/90thDivisionFolders/mervinbooks/790/790Ord/790O01.htm), 10.

33. 21 July 1944, Station: St. Jores, France, Organization: 790th Ord Co; Company Morning Reports Adjutant General's Office 1917-, Record Group 407; National Archives and Records Administration, Washington, D.C.

34. 28 July 1944, Station: Gorges, France; 29 July 1944, Station: Periers, France, Organization: 790th Ord Co; Company Morning Reports Adjutant General's Office 1917-, Record Group 407; National Archives and Records Administration, Washington, D.C.

35. 3 Aug 1944, Station: St. Osvin, Organization: 790th Ord Co; Company Morning Reports Adjutant General's Office 1917-, Record Group 407; National Archives and Records Administration, Washington, D.C.; 790th Ordinance Light Maintenance Company, *90th Division Association* (http://www.90thdivisionassoc.org/90thDivisionFolders/mervinbooks/790/790Ord/790O01.htm), 12.

36. 6 Aug 1944, Station: Landivy, Organization: 790th Ord Co; Company Morning Reports Adjutant General's Office 1917-, Record Group 407; National Archives and Records Administration, Washington, D.C.

37. 9 Aug 1944, Station: Le Mans, France, Organization: 790th Ord Co; Company Morning Reports Adjutant General's Office 1917-, Record Group 407; National Archives and Records Administration, Washington, D.C.

38. 790th Ordinance Light Maintenance Company, *90th Division Association* (http://www.90thdivisionassoc.org/90thDivisionFolders/mervinbooks/790/790Ord/790O01.htm), 13.

39. 11 Aug 1944, Station: Ballon, France, Organization: 790th Ord Co; Company Morning Reports Adjutant General's Office 1917-, Record Group 407; National Archives and Records Administration, Washington, D.C.

40. 15 Aug 1944, Station: Chaillous, Organization: 790th Ord Co; Company Morning Reports Adjutant General's Office 1917-, Record Group 407; National Archives and Records Administration, Washington, D.C.

41. 27 Aug 1944, Station: Nangis, France, Organization: 790th Ord Co; Company Morning Reports Adjutant General's Office 1917-, Record Group 407; National Archives and Records Administration, Washington, D.C.

42. 30 Aug 1944, Station: Chenay, France, Organization: 790th Ord Co; Company Morning Reports Adjutant General's Office 1917-, Record Group 407; National Archives and Records Administration, Washington, D.C.

43. 6 Sept 1944, Station: Etain, France, Organization: 790th Ord Co; Company Morning Reports Adjutant General's Office 1917-, Record Group 407; National Archives and Records Administration, Washington, D.C.

44. 10 Sept 1944, Station: Lixieres, 1 mi N. 6075 Verdun. Organization: 790th Ordnance L. M. Co.; Company Morning Reports Adjutant General's Office 1917-, Record Group 407; National Archives and Records Administration, Washington, D.C.

45. 12 Sept 1944, Station: Fontoy, France, Organization: 790th Ord Co; Company Morning Reports Adjutant General's Office 1917-, Record Group 407; National Archives and Records Administration, Washington, D.C.

46. 14 Sept 1944, Station: Briey, France, Organization: 790th Ord Co; Company Morning Reports Adjutant General's Office 1917-, Record Group 407; National Archives and Records Administration, Washington, D.C.

47. 26 Sept 1944 – 31 Oct 1944, Station: Giraumont, France, Organization: 790th Ord Co; Company Morning Reports Adjutant General's Office 1917-, Record Group 407; National Archives and Records Administration, Washington, D.C.

48. 790th Ordinance Light Maintenance Company, 90th Division Association (http://www.90thdivisionassoc.org/90thDivisionFolders/mervinbooks/790/790Ord/790O01.htm), 17.

49. Blumenson, Martin. The Patton Papers 1940-1945. Boston: Houghton Mifflin Company, 1974, 589.

50. 3 Nov 1944, Station: Piennes, France, Organization: 790th Ord Co; Company Morning Reports Adjutant General's Office 1917-, Record Group 407; National Archives and Records Administration, Washington, D.C.

51. 9 Nov 1944, Station: Hettange Grande, France, Organization: 790th Ord Co; Company Morning Reports Adjutant General's Office 1917-, Record Group 407; National Archives and Records Administration, Washington, D.C.

52. 18 Nov 1944, Station: Thionville, France, Organization: 790th Ord Co; Company Morning Reports Adjutant General's Office 1917-, Record Group 407; National Archives and Records Administration, Washington, D.C.

53. 790th Ordinance Light Maintenance Company, *90th Division Association* (http://www.90thdivisionassoc.org/90thDivisionFolders/mervinbooks/790/790Ord/790O01.htm), 17.

54. 5 Dec – 23 Dec 1944, Station: Veckring, France, Organization: 790th Ord Co; Company Morning Reports Adjutant General's Office 1917-, Record Group 407; National Archives and Records Administration, Washington, D.C.

55. 790th Ordinance Light Maintenance Company, *90th Division Association* (http://www.90thdivisionassoc.org/90thDivisionFolders/mervinbooks/790/790Ord/790O01.htm), 18.

56. 18 Dec 1944, Station: Veckring, WQ 0183 Nord de Guerre. Organization: 790th Ordnance L. M. Co.; Company Morning Reports Adjutant General's Office 1917-, Record Group 407; National Archives and Records Administration, Washington, D.C.

57. Blumenson, Martin. *The Patton Papers 1940-1945. Boston: Houghton Mifflin Company, 1974, 602 and 604.*

58. Conn, Stetson, ed. *U.S. Army in World War II The Ardennes: Battle of the Bulge The European Theater. Minnetonka: National Historical Society, 1995, reprinted from 1965 original CMH Pub 7-8; 649-650.*

59. 23 Dec 1944, Station: Elzange, France, Organization: 790th Ord Co; Company Morning Reports Adjutant General's Office 1917-, Record Group 407; National Archives and Records Administration, Washington, D.C.

60. 29 Dec 1944, Station: Veckring, WQ 0183 Nord de Guerre. Organization: 358th Infantry Regt Co F Morning Reports Adjutant General's Office 1917-, Record Group 407; National Archives and Records Administration, Washington, D.C.

61. Patton's yule prayer: Good war weather. 1945. *Chicago Daily Tribune (1923-1963), Jan 18, 1945. http://search.proquest.com/docview/177040554?account id=38403 (accessed March 19, 2013).*

62. 1 Jan 1945, Station: Scheuerwald, Germany, Organization: 358th Infantry Regt Co F Morning Reports Adjutant General's Office 1917-, Record Group 407; National Archives and Records Administration, Washington, D.C.

63. 3d army battles blizzard as well as nazis in bulge. 1945. *Chicago Daily Tribune (1923-1963), Jan 04, 1945. http://search.proquest.com/docview/176973582?accou ntid=38403 (accessed January 7, 2013).*

64. Battleground a 'white hell' to doughboys. 1945. *Chicago Daily Tribune (1923-1963), Jan 05, 1945. http://search.proquest.com/docview/177039446?account id=38403 (accessed January 6, 2013).*

65. Battleground a 'white hell' to doughboys. 1945. Chicago Daily Tribune (1923-1963), Jan 05, 1945. http://search.proquest.com/docview/177039446?account

id=38403 (accessed January 6, 2013), Chicago Daily Tribune, Chicago, Illinois, digital images (http://proquest.com).

66. After Action Report 90th Division January 1945, *90th Division Association* (http://www.90thdivisionassoc.org/afteractionreports/PDF/Jan-45.pdf), 1.

67. After Action Report 90th Division January 1945, *90th Division Association* (http://www.90thdivisionassoc.org/afteractionreports/PDF/Jan-45.pdf), 1.

68. 6 Jan 1945, Station: Waldwisse, France, Organization: 358th Infantry Ret Co F Morning Reports Adjutant General's Office 1917-, Record Group 407; National Archives and Records Administration, Washington, D.C.

69. 7 Jan 1945, Station: Nagam, Luxembourg, Organization: 358th Infantry Regt Co F Morning Reports Adjutant General's Office 1917-, Record Group 407; National Archives and Records Administration, Washington, D.C.

70. After Action Report 90th Division January 1945, *90th Division Association* (http://www.90thdivisionassoc.org/afteractionreports/PDF/Jan-45.pdf), 2.

71. 9 Jan 1945, Station: Rambrouch, Luxembourg, Organization: 358th Infantry Regt Co F Morning Reports Adjutant General's Office 1917-, Record Group 407; National Archives and Records Administration, Washington, D.C.

72. AAR January 1945 90th pg. 7. 11 Jan 1945, Station: Bavigne, Luxembourg, Organization: 358th Infantry Regt Co F Morning Reports Adjutant General's Office 1917-, Record Group 407; National Archives and Records Administration, Washington, D.C.

73. United States Army, *Peragimus "We Accomplish"*. A brief history of the 358th Infantry. (Washington, D.C. Undated,) 45.

74. 17 Jan 1945, Station: 1 mi E Niederwampach, Luxemburg, Organization: Co F, 358th Inf Regt.; Company Morning Reports Adjutant General's Office 1917-, Record Group 407; National Archives and Records Administration, Washington, D.C.

75. United States Army, Individual Deceased Personnel File, U.S. Army Human Resources Command, 200 Stovall Street Alexandria, VA 22332-0400, Report of Death for James F Privoznik, serial no. 36640529, dated 3 Feb 1945, stamped by Commanding Office of Graves Registration Company Mar 1945.

76. LIST OF 1,999 YANKS KILLED IS ANNOUNCED. 1945. *Chicago Daily Tribune (1923-1963)*, Mar 08, 1945. *http://search.proquest.com/docview/17705268 8?accountid=38403 (accessed September 16, 2013)*.

77. United States Army, Individual Deceased Personnel File, U.S. Army Human Resources Command, 200 Stovall Street Alexandria, VA 22332-0400, Report of

Burial for James F Privoznik, serial no. 36640529, dated 17 Jan 1945, stamped Commanding Office of Graves Registration Company Mar 1945. Memo on cause of death of Michael Kokoska, serial no. 275180, 21 Feb. 1919; General Records 92.8.1; Records of the Quartermaster General's Office, Record Group 92; National Archives, Washington, D.C,

78. National Museum of Military History - Diekirch, National Museum of Military History - Diekirch, National Museum of Military History - Diekirch, (http://www. mnhm.lu/), "Brief History of the Luxembourg American Cemetery" as narrated by the cemetery superintendent.

79. United States Army, Individual Deceased Personnel File, U.S. Army Human Resources Command, 200 Stovall Street Alexandria, VA 22332-0400, Letter dated 19 Apr 1945 requesting personal effects for James F Privoznik, serial no. 36640529.

80. United States Army, Individual Deceased Personnel File, U.S. Army Human Resources Command, 200 Stovall Street Alexandria, VA 22332-0400, Letter from the Quartermaster General dated 14 May 1945 in regards to personal effects of James F Privoznik, serial no. 36640529.

81. Davis, R. Warren. *The History of the Luxembourg American Military Cemetery. Luxembourg: 1965, 2.*

82. Davis, R. Warren. *The History of the Luxembourg American Military Cemetery. Luxembourg: 1965, 2.*

83. Davis, R. Warren. *The History of the Luxembourg American Military Cemetery. Luxembourg: 1965, 2.*

84. United States Army, Individual Deceased Personnel File, U.S. Army Human Resources Command, 200 Stovall Street Alexandria, VA 22332-0400, Letter dated 24 May 1945 from Quartermaster to Mary Privoznik regarding personal effects of James F Privoznik, serial no. 36640529.

85. Longfellow, Henry Wadsworth "Decoration Day," Henry Wadsworth Longfellow [online resource], Maine Historical Society, Accessed January 22, 2104. http://www.hwlongfellow.org

86. The Bible Gateway.com, "2 Corinthians 5:1-9," website (http://www.biblegateway.com/passage/?search=2+Corinthians+5%3A1-9 : accessed 3 January 2014.)

87. United States Army, Individual Deceased Personnel File, U.S. Army Human Resources Command, 200 Stovall Street Alexandria, VA 22332-0400, Letter dated 7 Dec 1945 to Quartermaster from Mary Privoznik regarding personal effects of James F Privoznik, serial no. 36640529.

88. United States Army, Individual Deceased Personnel File, U.S. Army Human Resources Command, 200 Stovall Street Alexandria, VA 22332-0400, Letter dated 18 Dec 1945 from Quartermaster to Mary Privoznik regarding personal effects of James F Privoznik, serial no. 36640529.

89. Davis, R. Warren. *The History of the Luxembourg American Military Cemetery. Luxembourg: 1965, 3.*

90. United States Army, Individual Deceased Personnel File, U.S. Army Human Resources Command, 200 Stovall Street Alexandria, VA 22332-0400, Letter dated 26 Sept 1946 from Quartermaster to Mary Privoznik regarding the grave location of James F Privoznik, serial no. 36640529.

91. United States Army, Individual Deceased Personnel File, U.S. Army Human Resources Command, 200 Stovall Street Alexandria, VA 22332-0400, Letter dated 12 Jan 1947 to Quartermaster from Mary Privoznik regarding personal effects of James F Privoznik, serial no. 36640529.

92. United States Army, Individual Deceased Personnel File, U.S. Army Human Resources Command, 200 Stovall Street Alexandria, VA 22332-0400, Letter dated 28 January 1947 from Quartermaster to Mary Privoznik regarding the grave location of James F Privoznik, serial no. 36640529.

93. United States Army, Individual Deceased Personnel File, U.S. Army Human Resources Command, 200 Stovall Street Alexandria, VA 22332-0400, Letter dated 19 February 1947 from Quartermaster to Mary Privoznik regarding the grave location of James F Privoznik, serial no. 36640529.

94. United States Army, Individual Deceased Personnel File, U.S. Army Human Resources Command, 200 Stovall Street Alexandria, VA 22332-0400, Letter dated 31 July 1947 from Quartermaster to Mary Privoznik regarding the final disposition of James F Privoznik, serial no. 36640529.

95. Davis, R. Warren. The History of the Luxembourg American Military Cemetery. Luxembourg: 1965, 4.

96. United States Army, Individual Deceased Personnel File, U.S. Army Human Resources Command, 200 Stovall Street Alexandria, VA 22332-0400, Disinterment Directive for James Privoznik, serial no. 36640529, Directive dated 15 Mar 1948, disinterment 24 May 1948.

97. Davis, R. Warren. The History of the Luxembourg American Military Cemetery. Luxembourg: 1965, 5.

98. United States Army, Individual Deceased Personnel File, U.S. Army Human Resources Command, 200 Stovall Street Alexandria, VA 22332-0400, Disinter-

ment Directive for James Privoznik, serial no. 36640529, Directive dated 15 Mar 1948, disinterment 24 May 1948.

99. United States Army, Individual Deceased Personnel File, U.S. Army Human Resources Command, 200 Stovall Street Alexandria, VA 22332-0400, Letter dated 11 Mar 1949 from Quartermaster to Mary Privoznik regarding the final burial and grave location of James F Privoznik, serial no. 36640529.

100. General Order 623 dated 16 August 1945, 90th Division Association(http://www.90thdivisionassoc.org/afteractionreports/PDF/1945%20GO/90th%20GO%2045%20623.pdf).

101. General Order 623 dated 16 August 1945, 90th Division Association(http://www.90thdivisionassoc.org/afteractionreports/PDF/1945%20GO/90th%20GO%2045%20623.pdf).

102. Davis, R. Warren. The History of the Luxembourg American Military Cemetery. Luxembourg: 1965, 2.

103. Account of cemetery visit written by Patricia Holik, 29 Aug 2013.

Graves Registration Notes

1. Shomon, Joseph James. Crosses in the Wind,(Netherlands: Keulers, Geleen: 1947, 1991), 160.

2. History, website American Battle Monuments Commission, (http://abmc.gov/commission/history.php 6 September 2013).

3. Richardson, Eudora Ramsay, and Allan, Sherman, Quartermaster Supply in the European Theater of Operations in World War II Volume VII Graves Registration. (Camp Lee, VA: The Quartermaster School, 1948), 1.

4. Ibid.

5. Ibid.

6. Account of cemetery visit written by Patricia Holik, 29 Aug 2013.

7. Department of the Army. Field Manual 10-29 Quartermaster Graves Registration Company. (Washington, D.C.: United States Government Printing Office, 1952), 30-31.

8. Department of the Army. Field Manual 10-29 Quartermaster Graves Registration Company. (Washington, D.C.: United States Government Printing Office, 1952), 31.

9. Department of the Army. Field Manual 10-29 Quartermaster Graves Registration Company. (Washington, D.C.: United States Government Printing Office, 1952), 31-32.

10. Department of the Army. Field Manual 10-29 Quartermaster Graves Registration Company. (Washington, D.C.: United States Government Printing Office, 1952), 32.

11. Department of the Army. Field Manual 10-29 Quartermaster Graves Registration Company. (Washington, D.C.: United States Government Printing Office, 1952), 27-28.

12. Department of the Army. Field Manual 10-29 Quartermaster Graves Registration Company. (Washington, D.C.: United States Government Printing Office, 1952), 29-30.

13. Department of the Army. Field Manual 10-29 Quartermaster Graves Registration Company. (Washington, D.C.: United States Government Printing Office, 1952), 30.

14. Department of the Army. Field Manual 10-29 Quartermaster Graves Registration Company. (Washington, D.C.: United States Government Printing Office, 1952), 30.

15. Department of the Army. Field Manual 10-29 Quartermaster Graves Registration Company. (Washington, D.C.: United States Government Printing Office, 1952), 36.

16. Department of the Army. Field Manual 10-29 Quartermaster Graves Registration Company. (Washington, D.C.: United States Government Printing Office, 1952), 37.

17. Department of the Army. Field Manual 10-29 Quartermaster Graves Registration Company. (Washington, D.C.: United States Government Printing Office, 1952), 37.

18. Department of the Army. Field Manual 10-29 Quartermaster Graves Registration Company. (Washington, D.C.: United States Government Printing Office, 1952), 37-38.

19. Department of the Army. Field Manual 10-29 Quartermaster Graves Registration Company. (Washington, D.C.: United States Government Printing Office, 1952), 38.

20. Crosses at Normandy, Jun 1944, digital story, U.S. Army Quartermaster Foundation (http://www.qmfound.com/crosses.htm 6 September 2013); citing story of Colonel Elbert E. Legg.

21. Crosses at Normandy, Jun 1944, digital story, U.S. Army Quartermaster Foundation (http://www.qmfound.com/crosses.htm 6 September 2013); citing story of Colonel Elbert E. Legg.

22. Department of the Army. Field Manual 10-63 Graves Registration. (Washington, D.C.: United States Government Printing Office, 1945), 14-15.

23. Department of the Army. Field Manual 10-63 Graves Registration. (Washington, D.C.: United States Government Printing Office, 1945), 16-18.

24. Account of cemetery visit written by Patricia Holik, 29 Aug 2013.

25. Shomon, Joseph James. Crosses in the Wind,(Netherlands: Keulers, Geleen: 1947, 1991), 91.

26. Shomon, Joseph James. Crosses in the Wind,(Netherlands: Keulers, Geleen: 1947, 1991), 137-138.

27. Shomon, Joseph James. Crosses in the Wind,(Netherlands: Keulers, Geleen: 1947, 1991), 15.

28. Department of the Army. Field Manual 10-63 Graves Registration. (Washington, D.C.: United States Government Printing Office, 1945), 23-24.

29. Shomon, Joseph James. Crosses in the Wind,(Netherlands: Keulers, Geleen: 1947, 1991), 93.

30. Request for Disposition of Remains Dated 31 July 1947 - Individual Deceased Personnel File James Privoznik, Serial No. 36640529; Records of the Quartermaster General's Office, Record Group 92; National Archives, Washington D.C.

31. Department of the Army. Field Manual 10-29 Quartermaster Graves Registration Company. (Washington, D.C.: United States Government Printing Office, 1952), 52-53.

32. Shomon, Joseph James. Crosses in the Wind,(Netherlands: Keulers, Geleen: 1947, 1991), 66-67.

33. Richardson, Eudora Ramsay, and Allan, Sherman, Quartermaster Supply in the European Theater of Operations in World War II Volume VII Graves Registration. (Camp Lee, VA: The Quartermaster School, 1948), 87.

34. Richardson, Eudora Ramsay, and Allan, Sherman, Quartermaster Supply in the European Theater of Operations in World War II Volume VII Graves Registration. (Camp Lee, VA: The Quartermaster School, 1948), 88.

35. Shomon, Joseph James. Crosses in the Wind,(Netherlands: Keulers, Geleen: 1947, 1991), 147.

36. WAR-DEAD COFFINS ON WAY TO EUROPE. 1947. New York Times (1923-Current file), May 15, 1947. http://search.proquest.com/docview/107912796 by?accountid=38403 (accessed August 27, 2013).

37. Ibid.

Bibliography

90th Division Association http://www.90thdivisionassoc.org/ : 2013.

"1910 United States Federal Census, Roll T624_254 : 1910." Database Ancestry.com. http://www.ancestry.com : 2010.

"1920 United States Federal Census, Roll T625_388 : 1920." Database Ancestry.com. http://www.ancestry.com : 2010.

"1930 United States Federal Census, Roll 498 ; 1930." Database Ancestry.com. http://www.ancestry.com : 2010.

American Battle Monuments Commission. http://www.90thdivisionassoc.org/ : 2013.

American Battle Monuments Commission Archives. Luxembourg City, Luxembourg.

Army Mortuary Affairs History Page. http://www.qmfound.com/mortuary-affairs.htm : 2013.

Astor, Gerald. A blood-Dimmed Tide. The Battle of the Bulge by the Men Who Fought It. New York: Donald I Fine, Inc., 1992.

Atkinson, Rick. *The Guns at Last Light.* New York: Henry Holt & Company, 2013.

Badger, Jeffrey. *Finding Granddad's War.* Provo: Ancestry, 2008.

Baisden, Charles. *Flying Tiger to Air Commando.* Atglen, PA: Schiffer Military History, 1999.

Balkoski, Joe. *Beyond the Beachhead.* Mechanichsburg: Stackpole Books, 1999.

Barnes, G. M. Weapons of World War II. Birmingham: Palladium Press, 2013.

Blumenson, Martin. The Patton Papers 1940-1945. Boston: Houghton Mifflin Company, 1974.

Bond, Charles R., Jr. and Terry Anderson. *A Flying Tiger's Diary.* Texas: Texas A&M University Press, 1984.

Brouk, Robert Artifact Collection. Owned by Jennifer Holik, [Address for private use] Woodridge, Illinois. 2010.

Brouk, Robert Book Research Files. Privately held by Jennifer Holik, [Address for private use] Woodridge, Illinois. 2010.

Brouk, Robert. Photograph. 1935. 1935 Morton Yearbooks. Morton East High School Archives. Cicero, Illinois.

Budreau, Lisa M. *Bodies of War.* New York: New York University Press, 2010.

Camp Wolters History. http://www.fortwolters.com/camp_wolters_ guide.htm : 2013.

Cavanagh, William C.C. A Tour of the Bulge Battlefield. South Yorkshire: Pen and Sword Books, Ltd., 2001.

Center of Military History. *Order of Battle of the United States Land Forces in the World War, vol. 1, American Expeditionary Forces: General Headquarters, Armies, Army Corps, Services of Supply, Separate Forces* (1937. Reprint, Washington: U.S. G.P.O., 1931-1949), 1366.

Center of Military History. *Order of Battle of the United States Land Forces in the World War, vol. 2, American Expeditionary Forces: Divisions* (1937. Reprint, Washington: U.S. G.P.O., 1931-1949), 1366.

Center of Military History. *Order of Battle of the United States Land Forces in the World War, vol. 3 part 1, Zone of the Interior: Organization and Activities of the War Department* (1937. Reprint, Washington: U.S. G.P.O., 1931-1949), 1366.

Center of Military History. *Order of Battle of the United States Land Forces in the World War, vol. 3 part 2, Zone of the Interior: Territorial Departments, Tactical Divisions Organized in 1918, Posts, Camps, and Stations* (1937. Reprint, Washington: U.S. G.P.O., 1931-1949), 1366.

Center of Military History. *Order of Battle of the United States Land Forces in the World War, vol. 3 part 3, Zone of the Interior: Directory of Troops* (1937. Reprint, Washington: U.S. G.P.O., 1931-1949), 1366.

Chennault, Claire L., Anna. *Chennault and the Flying Tigers.* New York: Paul S. Eriksson, Inc., 1963.

Cohen, Stan. The Tree Army. A Pictorial History of the Civilian Conservation Corps, 1933-1942. Missoula: Pictorial Histories Publishing Company, 1980.

Cole, Hugh M. The Lorraine Campaign. Washington, D.C.: Department of the Army, 1950.

Conn, Stetson, ed. U.S. Army in World War II The Ardennes: Battle of the Bulge The European Theater. Minnetonka: National Historical Society, 1995, reprinted from 1965 original CMH Pub 7-8.

Controvich, James. United States Air Force and its Anticedents Published and Printed Unit Histories: A Bibliography. Maxwell Air Force Base: Air Force Historical Research Agency, 2001.

Davis, Virginia S. (Scharer). "Red Hat Mommas of Pinnacle Peak." MS. Phoenix, Arizona, 2010. Privately held by Virginia S. Davis, [Address for private use,] Phoenix, Arizona. 2010.
Davis, Virginia S. (Scharer). "Memoir 1918 – 2010." MS. Phoenix, Arizona, 2010. Privately held by Virginia S. Davis, [Address for private use,] Phoenix, Arizona. 2010.

Davis, Virginia S. (Scharer). Photographs. ca. 1941 - 1942. Privately held by Virginia S. Davis, [Address for private use,] Phoenix, Arizona. 2010.

Davis, R. Warren. The History of the Luxembourg American Military Cemetery. Luxembourg: 1965.

Department of the Army. Field Manual 10-9 Ordnance Field Manual. Washington, D.C.: United States Government Printing Office, 1942.

Department of the Army. *Field Manual 10-63 Graves Registration.* Washington, D.C.: United States Government Printing Office, 1952.

Department of the Army. *Field Manual 10-29 Quartermaster Graves Registration Company.* Washington, D.C.: United States Government Printing Office, 1952.

Department of the Army. Technical Manual 10-240 Deceased Personnel in the United States, Excluding Alaska. Washington, D.C.: United States Government Printing Office, 1947.

Department of the Army. Technical Manual 10-285 Deceased Personnel. Washington, D.C.: United States Government Printing Office, 1947.

Department of the Army. Technical Manual 10-285 Deceased Personnel. Washington, D.C.: United States Government Printing Office, 1947.

Department of the Navy. Disposition of Navy, Marine Corps and Coast Guard World War II Dead. Washington D.C.: Navy Department, undated.

Dickon, Chris. *The Foreign Burial of American War Dead.* Jefferson, NC: McFarland & Company, Inc., Publishers, 2011.

Doubler, Michael D. Closing with the Enemy How GIs Fought the War in Europe, 1944-1945. Kansas: University Press of Kansas, 1994.

Dupra, Lyle E. *We Delivered! The U.S. Navy Armed Guard in World War II.* Manhattan, KS: Sunflower University Press, 1997.

Ewing, Joseph H. *The 29th. A Short History of a Fighting Division.* Available through GoogleBooks: http://bit.ly/173ynpm without photos.

Florida Office of Vital Statistics. Death Certificates. Bureau of Vital Records, Tallahassee.

Flying Tigers: American Volunteer Group, discussion list, 2003-2010. http://www.flyingtigersavg.com/ : 2010.

Gawne, Jonathan. *Finding Your Father's War.* Philadelphia: Casemate, 2013.

Ginzberg, Eli. *The Lost Divisions.* New York: Columbia University Press: 1959.

Green, Constance McLaughlin, and Thomson, Harry C., and Roots, Peter C. The Technical Services The Ordnance Department: Planning Munitions for War. Washington D.C.: Center of Military History, 1990.

Greenfield, Kent Roberts, Palmer, Robert R., Wiley, Bell I., of the Historical Section Army Ground Forces. *U.S. Army in World War*

II The Army Ground Forces. The Organization of Ground Combat Troops. Washington, D.C. , Center of Military History United States Army: 1947.

Griffith Jr., Robert K.. *Men Wanted For The U.S. Army. America's Experience with an All-Volunteer Army Between the World Wars.* Westport: Greenwood Press:1982.

Hawthorne Works Museum. Hello Charley 1963. Pamphlet. Cicero, IL.: 1963.

Hawthorne Works Museum. *Microphone*, September 1942. Newsletter. Cicero, IL : 1942.

Hawthorne Works Museum. *Microphone*, December 1942. Newsletter. Cicero, IL : 1942.

Holik, Jennifer, transcriber. "What's Next Diary of Robert R. Brouk From April 1941 – July 4, 1942." MS. 1941-1942. Copy held by Jennifer Holik, [Address for private use,] Woodridge, Illinois. 2010.

Hotz, Robert, Editor. *Way of a Fighter, The Memoirs of Claire Lee Chennault.* NY: G.P. Putnam's Sons, 1949.

Illinois, Berwyn. *The Berywn Life,* 1938–1945. Scattered issues.

Illinois, Chicago, City of. Probate case files. Circuit Clerk's Office, Chicago.

Illinois, Chicago. *Chicago Daily Tribune,* 1930–1943.

Illinois, Chicago. *The Herald-American,* 1942. Scattered issues.

Illinois, Cicero. *The Cicero Life.* 1943. Scattered issues.

Illinois, Cicero. *Morton Collegian,* 1936-1937. Scattered issues.

"J. Sterling Morton Year Book 1935." Database Ancestry.com. http://www.ancestry.com : 2010.

Joint War History Commissions of Michigan and Wisconsin. The 32nd Division in the World War 1917-1919. Milwaukee: Wisconsin Printing Company, 1920.

Kerner, M.D., John A. Combat Medic World War II. Berkley: Creative Arts Book Company, 2002.

Kleber A.G.D., Col. Victor. *Selective Service in Illinois, 1940-1947.* Illinois: 1948.

Knox, Debra Johnson. World War II Military Records. Spartanburg: Military Information Enterprises, Inc., 2003.

Knox, Lt. Col. Richard S., and Knox, Debra Johnson. How to Locate Anyone Who Is or Has Been In the Military. Spartanburg: MIE Publishing, 1999.

Koskimaki, George. The Battered Bastards of Bastogne. Havertown: Casemate, 2003.

Lantz, Catherine, and Dennis M. Schlagheck. Images of America: Hawthorne Works. Charleston SC: Arcadia, 2014. Print.

Leatherwood, Jeffrey M. Nine from Aberdeen. Newcastle upon Tyne: UK: Cambridge Scholars Publishing, 2012.

Lemmon, Sarah McCulloh. North Carolina's Role in World War II. Raleigh: Division of Archives and History North Carolina Department of Cultural Resources, 1995.

Losonsky, Frank and Terry Losonsky. *Flying Tiger A Crew Chief's Story.* Atglen, PA: Schiffer Military History, 1996.

Mayo, Lida. The Ordnance Department on Beachhead and Battlefront. Washington D.C.: Office of the Chief of Military History, 1968.

McManus, John C. The Deadly Brotherhood. Novato: Presido Press, 1998.

McMillan, Woody. In The Presence of Soldiers. Nashville: Horton Heights Press, 2010.

Military, Compiled Army Air Force Accident Report 43-12-19-12. World War II. Records of the Army Air Force, 1942.

Mireless, Anthony J. *Volume 1: Introduction, January 1941 - June 1943 "Fatal Army Air Forces Aviation Accidents in the United States, 1941-1945".* Jefferson, NC: McFarland & Company, Inc., 2006.

Morton High School Archives. Yearbook. ca. 1935. Held by Morton High School, [2400 Home Avenue,] Berwyn, Illinois, 1935.

Morton Junior College Archives. Pioneer Yearbook. ca. 1936. Held by Morton Junior College Library, [3801 S. Central Avenue,] Cicero, Illinois, 1936.

Morton Junior College Archives. Pioneer Yearbook. ca. 1937. Held by Morton Junior College Library, [3801 S. Central Avenue,] Cicero, Illinois, 1937.

Moser, Don, and the Editors of Time-Life Books. China-Burma-India. Time-Life Books, Inc., 1978.

Neagles, James . *U.S. Military Records: A Guide to Federal & State Sources.* Provo: Ancestry Publishing, 1994.

Neill, George W. Infantry Soldier. Holding the Line at the Battle of the Bulge. Norman: University of Oklahoma Press, 2000.

"New York Passenger Lists, Roll T715_99: 1820-1957." Database Ancestry.com. http://www.ancestry.com : 2010.

Office of the Quartermaster General. History of the American Graves Registration Service. *Q.M.C. in Europe Volume I to September 1920, Volume II, and Volume III.* Consolidated reprint of Volumes I, II, and III. Undated.

"Old Ship Picture Galleries." Website http://www.photoship.co.uk : 2010.

Palmer, Robert R., Wiley, Bell I., Keats, William R. of the Historical Section Army Ground Forces. *U.S. Army in World War II The Army Ground Forces. The Procurement and Training of Ground Combat Troops.* Washington, D.C., Center of Military History United States Army: 2003.

Pistole, Larry M. *The Pictorial History of the Flying Tigers.* VA: Publisher's Press, Inc., 1981.

Reynolds CB, Major General Michael. *Voices from the Battle of the Bulge.* UK: David and Charles, 2004.

Richardson, Eudora Ramsay, and Allan, Sherman. *Quartermaster Supply in the European Theater of Operations in World War II*

Volume III and IV Outfitting the Soldier and Fuels and Lubricants. Camp Lee, VA: The Quartermaster School, 1948.

Richardson, Eudora Ramsay, and Allan, Sherman. *Quartermaster Supply in the European Theater of Operations in World War II Volume VI Salvage and Services.* Camp Lee, VA: The Quartermaster School, 1948.

Richardson, Eudora Ramsay, and Allan, Sherman. *Quartermaster Supply in the European Theater of Operations in World War II Volume VII Graves Registration.* Camp Lee, VA: The Quartermaster School, 1948.

Ross, William and Romanus, Charles. *The Technical Services The Quartermaster Corps: Operations in the War Against Germany.* Washington, D.C.: Office of the Chief of Military History Department of the Army, 1965.

San Diego Air and Space Museum Library and Archives. Photographs. 1942. Held by the San Diego Air and Space Museum Library and Archives, [2001 Pan American Plaza,] San Diego, California. 2010.

Schultz, Duane. *The Maverick War.* New York: St. Martin's Press, 1987.

Selective Service System. *Registration and Selective Service.* Washington: Government Printing Office, 1946.

Shilling, Erik. *Destiny: A Flying Tiger's Rendezvous with Fate.* Privately Published, 1993.

Shomon, Joseph James. *Crosses in the Wind.* New York: Stratford House, Inc., 1947.

Sledge, Michael. *Soldier Dead. How We Recover, Identify, Bury, and Honor Our Military Fallen.* New York: Columbia University Press, 2005.

Smith, Eddie L. And Patrick, Ben. Voices from the Field. Oxford, NC: Oxford Orphanage School of Printing, 1992.

Smith, R.T. Photograph. 1942. Digital image. Privately held by Brad

Smith, [Address for private use,] Berkeley, California. 2010. "Social Security Death Index." Database Ancestry.com. http://www. ancestry.com : 2010.

Steere, Edward. *The Graves Registration Service in World War II.* Washington D.C.: U.S. Government Printing Office, 1951. Available online: http://www.bentprop.org/grs/GRS_in_WW-II.pdf Steere, Edward and Boardman, Thayer M. *Final Disposition of World War II Dead 1945-1951.* Washington D.C.: Historical Branch of the Office of the Quartermaster General, 1957. Available online: http://www.bentprop.org/grs/

Torrance, Duncan Leitch. *Desert to Danube.* Northumberland TD: Duncan Leitch Torrance, 2010.

United States Army. Individual Deceased Personnel File. Military Textual Reference Branch. National Archives, College Park, MD.

United States Army. *Peragimus* "We Accomplish". A brief history of the 358th Infantry. Washington, D.C. Undated.

United States Army. World War I Burial File. Military Textual Reference Branch. National Archives, College Park, MD.

Van Ells, Mark D. To Hear Only Thunder Again. America's World War II Veterans Come Home. Oxford: Lexington Books, 2001.

Warnock, Bill. The Dead of Winter. New York: Penguin, 2005.

Wasch, Diane Shaw; Bush, Perry; Landreth, Keith; Glass Ph.D., James. World War II and the U.S. Army Mobilization Program: A History of 700 and 800 Series Cantonment Construction. Washington D.C.: U.S. Department of Defense and U.S. Department of the Interior, n.d.

World War II U.S. Medical Research Centre. http://www.med-dept. com/index.php : 2013.

Zaloga, Steven J. Battle of the Bulge 1944 (2) Bastogne. New York: Osprey, 2002.

Websites

Need a reliable researcher at the National Personnel Records Center in St. Louis? Visit my author page for the contact information of Norm Richards.
http://jenniferholik.com/resources.html

29th Infantry Division Historical Society
http://www.29infantrydivision.org/

29th Infantry Division Morning Reports
http://www.29idmorningrpt.com/

90th Division Association
http://90thdivisionassociation.org

Army Mortuary Affairs History Page
http://www.qmfound.com/mortuary-affairs.htm

Camp Butner Society FaceBook Page
https://www.facebook.com/CampButnerSociety?ref=br_tf

Flying Tigers Association
http://flyingtigersavg.com/

Fort Wolters (For Camp Wolters WWII Booklet)
www.fortwolters.com/camp

Maine Historical Society. Henry Wadsworth Longfellow [online resource], Maine Historical Society, Accessed January 22, 2014. http://www.hwlongfellow.org

Maryland Military Historical Society - 29th Infantry Division
http://www.marylandmilitaryhistory.org/research.php

Newsobserver.com "History Buffs, Soldiers Plan Museum for Camp Butner"
http://www.newsobserver.com/2013/11/30/3416989/history-buffs-soldiers-plan-museum.html

The Volunteer State Goes to War: A Salute to Tennessee Volunteers
http://www.tn.gov/tsla/exhibits/veterans/ww2.htm

WW2 US Medical Research Centre
http://www.med-dept.com

If you would like some writing prompts to get the creative juices flowing, be sure to check out the Military Memories writing prompts on my blog starting May 1, 2014. http://blog.generationsbiz.com

Index

About the Author

About The Author

Jennifer is a genealogi-
cal, historical, and military
researcher. Through her business Generations, she lectures
throughout the Chicagoland
area on World War II records
and stories, women during
World War II , kids genealogy,
and Italian genealogy.

As a researcher and writer
she can help you research and
piece together the stories of
your ancestors, particularly if
they served during World War II.

Jennifer is on the faculty of the National Institute of Genealogical Studies. She volunteers as the Genealogy Department Manager
at Casa Italia in Stone Park, Illinois. There she hosts monthly
genealogy and writing programs and works in the Italian American
Veterans Museum.

You can learn more at http://jenniferholik.com

Coming Fall 2014!

A new book series that will help you navigate World War II military records. Four books will be released starting this fall through
summer 2015 along with a big surprise! Sign up for my newsletter
at http://jenniferholik.com to stay in touch and receive details about
these books, pre-sales, special offers, and tips on researching and
writing your military ancestor stories.

Books By Author

All books and associated guides can be purchased through the author's website or on Amazon.com

The Tiger's Widow (August 2014)

Love knows no boundaries of time and space or life and death. It exists forever in our hearts as we remember and honor those who have gone before us. Through those memories we pass life lessons on to the next generation. We teach others there is light after darkness, hope after despair, and love is the glue that puts shattered hearts back together. This is a story of five hearts separated by time and space; hearts which would meet in the perfect moment. It is a story about never ending love that lived on even after death.

Join me on a journey that spans 72 years and several continents. This is the story of the life of Virginia Scharer Brouk, the wife of Flying Tiger, Robert Brouk. Virginia picked up the pieces of her life and joined the Women's Army Auxiliary Corps, later known as the Women's Army Corps (WAC,) to take up the fight after Robert was killed in a plane crash. Virginia's story is of life, loss, war, and the connection of hearts filled with love.

To Soar with the Tigers

This is the story of Flying Tiger Robert Brouk, a Flight Leader in the 3rd Squadron of the American Volunteer Group. In the months prior to Pearl Harbor, until the disbandment of the American Volunteer Group in July 1942, the Flying Tigers valiantly fought the Japanese over the skies of Burma and China. This story contains Robert's complete war diary. The diary outlines his dramatic experiences from the moment he enlisted in the American Volunteer Group to its disbandment. His story also contains snapshots of the life he led upon his return to his home in Cicero, Illinois; a graphic account of his untimely death; and accounts of how Robert has been remembered through the years.

Branching Out: Genealogy for Students 1st-3rd Grade
Branching Out: Genealogy for Students 4th-8th Grade
Branching Out: Genealogy for High School Students
Branching Out: Genealogy for Adults

Are you looking for a how-to genealogy book that introduces the basics of research through easy to learn lessons? Then look no further. In Branching Out, a new series available from Generations, author and professional genealogist Jennifer Holik provides adults with the tools they need to learn how to research their family history. Through thirty fun and educational lessons, you will learn the foundations of genealogy and how to begin research. Each lesson contains a clearly defined goal, all necessary vocabulary, additional reading assignments, and lesson and homework assignments to extend understanding of the concept.

Engaging the Next Generation: A Guide for Genealogy Societies and Libraries

Engaging the Next Generation is written specifically for groups looking to create youth programs. This is a two-part book featuring one-hour and half-day youth program examples and the complete 4th-8th grade Branching Out set of thirty lessons. Part I allows genealogy societies and libraries to create youth programs based on example outlines, example speaking text, and project ideas in the book. Part II allows genealogy societies and libraries to build larger programs using the thirty lessons provided in the Branching Out series. Part II can also be used to teach beginning genealogy in public schools.

CPSIA information can be obtained at www.ICGtesting.com
Printed in the USA
LVOW10s1926010115

MAR 1 9 2015

421094LV00015B/788/P